W9-ABB-977

The Letters of Theodore Roosevelt and Brander Matthews

The Letters of
Theodore Roosevelt
and Brander Matthews

Edited by

Lawrence J. Oliver

The University of Tennessee Press
Knoxville

Matthews's letters to Roosevelt printed by permission of Columbia University Libraries.

Letter from Matthews to Roosevelt dated November 20, 1905, from the Scribner Archives at Princeton University, published with permission of the Manuscripts Division, Department of Rare Books and Special Collections, Princeton University Libraries.

Roosevelt's letters to Matthews courtesy of the Library of Congress.

Letter from Roosevelt to Matthews dated April 17, 1918, from the James Weldon Johnson Collection, Yale Collection of American Literature, published with permission of the Beinecke Rare Book and Manuscript Library, Yale University.

The paper in this book meets the minimum requirements of the American National Standard for Permanence of Paper for Printed Library Materials.   ∞   The binding materials have been chosen for strength and durability.

Library of Congress Cataloging-in-Publication Data

Roosevelt, Theodore, 1858-1919
    The letters of Theodore Roosevelt and Brander Matthews / edited by
Lawrence J. Oliver.— 1st edition.
        p.   cm.
    Includes bibliographical references and index.
    ISBN 0-87049-894-0 (cloth: alk. paper)
    1. Roosevelt, Theodore, 1858-1919—Correspondence.
    2. Matthews, Brander, 1852-1929—Correspondence.
    3. Presidents—United States—Correspondence.
    4. Critics—United States—Correspondence.
    I. Matthews, Brander, 1852-1929. I. Oliver, Lawrence J., 1949-
III. Title.
E757.A4R66   1995
973.91′1′092—dc20
{B}   94-18766
                                       CIP

For my parents

Contents

Acknowledgments xv
Introduction xvii
Editorial Statement xxix
Abbreviations xxxi

CORRESPONDENCE

1888–1890

Roosevelt to Matthews, 1 October 1888 3
Roosevelt to Matthews, 5 October 1888 4
Roosevelt to Matthews, 31 July 1889 5
Roosevelt to Matthews, 7 November 1889 7
Roosevelt to Matthews, 29 December 1889 7
Roosevelt to Matthews, 13 January 1890 9
Roosevelt to Matthews, 10 February 1890 10
Roosevelt to Matthews, 14 April 1890 12
Roosevelt to Matthews, 28 April 1890 13
Roosevelt to Matthews, 3 May 1890 14
Roosevelt to Matthews, 20 June 1890 15
Roosevelt to Matthews, 12 July [1890] 16
Roosevelt to Matthews, 3 August 1890 17
Roosevelt to Matthews, 21 October [1890] 19
Roosevelt to Matthews, 21 November 1890 20
Roosevelt to Matthews, 28 December 1890 21

1891

Roosevelt to Matthews, 1 January 1891 23
Roosevelt to Matthews, 29 January 1891 24
Roosevelt to Matthews, 27 March 1891 24
Roosevelt to Matthews, 31 March 1891 25
Roosevelt to Matthews, 21 April 1891 25
Roosevelt to Matthews, 23 June 1891 26
Roosevelt to Matthews, 9 November 1891 27
Roosevelt to Matthews, 8 December 1891 28
Roosevelt to Matthews, 15 December 1891 29

1892

Roosevelt to Matthews, 2 January [1892]   30
Roosevelt to Matthews, 25 February 1892   31
Roosevelt to Matthews, 27 February 1892   32
Roosevelt to Matthews, 8 April 1892   33
Roosevelt to Matthews, 15 April 1892   34
Roosevelt to Matthews, 26 April 1892   35
Roosevelt to Matthews, 31 May 1892   36
Roosevelt to Matthews, 12 June 1892   37
Roosevelt to Matthews, 27 June 1892   37
Roosevelt to Matthews, 27 July 1892   39
Roosevelt to Matthews, 1 October 1892   40
Roosevelt to Matthews, 3 October 1892   42
Roosevelt to Matthews, 20 October 1892   43
Roosevelt to Matthews, 23 October 1892   44
Roosevelt to Matthews, [October–November 1892?]   44
Roosevelt to Matthews, 6 December 1892   45
Roosevelt to Matthews, 13 December 1892   47

1893

Roosevelt to Matthews, 4 January 1893   49
Roosevelt to Matthews, 8 February 1893   50
Roosevelt to Matthews, 14 February 1893   52
Roosevelt to Matthews, 17 February 1893   53
Roosevelt to Matthews, 16 March [1893]   54
Roosevelt to Matthews, 30 March 1893   55
Roosevelt to Matthews, 6 April [1893]   56
Roosevelt to Matthews, 7 May 1893   57
Roosevelt to Matthews, [8?] June 1893   58
Roosevelt to Matthews, 2[9?] [June 1893]   59
Roosevelt to Matthews, 26 August 1893   60
Roosevelt to Matthews, 16 October 1893   61
Roosevelt to Matthews, 24 October 1893   62
Roosevelt to Matthews, 1 November 1893   63
Roosevelt to Matthews, 5 November 1893   63
Roosevelt to Matthews, 18 December 1893   64
Roosevelt to Matthews, 21 December 1893   65
Roosevelt to Matthews, 27 December 1893   66
Roosevelt to Matthews, 31 December 1893   67

1894

Roosevelt to Matthews, 2 January 1894   68
Roosevelt to Matthews, 15 January 1894   68
Roosevelt to Matthews, 30 January 1894   70
Roosevelt to Matthews, 1 February 1894   71
Roosevelt to Matthews, 4 February 1894   72
Roosevelt to Matthews, 7 February 1894   72
Roosevelt to Matthews, 8 February 1894   74
Roosevelt to Matthews, 14 February 1894   74
Roosevelt to Matthews, 7 March 1894   75
Roosevelt to Matthews, 20 March 1894   76
Roosevelt to Matthews, 3 April 1894   76
Roosevelt to Matthews, 5 May 1894   78
Roosevelt to Matthews, 10 May 1894   79
Roosevelt to Matthews, 21 May 1894   80
Roosevelt to Matthews, 29 June 1894   82
Roosevelt to Matthews, 25 August 1894   84
Roosevelt to Matthews, 13 October 1894   86
Roosevelt to Matthews, 24 October 1894   87
Roosevelt to Matthews, 7 December 1894   88
Roosevelt to Matthews, 9 December 1894   90
Roosevelt to Matthews, 22 December 1894   91

1895

Roosevelt to Matthews, 2 January 1895   93
Roosevelt to Matthews, 11 February 1895   94
Roosevelt to Matthews, 23 February 1895   95
Roosevelt to Matthews, 9 March 1895   96
Roosevelt to Matthews, 19 March 1895   96
Roosevelt to Matthews, 6 April 1895   97
Roosevelt to Matthews, 13 May 1895   98
Roosevelt to Matthews, 18 October 1895   99
Roosevelt to Matthews, 11 November 1895   99
Roosevelt to Matthews, 6 December 1895   100

1896–1897

Roosevelt to Matthews, 3 January 189[6]   101
Roosevelt to Matthews, 4 May 1896   101
Roosevelt to Matthews, 1 July 1896   102
Roosevelt to Matthews, 2 November 1896   103

Roosevelt to Matthews, 28 January 1897   103
Roosevelt to Matthews, 11 February 1897   104
Roosevelt to Matthews, 6 March 1897   105
Roosevelt to Matthews, 10 June 1897   105
Roosevelt to Matthews, 14 June 1897   106
Roosevelt to Matthews, 4 September 1897   107
Roosevelt to Matthews, 27 September 1897   108
Roosevelt to Matthews, 26 October 1897   109
Roosevelt to Matthews, 4 November 1897   110
Roosevelt to Matthews, 29 November 1897   110
Roosevelt to Matthews, 20 December 1897   111
Roosevelt to Matthews, 27 December 1897   111

1898–1899

Roosevelt to Matthews, 28 February 1898   113
Roosevelt to Matthews, 14 August 1898   113
Roosevelt to Matthews, 27 December 1898   114
Roosevelt to Matthews, 27 May 1899   114
Roosevelt to Matthews, 29 August 1899   115

1900–1901

Roosevelt to Matthews, 25 January 1900   116
Matthews to Roosevelt, 15 April 1900   116
Roosevelt to Matthews, 30 April 1900   118
Matthews to Roosevelt, 2 December 1900   119
Roosevelt to Matthews, 4 December 1900   120
Matthews to Roosevelt, 27 December 1900   121
Roosevelt to Matthews, 31 December 1900   121
Matthews to Roosevelt, 22 September 1901   121
Matthews to Matthews, 25 September 1901   122
Roosevelt to Matthews, 26 October 1901   122
Matthews to Roosevelt, 29 December 1901   123
Roosevelt to Matthews, 31 December 1901   124

1902–1903

Roosevelt to Matthews, 19 February 1902   126
Matthews to Roosevelt, 26 February 1902   126
Roosevelt to Matthews, 27 February 1902   127
Roosevelt to Matthews, 13 June 1902   127
Matthews to Roosevelt, 26 July 1902   128
Matthews to Roosevelt, 25 August 1902   129
Matthews to Roosevelt, 4 February 1903   129

Matthews to Roosevelt, 7 February 1903   130
Roosevelt to Matthews, 31 March 1903   130
Matthews to Roosevelt, 10 July 1903   131
Roosevelt to Matthews, 11 July 1903   132
Roosevelt to Matthews, 25 July 1903   133
Roosevelt to Matthews, 27 July 1903   134
Roosevelt to Matthews, 30 July 1903   135
Matthews to Roosevelt, 3 August 1903   135
Roosevelt to Matthews, 1 September 1903   136
Roosevelt to Matthews, 5 October 1903   137
Matthews to Roosevelt, 7 October 1903   137
Roosevelt to Matthews, 8 October 1903   138

1904

Matthews to Roosevelt, 25 January 1904   139
Roosevelt to Matthews, 27 January 1904   140
Matthews to Roosevelt, 29 January 1904   140
Roosevelt to Matthews, 1 February 1904   141
Matthews to Roosevelt, 5 February 1904   141
Roosevelt to Matthews, 8 February 1904   142
Matthews to Roosevelt, 22 February 1904   142
Roosevelt to Matthews, 23 February 1904   143
Matthews to Roosevelt, 10 April 1904   144
Roosevelt to Matthews, 11 April 1904   145
Matthews to Roosevelt, 12 April 1904   145
Roosevelt to Matthews, 13 April 1904   146
Matthews to Roosevelt, 20 May 1904   146
Roosevelt to Matthews, 21 May 1904   147
Roosevelt to Matthews, 7 June 1904   147
Matthews to Roosevelt, 8 June 1904   148
Matthews to Roosevelt, 27 November 1904   150
Roosevelt to Matthews, 29 November 1904   151
Matthews to Roosevelt, 1 December 1904   151
Roosevelt to Matthews, 2 December 1904   152
Matthews to Roosevelt, 10 December 1904   152
Roosevelt to Matthews, 12 December 1904   153

1905

Matthews to Roosevelt, 1 January 1905   154
Roosevelt to Matthews, 3 January 1905   155
Matthews to Roosevelt, 4 January 1905   155
Roosevelt to Matthews, 7 January 1905   156

Matthews to Roosevelt, 1 February 1905   156
Roosevelt to Matthews, 3 February 1905   157
Matthews to Roosevelt, 16 March 1905   157
Roosevelt to Matthews, 18 March 1905   159
Roosevelt to Matthews, 20 March 1905   159
Matthews to Roosevelt, 11 June 1905   159
Roosevelt to Matthews, 12 June 1905   161
Matthews to Roosevelt, 31 August 1905   161
Roosevelt to Matthews, 2 September 1905   162
Matthews to Roosevelt, 20 November 1905   163
Roosevelt to Matthews, 21 November 1905   164
Matthews to Roosevelt, 26 November 1905   165

1906

Matthews to Roosevelt, 1 January 1906   166
Roosevelt to Matthews, 2 January 1906   167
Matthews to Roosevelt, 1 February 1906   167
Roosevelt to Matthews, 2 February 1906   168
Matthews to Roosevelt, 6 March 1906   169
Roosevelt to Matthews, 7 March 1906   170
Roosevelt to Matthews, 20 March 1906   170
Matthews to Roosevelt, 22 April 1906   171
Roosevelt to Matthews, 23 April 1906   172
Matthews to Roosevelt, 16 May 1906   172
Roosevelt to Matthews, 17 May 1906   173
Roosevelt to Matthews, 22 August 1906   173
Matthews to Roosevelt, 22 September 1906   174
Roosevelt to Matthews, 24 September 1906   175
Roosevelt to Matthews, 27 September 1906   175
Roosevelt to Matthews, 16 December 1906   175

1907

Roosevelt to Matthews, 8 January 1907   177
Matthews to Roosevelt, 9 January 1907   177
Roosevelt to Matthews, 1 April 1907   178
Matthews to Roosevelt, 2 April 1907   178
Matthews to Roosevelt, 6 May 1907   179
Roosevelt to Matthews, 7 May 1907   180
Roosevelt to Matthews, 12 May 1907   180
Roosevelt to Matthews, 20 July 1907   181
Roosevelt to Matthews, 2 September 1907   181

Matthews to Roosevelt, 26 September 1907   182
Roosevelt to Matthews, 27 September 1907   183
Matthews to Roosevelt, 25 November 1907   183
Matthews to Roosevelt, 10 December 1907   184
Matthews to Roosevelt, 15 December 1907   185
Roosevelt to Matthews, 18 December 1907   186

1908–1910

Roosevelt to Matthews, 1 September 1908   187
Roosevelt to Matthews, 2 November 1908   187
Roosevelt to Matthews, 15 December 1908   188
Matthews to Roosevelt, 16 December 1908   189
Roosevelt to Matthews, 4 January 1909   190
Roosevelt to Matthews, 15 March 1909   190
Matthews to Roosevelt, 21 June 1910   191
Roosevelt to Matthews, 6 October 1910   192

1911–1912

Matthews to Roosevelt, 26 May 1911   193
Matthews to Roosevelt, 18 June 1911   193
Roosevelt to Matthews, 21 June 1911   194
Roosevelt to Matthews, 30 June 1911   195
Matthews to Roosevelt, 19 October 1911   195
Roosevelt to Matthews, 20 October 1911   196
Matthews to Roosevelt, 4 January 1912   196
Roosevelt to Matthews, 5 January 1912   196
Matthews to Roosevelt, 2 December 1912   197
Roosevelt to Matthews, 6 December 1912   198

1913–1914

Matthews to Roosevelt, 3 January 1913   199
Roosevelt to Matthews, 7 January 1913   200
Matthews to Roosevelt, 16 February 1913   200
Roosevelt to Matthews, 18 February 1913   201
Matthews to Roosevelt, 19 February 1913   202
Roosevelt to Matthews, 26 February 1913   202
Matthews to Roosevelt, 27 September 1913   203
Roosevelt to Matthews, 15 October 1913   204
Roosevelt to Matthews, 25 May 1914   205
Matthews to Roosevelt, 24 November 1914   205
Matthews to Roosevelt, 8 December 1914   206

1915–1916

Roosevelt to Matthews, 3 February 1915   207
Matthews to Roosevelt, 7 February 1915   207
Matthews to Roosevelt, 23 March 1915   208
Roosevelt to Matthews, 4 October 1915   210
Matthews to Roosevelt, 6 October 1915   211
Roosevelt to Matthews, 10 January 1916   211
Matthews to Roosevelt, 16 January 1916   212
Roosevelt to Matthews, 18 January 1916   213

1917–1918

Matthews to Roosevelt, 8 January 1917   214
Matthews to Roosevelt, 11 March 1917   215
Roosevelt to Matthews, 15 March 1917   215
Matthews to Roosevelt, 31 August 1917   216
Roosevelt to Matthews, 4 September 1917   216
Matthews to Roosevelt, 19 September 1917   217
Matthews to Roosevelt, 2 April 1918   217
Roosevelt to Matthews, 4 April 1918   218
Matthews to Roosevelt, 12 April 1918   218
Roosevelt to Matthews, 17 April 1918   219
Matthews to Roosevelt, 20 July 1918   219
Roosevelt to Matthews, 24 July 1918   220
Matthews to Roosevelt, 6 September 1918   221
Roosevelt to Matthews, 13 September 1918   221
Matthews to Roosevelt, 20 September 1918   222
Matthews to Roosevelt, 29 October 1918   222
Roosevelt to Matthews, 4 November 1918   223

UNDATED

Roosevelt to Matthews, 17 March [ca. 1890]   224
Roosevelt to Matthews, 21 March [ca. 1890]   224
Roosevelt to Matthews, 19 November [1892?]   225
Roosevelt to Matthews, 5 October [ca. 1895]   226

Selected Bibliography   227
Index   233

Acknowledgments

Editing a large collection of letters such as that contained in this volume engenders feelings of dependency in the editor. During the research for and preparation of this book, I was fortunate to be able to depend on the cooperation, advice, and knowledge of many individuals, whom I take great pleasure in acknowledging here.

I would not have undertaken the project at all had I not received permission from Columbia University Libraries to publish letters in the Brander Matthews Papers, Rare Book and Manuscript Library, Columbia University, New York City. Bernard Crystal, curator for rare books and manuscripts at Columbia's Butler Library, and his staff processed my request for microfilm of the letters; and they were very helpful and hospitable during the week that I spent doing research at the Butler Library. I also wish to thank Yale University Library for permission to publish a letter by Roosevelt in the James Weldon Johnson Collection, Beinecke Rare Book and Manuscript Library; Princeton University Libraries for permission to publish a letter by Matthews in the Scribner Archives, Rare Books and Special Collections; and Fred Baum, senior reference librarian at the Library of Congress, for informing me that Roosevelt's letters are in the public domain.

As I formulated my editorial principles during the initial stage of the project, I profited greatly from the knowledge and experience of other documentary editors, especially Robert C. Leitz, Jr., who critiqued an early draft of sample letters, and who shared his expertise with me many times thereafter. The readers' reports furnished to the University of Tennessee Press by Louis J. Budd and Joseph R. McElrath, Jr., offered many helpful suggestions for revising the manuscript and noted errors in it that otherwise might have gone undetected. I have also profited from the assistance rendered by several colleagues here at Texas A&M University. Kenneth M. Price and Dennis Berthold read portions of the manuscript; Jeffrey Cox and Hamlin Hill each spared me a trip to the library by identifying a literary reference; and Nathan Bracher helped me with troublesome French translations. While researching the hundreds of annotations accompanying the letters within, I depended heavily on librarians and support staff here at Texas A&M University. I especially wish to express my appreciation to the department of Interlibrary Loan Services, which processed literally hundreds of my requests for materials.

I am deeply indebted as well to librarians at other institutions, particularly Wallace Finley Dailey, curator of the Theodore Roosevelt Collection, Houghton Library, Harvard University. He answered many questions and provided invaluable information and documents, often after I had exhausted all my leads and had arrived at an apparent dead end while tracking an elusive reference. Ernest J. Emrich, manuscript reference librarian at the Library of Congress, graciously checked my transcriptions of several photocopied Roosevelt letters against the originals at the Library of Congress. I also received assistance from Amy Verone, curator of the Theodore Roosevelt Library at Sagamore Hill, and from Kathleen Young, museum technician there; from Melanie Yolles, manuscript specialist, New York Public Library; and from Maggie Kruesi, manuscript librarian, Van Pelt Library, University of Pennsylvania.

I wish also to thank Texas A&M University for granting me Development Leave for one full semester to work on this book, and also to the Department of English for allowing me a teaching reduction during another semester. My research for the project was supported financially by a grant from Texas A&M's Center for Presidential Studies and by a Texas A&M Faculty Mini-Grant.

Finally, I thank my wife, Mary Jane, and my two sons, Cory and Craig, for their understanding and patience.

Introduction

In his numerous essays and addresses written before, during, and after his presidency, Theodore Roosevelt warned his fellow Americans that they were losing the frontier spirit that had made the nation great. The enemies of "true Americanism" were everywhere—in the union halls, the Wall Street offices, the women's suffrage movement, the immigrant enclaves in the ghettos, and the eastern literary establishment. Roosevelt reserved some of his most vituperative remarks for that establishment: too many writers, critics, and professors were, he snarled, "over-civilized, over-sensitive, over-refined"; they had lost the "manly courage by which alone [one] can conquer in the keen struggle of our national life." Their criticism of American culture was perhaps not treasonous according to the law, but it certainly was unpatriotic, and, he said, "one may fall very short of treason and yet be an undesirable citizen."[1]

As Daniel Aaron observes in "Theodore Roosevelt as Cultural Artifact," much of Roosevelt's inexhaustible energy was devoted to a "campaign of self-promotion, a sustained 'Song of Myself.'"[2] And the self that Roosevelt delighted in representing to a public anxious about the alleged feminization and overcivilization of American culture was that of the Hunter-Soldier. Roosevelt projects this "manly" image in his "rough writing" attacks on effete easterners, and in the many photographs of him in cowboy or military attire, posing sternly, rifle in hand, sometimes amid animal carcasses he had bagged or thieves he had captured.[3] This "western" image of Roosevelt captivated the imagination of the country during the Progressive era, and it continues to appeal to an American public disposed toward tough rhetoric from the "bully pulpit." (Even former President George Bush, the Yale graduate who promised to usher in a "kinder and gentler nation," once suggested that he might "turn out to be a Teddy Roosevelt.")[4]

But as anyone familiar with Roosevelt's life and writings knows, Roosevelt—who, it is often forgotten, was a Harvard-educated member of the New York gentry—was one of America's most scholarly presidents. Author of more than fifty books and hundreds of essays and reviews, he worked as assiduously to make his mark as a writer and critic as he did as a politician. Throughout his professional life, and especially during his years in the White House, Roosevelt's large circle of intimate friends included many of his era's most notable writers, critics, and academics: Henry Adams, Hamlin Garland, W. D. Howells, Rudyard

Kipling, Owen Wister, and Edith Wharton—to name but a few. None of these luminaries, however, had a closer literary relationship with Roosevelt than Brander Matthews (1852–1929). An influential literary critic and professor at Columbia University (Columbia College until 1912), Matthews has, until very recently, rested in obscurity since his death.[5]

Ironically, Matthews epitomized the "overcivilized" easterner so often verbally abused by Roosevelt. Son of a wealthy cotton speculator whose extensive property holdings included the present site of the Empire State Building, young Matthews was, as he remarks in his auto-biography, raised to be a "professional millionaire."[6] When the Panic of 1873 ruined his father, Edward Matthews, Brander was forced to earn his own way in the world, first as a drama critic and then as a professor of literature at Columbia (from 1891 to 1924). But by 1873, twenty-one-year-old Brander already had enjoyed all the advantages of a young American aristocrat. He spent his childhood in a mansion on fashionable Fifth Avenue, where many prominent writers, businessmen, and politicians came to visit his father; he traveled extensively in Europe, gaining there the fluency in French and the deep knowledge of Continental literature that he would later exploit as a literary critic and professor; and, after being educated in exclusive private academies, he earned undergraduate and law degrees at Columbia.

If the Panic of 1873 destroyed Edward Matthews's hope that his son would live his adult life as a professional millionaire who could devote his energies to politics instead of making money, the financial collapse did not by any means remove Brander from the ranks of the privileged. The income he received from his hundreds of essays and reviews in such periodicals as the *Nation*, the *Atlantic*, the *Century*, and *Harper's Monthly* and from the sales of the more than seventy books he authored or edited was substantial. His textbook *An Introduction to the Study of American Literature* (1896) alone sold over a quarter of a million copies. Added to his Columbia salary and a significant inheritance from his mother (the daughter of a New Orleans aristocrat), his publishing earnings allowed him to maintain his status in New York City's upper echelons.

Matthews fully enjoyed his privileged position. As one of his friends expressed it, Matthews was a "most clubbable man."[7] He belonged to virtually all the exclusive clubs and literary societies of London, Paris, and New York City. He helped found the Dunlap Society, the Authors Club (New York City's first distinctively literary club), the National Institute of Arts and Letters, and its offshoot, the American Academy of Arts and Letters. He served as president of the institute (1912–14) and chancellor of the academy (1920–24); he also presided over the Modern Language Association (1910–11). During his many sojourns in France, he was frequently in attendance at the Théâtre Français and the Opéra-Comique; in 1907, the French awarded him the Legion of Honor for his services to their literature. When summering in England, he often passed his evenings at the Rabelais, Savile, or the Athenaeum clubs. (His membership in the Athenaeum was sponsored by Matthew Arnold.) Matthews's active participation in these and other clubs and organizations, and his influential status as a critic and writer, brought him into contact with many of the age's most prominent personages on both sides of the Atlantic. He developed close friendships with Andrew Carnegie, Constant Coquelin, Kate Field, W. D. Howells, James Weldon Johnson, Rudyard Kipling, Henry Cabot Lodge, Charles Scribner, Mark Twain, and, last but certainly not least, Theodore Roosevelt.

When and under what circumstances Roosevelt and Matthews first met remains a mystery, but apparently they had become friends long before 1 October 1888, the date of the earliest extant letter in their correspondence (and the opening letter of this edition). They may have made each other's acquaintance as early as 1884, for in November of that year Roosevelt participated in a panel discussion sponsored by the Nineteenth Century Club, a New York City debating society in which Matthews was active.[8] Or perhaps the two men were first introduced at the Century Club or at one of the other elite clubs that Roosevelt, despite all his denunciations of the "overcivilized" life, visited as regularly as Matthews. In any case, in 1888 Matthews, as literary advisor to the American branch of the English publishing firm Longmans, Green, & Company, solicited from Roosevelt a history of New York City, to be part of the "Historic Towns" series, under the general editorship of the historian E. A. Freeman. (Matthews also persuaded Roosevelt's close friend and political ally Henry Cabot Lodge to write a history of Boston for the series.)

As he remarked in his letter to Matthews of 5 October 1888, Roosevelt in the late 1880s was a "'literary feller,' not a politician." With the Democrats in the White House, Republican Roosevelt's political prospects seemed less promising than his literary ones. If he was not then a famous writer, he nonetheless had made significant progress in his quest, begun while he was a student at Harvard, to become a respected author. His first book, *The Naval War of 1812* (1882) had been well received, and his next two books—*Hunting Trips of a Ranchman* (1885) and *Thomas Hart Benton* (1887)—were moderately successful.[9] Moreover, severe financial pressures (an especially hard winter had decimated the cattle herd on his Dakota ranch) demanded that Roosevelt earn money somehow. Thus, though he had just completed *Gouverneur Morris* (1888) and *Ranch Life and the Hunting Trail* (1888) and was feeling overburdened with the research and writing of *The Winning of the West* (which was under contract with Putnam's publishing firm), Roosevelt accepted Matthews's offer to write the history.

New York was published in 1890; in the preface Roosevelt expresses particular thanks to Matthews, "who indeed is responsible for my undertaking to write the book at all."[10] Shortly after the book appeared, Matthews gave it a flattering review in the *Century*.[11] Upon reading the review, Roosevelt wrote to thank Matthews, adding that his critique "touched on the very points I desired to see emphasized, and it appeared in the magazine which of all others I should have chosen. So I have cause to be greatly obliged to you."[12] This was not the last time that Matthews publicly praised Roosevelt's writings, nor the final expression of appreciation that Roosevelt extended to Matthews. Despite Matthews's efforts to promote *New York*, it did not sell well; Matthews attributed the weak sales to the fact "that in 1890 [Roosevelt] was not yet a celebrity."[13]

By the end of the decade, Roosevelt's military and political exploits had, of course, made him into a celebrity, and by the time of his death in 1919, he had become the monumental figure that he remains today. (As one of the four presidents whose visages are permanently inscribed in the granite of Mt. Rushmore, Roosevelt became a monument in the most literal sense.) No one worked more energetically than Matthews to construct Roosevelt as American culture's quintessential political leader *and* man of letters. During their long friendship, Matthews often cited in his writings Roosevelt's political and literary achievements. In addition to his attempts to promote *New York,* he lavished praise upon Roosevelt's *Autobiography* (1913) and *History as Literature and Other Essays* (1913) in reviews in *The Bookman*. Roosevelt's autobiography, he proclaimed, was as important to American culture as was Benjamin Franklin's. The essays in *History as Literature,* he asserted, reveal historian Roosevelt's possession of the "interpreting imagination" which can survey the past in order to discover the universal laws of human history.[14]

In the years following Roosevelt's death, Matthews increased the frequency and intensity of his praises. For example, shortly after Roosevelt was buried, Matthews lionized him in an article in the *Outlook* magazine, declaring that Roosevelt was the equal of Jefferson and Lincoln in political skill, erudition, and moral character. In a commemorative tribute delivered in 1919 to the American Academy of Arts and Letters, of which Roosevelt had been a member, Matthews celebrated his deceased friend's political, oratorical, and literary skills. When Joseph Bishop's *Theodore Roosevelt and His Time* appeared in 1920, Matthews reviewed it in the *New York Times,* using the occasion to proclaim Roosevelt one of the nation's greatest presidents. Matthews's culminating tribute to Roosevelt is "Theodore Roosevelt as a Man of Letters," published in

1919 in *Munsey's Magazine*. Surveying the full field of Roosevelt's literary works, Matthews clearly aimed to secure him a space in the literary canon. He declares that Roosevelt's career was fuller and richer than Benjamin Franklin's; that his *Great Adventure* equals Lincoln's "Gettysburg Address" in its attainment of the "serener heights of pure literature"; that the author of the *Winning of the West* was a born storyteller as well as a "severely trained scientific investigator."[15] In 1926, "Theodore Roosevelt as a Man of Letters" was reprinted as the introduction to volume 12—*Literary Essays*—of the National Edition of Roosevelt's *Works*, where it continues to sustain Roosevelt's status as a "literary feller."

As noted above, the correspondence between Roosevelt and Matthews begins with a letter from Roosevelt to Matthews dated 1 October 1888; it ends with Matthews's letter to Roosevelt of 4 November 1918. The two men corresponded regularly during the 1890s and the early years of the new century; after Roosevelt left the White House, they corresponded less frequently. But there is no reason to believe that their friendship waned; it apparently remained strong until Roosevelt's death in 1919. The letters indicate that during the last decade of his life, Roosevelt, when he was not traveling the nation or the globe, often invited Matthews (and his wife) to visit Sagamore Hill or to lunch with him in New York City.

The primary repositories of Roosevelt's and Matthews's papers—the Theodore Roosevelt Papers in the Library of Congress and the Brander Matthews Papers at Columbia University—contain over 300 pieces of correspondence between the two men, 271 of which are collected in this volume. The Library of Congress collection does not contain any letters dated prior to 23 April 1897; but the Matthews Papers includes 116 letters that Roosevelt wrote to Matthews between 1 October 1888 and 7 April 1897. Since virtually all these letters respond to or solicit responses from Matthews, it is clear that a large number of letters from Matthews to Roosevelt (as well as some from Roosevelt to Matthews, since gaps in the chain exist) have been lost.

In the appendix of the selected edition, *The Letters of Theodore Roosevelt*, one of the editors correctly remarks that Roosevelt's correspondence with Matthews yields especially valuable information on "literary and historical matters."[16] Yet the eight volumes of letters include a mere thirty-five letters from Roosevelt to Matthews, only eight of them written after 1900. Thus, only a small percentage of the total correspondence—and no letters written by Matthews—have been previously published.

Whereas the small number of Roosevelt's letters to Matthews scattered throughout the thousands of other pieces of correspondence in *The*

Letters of Theodore Roosevelt suggests that Matthews was a minor figure in the great gallery of Roosevelt's personal and professional acquaintances, the letters collected in the present edition make clear that Matthews was, for three decades, one of Roosevelt's most trusted friends and confidantes, especially when Roosevelt assumed the role of "literary feller." Indeed, it is no exaggeration to claim that the Columbia professor was Roosevelt's literary mentor. Roosevelt held Matthews's critical and scholarly work in the highest regard, and he often addressed Matthews in the humble tones of an admiring student. Moreover, Roosevelt often sought the professor's advice before, during, and after composing a piece of writing. "The only thing that unnerves President Roosevelt is literary composition," *Critic* editor Joseph Gilder once remarked.[17] The truth of that observation is demonstrated by many of Roosevelt's letters to Matthews, including one in which he admits: "I struggle and plunge frightfully, and when written my words do'n't express my thought" (27 June 1892).

Matthews was an enthusiastic and dedicated tutor: he solicited manuscripts from Roosevelt; criticized his drafts; suggested where to publish finished works; and sent him numerous literary books and essays, including copies of almost every book and major essay that he (Matthews) published. Clearly, Matthews sought to shape Roosevelt's literary views (and at times his social and political views as well). Since Roosevelt was fiercely independent in his thinking, he did not always concur with Matthews's judgments or with those of the authors whom Matthews recommended. Matthews's literary taste was somewhat more tolerant than Roosevelt's, as demonstrated by the two men's sharp difference of opinion over the artistic merits of Émile Zola's naturalist fictions, which Matthews admired and Roosevelt detested. Nonetheless, if they did not always see eye-to-eye on the merits of a particular literary work, Matthews exerted an undeniable influence on Roosevelt's theory and practice of literary criticism. The literary essays comprising volume 12 of Roosevelt's *Works* (the volume with the introduction by Matthews), repeatedly echo words and ideas that have their source in Matthews's writings or in works that he suggested to Roosevelt. For example, "Nationalism in Literature and Art" (1916), one of Roosevelt's best-known literary pieces, shows striking parallels with Matthews's 1896 essay "American Literature" and with *An Introduction to the Study of American Literature,* a textbook that Roosevelt had urged Matthews to write. At Matthews's suggestion, Roosevelt reviewed the book in *The Bookman,* where he extolled it, asserting that it should be required reading not only for students of American literature but for "every American writer if he is going to do work that is really worth doing."[18] Roosevelt paid no other writer or critic a higher or, I believe, more sincere compliment.

If the Roosevelt-Matthews correspondence is most interesting for its literary focus, the topics covered are by no means restricted to the literary realm. Like Roosevelt, Matthews was a voracious reader interested in many fields of study. Thus we find Roosevelt stating in one letter that he wants to "see you at leisure, with nobody, not even [Richard Watson] Gilder or Howells or [Henry C.] Bunner at the table with us, and with *ample* time to discuss the twenty seven different subjects I have stored up" (1 Oct. 1892). In 1906, Roosevelt invited Matthews to the White House to "talk over everything from spelling to the Japanese" (17 May 1906). In other letters, the two men shared their ideas on a wide variety of social, political, and personal topics: political appointments and controversies; municipal, state, national, and international affairs; the so-called "Negro Problem"; British superciliousness and the "colonial" mentality of certain American intellectuals; the simplified-spelling movement; international copyright law; grammar and usage; and their shared love of New York City.

Directly or indirectly, many of the letters are concerned with Columbia University. Nicholas Murray Butler, the institution's president from 1902 to 1945, was an intimate friend and political supporter of Roosevelt, who had studied law there during 1880–1881. In addition to Butler, Matthews's colleagues at Columbia included several of the Progressive movement's most distinguished scholars: Felix Adler in social and political ethics; John W. Burgess in political science; Franz Boas in anthropology; Franklin H. Giddings in sociology; Edwin R. Seligman in economics. Matthews's ideology and the texts in which that ideology is inscribed were profoundly influenced by the economic, social, and political ideas advocated by these and other social-science faculty members.

Matthews's letters reveal him as a conduit through which ideas and theories formulated at Columbia flowed to Roosevelt, especially during his presidency. Matthews, for example, often sent Roosevelt copies of the *Political Science Quarterly,* which was housed in Columbia's political science department, calling to Roosevelt's attention those articles that Matthews thought would be most interesting and informative. To Matthews and Roosevelt, these articles exemplified the "progressive" ideas that would shape the new world order of their day; to most contemporary readers, the essays often exemplify the race, gender, and class prejudices which undergirded those ideas and which were responsible for the essentially conservative—and often reactionary—nature of the Progressive movement. For example, in 1904 Matthews sent President Roosevelt a copy of Burgess's "Germany, Great Britain, and the United States," in which the author insists that these three heirs of the "Teutonic genius and the Teutonic conscience" bear the moral obligation of extending their common culture into the "dark places of the earth for the enlightenment and advancement of the inhabitants" of the "dark" regions of the globe.[19] A year earlier, Matthews had sent Roosevelt a copy of "American People" by Giddings, head of Columbia's sociology department and president of the American Sociological Society. Like his colleague Burgess, Giddings devoutly believed that the Anglo-Teutonic race was morally obliged to dominate the "semi-civilized, barbaric, and savage" cultures. In "American People," he assured those who feared—as Roosevelt did—"race decadence" that the United States would remain "essentially English," its ability to convert "the most unpromising" foreigners as strong as ever.[20]

Not all the books and articles that Matthews recommended or sent to Roosevelt masked a racist ideology with progressive rhetoric, however; for the professor also sent to the White House works that challenged the theory of Anglo-Teutonic racial superiority to which Roosevelt subscribed. For example, Matthews sent a pamphlet by Boas denouncing race prejudice and irrational nationalism (7 Feb. 1915). Matthews also mailed and urged Roosevelt to read James Weldon Johnson's landmark novel *The Autobiography of an Ex–Colored Man* (2 Dec. 1912; 3 Jan. 1913). Since Thomas G. Dyer's *Theodore Roosevelt and the Idea of Race* (1980), the fullest account of Roosevelt's racial views we have, suggests that Roosevelt was unacquainted with Boas's work and makes no mention of his having read Johnson's novel, these letters are especially significant.

Other letters are equally important for what they reveal about Roosevelt's reading and his reactions to what he read. In fact, his correspondence with Matthews forms a virtual chronicle of his literary life from 1888 until his death. Roosevelt, as the reader of this edition will discover, devoured not only the major works of American and world literature, but the minor ones as well. The letters contain Roosevelt's and Matthews's opinions on a host of writers who, though obscure today, were important figures in American and European literary culture during the period 1880–1920. Since many of these writers do not appear in *The Letters of Theodore Roosevelt* nor in the Roosevelt biographies (which tend to emphasize his political rather than his literary life), the letters greatly enrich our knowledge of Roosevelt the literary and cultural critic.

The correspondence also demonstrates that, whatever differences Roosevelt and Matthews had regarding the relative merits of individual works, the two were deeply committed to the construction and institutionalization of an American literary canon that would engender a proper sense of "manly Americanism" in readers, especially students. In addition to encouraging and then publicly praising Matthews's textbook on American literature (which strikes a note of "true Americanism" at the outset), Roosevelt's letters indicate that he took a direct interest in Matthews's American literature classes at Columbia. Matthews often sent Roosevelt copies of course syllabi and exams; and in 1891 Roosevelt even visited Matthews's class to lecture on the novels of James Fenimore Cooper (9 Nov. 1891). In 1900, Roosevelt, then governor of New York, lent his support to Matthews's successful attempt to secure the appointment of William P. Trent, founder of the *Sewanee Review*, to the Columbia English Department. When one considers that American literature during this period was generally deemed a "subject fit for women but not for serious male scholars," Roosevelt's and Matthews's strenuous efforts to establish American literature in the academy are all the more remarkable.[21]

Roosevelt's defeat in the election of 1912 ended his political but not his literary career; nor did he cease engaging in "literary politics" with Matthews. In 1913, for instance, Matthews, acting as president of the National Institute of Arts and Letters, appealed to Roosevelt to deliver the keynote address at the institute's convention. The topic was to be "The West in Literature." "Nobody but you," Matthews wrote, "can say [the things that need to be said] as they ought to be said" (19 Feb. 1913). Roosevelt was forced to decline that invitation. But in 1916 he joined in an effort, led by Matthews, to prevent the Authors' League of America from affiliating with the American Federation of Labor.[22] Literary organizations such as the National Institute, Matthews had assured President Roosevelt in 1902, could "wield influence on the right side."[23] For more than three decades, the literary-minded politician and the politically minded professor often collaborated, publicly and privately, to ensure that American literature and literary criticism would promote what they perceived to be the "right side"; and the actions of these two "progressives" did indeed often place them on the right, or conservative, side of the political fence.

Thus, in addition to casting new light on Roosevelt, especially in his role of "literary feller," and on his remarkable friendship with Matthews, the letters in this volume demonstrate in fascinating detail that literature and politics were as inextricably connected in America a century ago as they are today.

NOTES

1. Theodore Roosevelt, *The Works of Theodore Roosevelt: National Edition*, ed. Hermann Hagedorn (New York: Scribner's, 1926), 13:17.
2. Daniel Aaron, "Theodore Roosevelt as Cultural Artifact," *Raritan* 9 (Winter 1990): 113.
3. After his death, articles eulogizing Roosevelt usually emphasized, visually as well as verbally, the image of Roosevelt the Hunter-Soldier. Hamlin

Garland's tribute, "Theodore Roosevelt," in *The Mentor* (2 Feb. 1920, 1–20), for example, includes a full-page photograph of Roosevelt in cowboy garb, packing a pistol; and another of him in his Rough Rider uniform, mounted on his horse. For a photograph of Deputy Sheriff Roosevelt, rifle in hand, standing guard over thieves he had captured, see Edmund Morris, *The Rise of Theodore Roosevelt* (New York: Coward, McCann and Geoghegan, 1979), 318.

4. Quoted in Aaron, "Theodore Roosevelt," iii.

5. See Lawrence J. Oliver, *Brander Matthews, Theodore Roosevelt, and the Politics of American Literature, 1880–1920* (Knoxville: Univ. of Tennessee Press, 1992).

6. Brander Matthews, *These Many Years: Recollections of a New Yorker* (New York: Scribner's, 1917), 7.

7. Clayton Hamilton, "Brander," *Scribner's Magazine* 86 (July–Dec. 1929): 85.

8. "On the Republican Party," *New York Times,* 12 Nov. 1884, 5.

9. On Roosevelt's early literary career, see Morris, *Rise of Theodore Roosevelt,* 368–93; and Aloysius A. Norton, *Theodore Roosevelt* (Boston: Twayne, 1980), 24–31. Norton notes that Matthews "aided greatly in [Roosevelt's] development as an author" (28).

10. Roosevelt, *Works,* 10:359.

11. [Matthews], "New York as a Historic Town," *Century Magazine* 41 (Jan. 1891): 476–77.

12. Roosevelt to Matthews, 1 Jan. 1891. References to subsequent letters in this volume will appear parenthetically within the text.

13. Quoted in Roosevelt, *Works,* 10:347.

14. Matthews, reviews of Roosevelt's *Theodore Roosevelt* and *History as Literature,* in *Bookman* 38 (Dec. 1913): 418–22.

15. Matthews, "Roosevelt as a Practical Politician," *Outlook,* 16 July 1919, 433–35; "Theodore Roosevelt," in *Commemorative Tributes of the American Academy of Arts and Letters, 1905–1941* (1942; rpt. ed. Freeport, N.Y.: Books for Libraries Press, 1968), 110–15; review of Joseph Bishop's *Theodore Roosevelt and His Time,* in *New York Times,* 3 Oct. 1920, sec. 3; "Theodore Roosevelt as a Man of Letters," *Munsey's Magazine* (Mar. 1919; rpt. in Roosevelt, *Works,* 12: ix–xx).

16. John M. Blum, "A Note on Method and Materials," *The Letters of Theodore Roosevelt,* ed. Elting E. Morison et al. (Cambridge, Mass.: Harvard Univ. Press, 1954), 8:1499.

17. Joseph B. Gilder, "A Man of Letters in the White House," *Critic* 29 (1901): 405.

18. Roosevelt, *Works,* 12:292.

19. John W. Burgess, "Germany, Great Britain, and the United States," *Political Science Quarterly* 19 (1904): 1–19.

20. Franklin H. Giddings, *Democracy and Empire* (New York: Macmillan, 1900), v; "The American People," *International Quarterly* 7 (June 1903): 281–99.

21. Elizabeth Renker, "Resistance and Change: The Rise of American Literature Studies," *American Literature* 64 (June 1992): 352.

22. See Oliver, *Brander Matthews*, 175–77.

23. Matthews to Roosevelt's secretary, 26 Apr. 1902, Theodore Roosevelt Papers.

Editorial Statement

This edition includes the complete texts of nearly all extant correspondence between Roosevelt and Matthews. I have not included the roughly thirty invitations, thank-you notes, and other less significant missives contained in the two major repositories of the two men's papers: the Brander Matthews Papers, Rare Book and Manuscript Library, Columbia University; and the Theodore Roosevelt Papers, Library of Congress. Texts of the letters in this edition were transcribed from microfilm of the holographs in the Matthews Papers and of holographs or carbon copies in the Roosevelt Papers. The location of the source letter, along with information regarding its number of pages, form, and previous publication, appears at the foot of the printed text of each letter in this edition, after the signature or postscript. A key to the symbols and abbreviations used in the source notes and annotations is provided below.

I have kept emendations to a minimum. Thus I have not corrected misspelled words, errors in punctuation and grammar, unconventional capitalization, idiosyncratic usages, and so on. Special note should be made of Roosevelt's and Matthews's unorthodox spelling practices. Like many progressivists, Roosevelt and Matthews were advocates of the "simplified spelling movement" of their day, and they therefore often employed simplified spellings (e.g., "thru" for "through") in their letters.

I have departed from the general rule of reproducing the text verbatim, however, by silently emending obvious slips of the pen, such as the repetition of a word ("and and") and typographical errors ("Bradner"). I have also silently inserted end punctuation where omitted, and have deleted from the transcription canceled versions of a word or phrase. If, however, the canceled word(s) seems significant—if, for example, the cancellation reflects a substantive change in the author's thought—I record the canceled word(s) in a footnote.

Where I have encountered difficulty deciphering a word or phrase, I have enclosed it in brackets with a question mark; completely illegible words are indicated by a bracketed question mark. All above-line insertions have been brought down to the printed line. The format of the letters has been standarized. Thus, placement of headings, salutations, paragraph indentations, complimentary closings, signatures, and postscripts have been regularized. I have not included inside addresses.

When Matthews did not use letterhead stationery and handwrote the return address, he capitalized only the first letter of each word; thus letters within bearing the shortened heading "681 West End Avenue" (as opposed to "681 WEST END AVENUE") indicate that the return address was handwritten rather than printed.

Letters are arranged chronologically. Several holographs bear the month and day but not the year in which they were written; where I have been able to determine the year with certainty, I have placed the letter in its appropriate chronological location in this edition and have enclosed the inserted year in brackets (e.g., July 12th [1890]). Letters for which I could not with confidence assign a date are placed in the "Undated" section following the final dated letter.

I have made every effort to identify the myriad references in the letters to people, events, and publications, and to provide necessary contextual information. In cases where I was unable to identify someone or something, or where the identification provided is conjectural, I have so indicated. I have aimed to make the explanatory notes informational rather than interpretive.

Sources cited frequently in the annotations are referred to by the author's last name (except when two authors have the same last name, in which case the first name is included) and short title of the work. The author's full name and the work's complete title and bibliographical information may be found in the bibliography.

Abbreviations

SAGAMORE HILL for
SAGAMORE HILL
OYSTER BAY,
LONG ISLAND, N.Y.

CIVIL SERVICE COMMISSION for
United States
Civil Service Commission,
Washington, D.C.

POLICE DEPARTMENT for
Police Department,
of the City of New York,
300 Mulberry Street,
New York,

NAVY DEPARTMENT for
NAVY DEPARTMENT,
WASHINGTON.

EXECUTIVE CHAMBER for
STATE OF NEW YORK
EXECUTIVE CHAMBER
ALBANY

EXECUTIVE MANSION for
EXECUTIVE MANSION,
WASHINGTON.

WHITE HOUSE for
WHITE HOUSE,
WASHINGTON.

The Outlook for

The Outlook
287 Fourth Avenue
New York

THE KANSAS CITY STAR for
THE KANSAS CITY STAR
New York Office
347 Madison Avenue

HEADINGS FOR MATTHEWS'S LETTERHEAD STATIONERY

681 WEST END AVENUE for
681 WEST END AVENUE,
N. W. CORNER 93rd ST.
NEW YORK.

337 WEST 87TH STREET for
337 WEST 87TH STREET
NEW YORK

NARRAGANSETT PIER for
SHINGLENOOK,
NARRAGANSETT PIER, R.I.

SOURCE NOTES AND ANNOTATIONS

als.	autograph letter, signed
ans.	autograph note, signed
apcs.	autograph postcard, signed
BM	Brander Matthews
BMP	Brander Matthews Papers
cc.	carbon copy, unsigned
ccs.	carbon copy, signed
LTR	*The Letters of Theodore Roosevelt*
pbd.	published
tls.	typed letter, signed
TR	Theodore Roosevelt
TRP	Theodore Roosevelt Papers
Works	*The Works of Theodore Roosevelt: National Edition*

CORRESPONDENCE

1888–1890

Headers for correspondence will read simply "To Matthews" or "To Roosevelt." Matthews's letters to Roosevelt prior to 15 Apr. 1900 have been lost.

To Matthews

HOTEL RYAN.
ST. PAUL, MINN.,
Oct 1st 1888[1]

My dear Matthews,

Being out on the range I have just received your very kind note; the first lull there comes in this blessed campaign, into which I find myself plunged head first the second I get out of the wilds, I shall call on you to thank you, for I presume it is to you that I owe the offer.[2] I should like much to do the work; and will undertake it with pleasure if a little lee way is allowed me to finish up some matters which I *must* get through first. I appreciate your kindness in the matter very much, I assure you— and I can answer for it that Lodge does to.[3]

Remember me to Mrs Matthews.[4]

Very sincerely yours
Theodore Roosevelt

BMP; 2 pp.; als.; pbd. *LTR*, 1:147.

1. TR by this time had become a well-known Republican politician on the national as well as the New York state political scene. He had spent three terms in the New York State Assembly (1882–84) and had served as a delegate to the 1884 Republican National Convention. After the sudden death of his first wife, Alice Hathaway Lee, and his mother in 1884, he bought a ranch in the Dakota territory and left politics behind for two years. In 1886 he returned to New York City to run for mayor, losing the election after a strong campaign.

   As the presidential contest of 1888 between Democratic incumbent Grover Cleveland (1837–1908) and Republican candidate Benjamin Harrison (1833–1901) was heating up, TR was on a hunting trip out west (from 21 Aug. to 5 Oct.). See next letter.

2. TR is responding to BM's offer to write a history of New York City for the American Historic Towns series being published by the American branch

of Longmans, Green, and Co., to which BM was literary advisor. Though TR was struggling to complete the first volume of *The Winning of the West* (his sixth book), under contract with G. P. Putnam's Sons, he accepted the offer.

    New York was published in 1891, TR noting in the preface that BM "indeed is responsible for my undertaking to write the book at all" (TR, *Works*, 10:359; see also BM's remarks quoted in *Works*, 10:347).

3. Henry Cabot Lodge (1850–1924), TR's intimate friend and staunch political ally in Republican Party causes. At the same time he solicited the history of New York from TR, BM had invited Lodge to write a history of Boston. Lodge accepted, and *Boston* was published by Longmans, Green in the same year as *New York*. Lodge and BM remained friends and correspondents; the BMP contain many letters from Lodge to BM.

4. Ada Smith Matthews (d. 1924). Daughter of a London physician, she was a successful London actress (under the stage name Ada Harland) when she met BM; she gave up her career to become his wife in 1873. According to Clayton Hamilton, a close friend of BM and Ada, the two were devoted to one another throughout their more than 50 years of marriage ("Brander," *Scribner's Magazine* 86 [July 1929]: 85). Curiously, BM makes but one reference to Ada in his autobiography (*Years*, 153).

To Matthews

Sagamore Hill
Oct 5th 88

My dear Matthews,

    Just a line to acknowledge your last note; I am now about to plunge into the campaign (mind you, however, I'm a "literary feller," not a politician, nowadays).[1] As soon as I get a spare hour I shall call on you; I want to express my acknowledgements in person; and there are several things I would like to talk over with you.

Yours sincerely
Theodore Roosevelt

BMP; 2 pp.; ans.

1. Despite his heavy literary commitments, TR embarked (on 7 Oct.) on a speaking tour of Illinois, Michigan, and Minnesota on behalf of Harrison. After his election, President Harrison appointed TR to the U.S. Civil Service Commission, TR assuming his duties in May 1889.

To Matthews

Civil Service Commission
July 31, 1889.

Dear Matthews,—

O, you Mugwumps![1] The way you go and arrogate all virtue to your-selves is enough to exasperate an humble party man like myself. Here am I, feebly trying to do my duty, threatened with overwhelming disaster by my own party men, who, as the last bitterest term of reproach, accuse me of being a mugwump; and now you want to join in and help foster the de-lusion. By the way, if you see our good friend Bunner,[2] give him the love of the "Bob-tailed" statesman.[3] Seriously, I have pretty hard work, and work of rather an irritating kind; but I am delighted to be engaged in it. For the last few years politics with me has been largely a balanc-ing of evils, and I am delighted to go in on a side where I have no doubt whatever, and feel absolutely certain that my efforts are wholly for the good; and you can guarantee I intend to hew to the line, and let the chips fly where they will. Just yesterday, in a brief interval of battling with the spoilsmen, I strolled into a club-room here—glad to get anywhere out of the Washington streets—and picked up a copy of Scribner's. As soon as I saw your article, I knew that you had written the piece about which you spoke to me two years ago.[4] On reading it, I was electrified when I struck the name of the fort. It may be prejudice on my part, but I really think it is one of the best of your stories, and I am very glad to have my name connected with it in no matter how small a way. I congratulate you on it very sincerely. Much obliged for the information about Emmetts book.[5] It has been wholly impossible for me to work at the volume on New York this summer as I had in-tended, but in the fall I shall take it up, and then I will get you to put me in the way of getting Emmetts volume of illustrations and documents.

I am going to spend six weeks after the 5th of August out West among the bears and cow-boys, as I think I have fairly earned a holiday.

Faithfully yours,
Theodore Roosevelt

BMP; 2 pp.; tls.; pbd. *LTR*, 1:177.

1. In 1884, reform-minded Republicans who were outraged by their party's nomination of the corrupt James G. Blaine for president broke ranks and threw their support to the Democratic nominee, Grover Cleveland, helping elect him. Loyal Republicans labeled the independents "mugwumps," a de-risive term for an arrogant, self-righteous person, a "boss." But as BM ex-plains in an essay (directed at a British audience) published shortly after the 1884 election, the term derives from the Algonquin word *mugquomp*, "great man" ("Mugwumps," *Saturday Review* [London] 58 [24 Nov. 1884]: 658–59).

To BM, the mugwumps were indeed "great men" who were leading the fight to purify a corrupt political system. TR initially opposed the nomination of Blaine, but (like Cabot Lodge) refused to join the mugwump revolt; many mugwumps therefore heaped contempt upon TR, who in turn became their bitter adversary. But TR's campaign against the spoils system during his six years as Civil Service Commissioner led some Republicans, most notably Postmaster General John Wanamaker, to accuse him of betraying the party and of engaging in mugwumpery. (See Morris, *Rise,* 247–68, 395–427.) In this letter TR apparently is responding to BM's suggestion that TR was a mugwump, or independent, at heart.

2. Henry Cuyler Bunner (1855–1896). Poet, critic, and editor (from 1878 until his death) of *Puck,* the first comic magazine to establish itself in the United States. The sharp-witted Bunner and BM were intimate friends, and they co-authored several short stories (see *Years,* 175–82). After Bunner's death, BM edited *The Poems of H. C. Bunner* (New York: Scribner's, 1896) and helped establish the H. C. Bunner Medal at Columbia. TR was equally fond of Bunner and frequently socialized with him and BM.

3. What TR means by the "Bob-tailed statesman" remark is unclear. The comment might refer in some way to BM's story "In a Bob-Tail Car," in BM, *A Family Tree and Other Stories* (New York: Longmans, Green, 1889), 209–19. Referring to the popular horse-drawn trams of the day, one of the story's characters remarks that a "bob-tail car is like a policeman; it is never here just when it is wanted. And yet it is a necessary evil—like the policeman again" (210).

4. BM, "Memories," *Scribner's Magazine* 6 (Aug. 1889): 168–75. Set at a fictional Fort Roosevelt, the story centers on an army officer who puts aside personal grief when duty calls. The piece is a veiled tribute to TR (see Oliver, *Brander Matthews,* 35–36).

5. Most likely Mary Louise Booth's *History of the City of New York* (1876), which TR cites in his preface to *New York* (*Works,* 1:359). Booth's was one of three multivolume histories of New York City in the private collection of Dr. Thomas Addis Emmet (1828–1919), a New York physician, historian, and bibliophile; Emmet added hundreds of original documents and illustrations to the histories, which he later (in 1896) donated to the New York Public Library. Melanie Yolles, manuscripts specialist at the New York Public Library, has noted that since the value of these histories "lay in the illustrative matter rather than in the text," they were considered works by Emmet (letter to editor, 26 Aug. 1992).

To Matthews

Civil Service Commission
Nov 7th 89

My dear Matthews,

I have just returned from a visit home (Oyster Bay, Long Island), where another small son and heir had arrived; and so I have but now received your letter.[1]

I most sincerely wish it were in my power to accept your very kind invitation, but next week we will have our hands full in prosecuting a case of political assessments (on the part of a Mahone Republican Club—you see me now with an impartial scythe); and to my great regret I can not leave.[2] If Mr. Longman comes to Washington be sure to [give?] him a line to me.[3]

I am going to be in New York for a flying visit on or about the 2d and 3d of December; can't we arrange to lunch together somewhere at that time? If convenient, I will write you as soon as I find out definitely the days I will be there. We will get Gilder too.[4]

Remember me warmly to Mrs. Matthews; and, with much regret, I am

Very sincerely yours
Theodore Roosevelt

BMP; 3 pp.; als.

1. Kermit Roosevelt, TR's second son, was born (prematurely) on 10 Oct. 1889.
2. William Mahone (1826–95) controlled the patronage of Virginia during the Harrison administration. TR's "scythe" was less sharp than he believed; the Civil Service Commission's attempts to prosecute the powerful Republican boss for illegal political assessments proved futile. See LTR, 1:201.
3. Probably Charles James Longman (1852–1934), member of Longmans, Green publishing house (see TR to BM, 1 Oct. 1888, n. 2). There is correspondence between him and BM in the BMP.
4. Richard Watson Gilder (1844–1909); the influential author, critic, and editor of the *Century Magazine* (1881–1909) was a close friend of both TR and BM, each of whom published in the *Century*.

To Matthews

Civil Service Commission
Dec 29th 89

Dear Matthews,

Many thanks for the America; I liked the review, for I like America, though I think it much too cranky.[1] I shall "peddle out" the pamphlets so as to most effectually corrupt our intelligent representatives at Washington.² I shall be back, to finish my investigation, on Jan 9th & 10th, and if I can get a moment will be in to see you.

Do you know where I can get both the numbers of Longmans—Lang's & yours?³ It wasn't in the Union League Club.⁴

Yours always
Theodore Roosevelt

BMP; 2 pp.; als.

1. The review (of a book concerned with American culture?) has not been identified. TR often found his fellow Americans to be "cranky" about social and political issues.

2. The pamphlets are probably BM's *Cheap Books and Good Books* (1888) and *American Authors and British Pirates* (1889), both published by the American Copyright League. As subsequent letters show, BM and TR were deeply engaged in the literary-political campaign for an international copyright act that would protect American authors from foreign book pirates; such protection, they believed, would not only profit individual authors but would spur the development of American literature. BM helped establish the American Copyright League in 1883, and he chaired the subcommittee on publicity. A member of the league, TR promoted BM's pamphlets and essays on copyright among members of Congress. The league's lobbying was ultimately successful; in 1891, Congress passed the Platt-Simmonds Act, generally referred to as the Copyright Act of 1891, a momentous event in American publishing history. See Oliver, *Brander Matthews*, 128–36.

3. Andrew Lang (1844–1912), Scotch critic, poet, essayist, and anthropologist. BM's "The Dramatization of Novels" appears in *Longman's Magazine* 14 (Oct. 1889): 588–603, his only essay in that magazine during 1889. In the next number, Lang, who had a regular column in *Longman's* titled "At the Sign of the Ship," took some friendly jabs at BM ("At the Sign of the Ship," *Longman's Magazine* 15 [Nov. 1889]: 109–110; see TR to BM, 10 Feb. 1890, n. 1). Though BM and TR often disagreed with Lang's opinions on American literature and culture, they greatly respected his literary talents; BM in fact considered him to be the "most versatile, the most fecund, and the most learned" of all his friends (*Years*, 263).

4. In 1863, Frederick Law Olmsted (1822–1903), the civic-minded designer of New York's Central Park and other municipal, state, and national parks and historical sites, established the Loyalist Club, the name later being changed to the Union League Club. Olmsted and the other founders aimed to unite influential men who were loyal to the Union and who supported emancipation of slaves. During the Gilded Age, the Union League Club was a favorite meeting place for the metropolitan gentry.

To Matthews

Civil Service Commission
Jan 13th 90

Dear Matthews,

First, I have been doing all I could to get Lodge for you; but I do'n't think he will come. He is not in the humour for much public speaking at this moment; and he is especially unwilling to talk about elections in the south in view of the action on his bill in the senate.[1] He does not feel that, under the circumstances, he would make a speech that would satisfy himself or you. What do you think of trying Murat Halstead in his place? Halstead has always made rather a specialty of the southern situation, from an extreme anti-southern standpoint.[2]

Next, I think you have written a really admirable article on the evolution of copyright; I wish that your different articles on the subject could be bound into one volume.[3] Our friends have injured their cause, in many cases, by their curiously unintelligent deification of the English attitude on the subject.[4] The truth is that at present while France is civilised in her position about copyright, the English are Barbarians, and we Americans downright savages. To me the worst practical effect of our conduct is the effect it has in perpetuating our condition of literary servitude.

Yours in haste
Theodore Roosevelt

BMP; 4 pp.; als.; pbd. *LTR*, 1:213.

1. As subsequent letters make clear, BM tried unsuccessfully to recruit Lodge to speak on the "Southern problem" to the Nineteenth Century Club. At this time, TR was a member and BM was the vice-president of the club, which had been founded in 1882 to stimulate debate on current topics of importance (see *Years*, 235–41). Lodge was in poor humor because the Senate recently had defeated the Federal Elections Bill of 1890, often referred to as the "Force Bill," which Lodge had introduced into the House. Designed to insure fair elections—especially in the South, where blacks had been disenfranchised—the bill was defeated by southern senators and by their northern colleagues who were willing to sacrifice blacks' rights in order to maintain peaceful relations with the South. See John G. Sproat, *"The Best Men": Liberal Reformers in the Gilded Age* (New York: Oxford Univ. Press, 1968), 41–42.

2. A staunch Republican and influential newspaper editor from Ohio, Murat Halstead (1829–1908) blamed the South for the Civil War and also for the racial problems besetting the region in his own day. See, e.g., his assault on "Southern pride and prejudice" in "The Revival of Sectionalism," *North American Review* 140 (Mar. 1885): 237–50. Halstead did not address the Nineteenth Century Club; but Col. Charles H. Jones, editor of the St. Louis *Re-*

public, did on 17 Mar. 1891. Entitled "The South and Its Problems," his speech was decidedly pro-southern; he condemned the Reconstruction policies of the Republican Party and advised the North not to interfere in the "race problem" ("The South and Its Problems," *New York Times,* 18 Mar. 1891, p. 2).

3. BM apparently sent TR the manuscript of "The Evolution of Copyright," which later appeared in the *Political Science Quarterly* 5 (Dec. 1890): 583–602. BM never gathered his several essays on the copyright issue into a volume, but he did include "Evolution" in his collection of essays *Books and Play-Books* (1895). In addition to tracing the history of copyright law from ancient times to 1890, the article makes a strong case for an international copyright act.

4. TR may have in mind their mutual friend Mark Twain, who, when asked by BM in 1887 to aid in the fight for an international copyright act, astonished BM by publishing an article in the *New Princeton Review,* which argued that existing British copyright law sufficiently protected American authors. BM's compelling response to Twain, in the same journal, caused a breach in their friendship for several years. The curious affair is detailed in Oliver, *Brander Matthews,* 130–33.

To MATTHEWS

Civil Service Commission
Feb 10th '90

Dear Matthews,

You evidently touched friend Andrew on the raw; but I wish your counter stroke had not been suppressed. I was looking forward to it.[1]

Work is progressing slowly but steadily on the "New York". It is about a quarter through. I find that I have got to make it sketchy to get it into the limits; and really so far I have done more rejecting than accepting material. There is some original matter which I should like to use, but can't, because it would make the book lopsided. Don't you find it harder to write when you have to condense? I knew about Adam's "Chapter of Erie", but I am much obliged to you for the hints about Parton and the Mag. of Am. Hist for '82.[2] I am not altogether satisfied with my work on the book. I have to do it at odd times, in the midst of the press of this civil service business; and so I do'n't feel atall that I can do the subject justice.

Can't you get down here some time this winter? I would like you to see some of our "men of action" in congress. They are not always polished, but they are strong, and as a whole I think them pretty good fellows. I swear by Tom Reed; and I tell you what, all copyright men ought to stand by him.[3] No one man can filibuster and beat a bill now.

A house may do well or ill; but at least it can do *something* under the new dispensation. Besides, I am tired of flabbiness, and I am glad to see a Republican of virility, who really does something![4] There is no great hardship in refusing to entertain purely filibustering and dilatory motions and in counting a man as present when he is present, even if he is at the moment howling out that he is "constructively" absent.

> Warm regards to Madame
>> Yrs faithfully
>> Theodore Roosevelt

BMP; 4 pp.; als.; pbd. *LTR*, 1:213–14.

1. Most likely Lang's good-humored attack on BM in the *Longman's Magazine* number that TR mentions in his letter of 29 Dec. 1889. Wrote Lang:

> Mr. Brander Matthews, in an article on Cooper in the *Century* [Sept. 1889, 796–98], admits that British criticism was once "even more ignorant and insular than it is to-day." This is a comfort. We are advancing. In the same essay Mr. Matthews remarks that Cooper was the first author who introduced the Red Man to literature. In my insular ignorance I had conceived that one Chateaubriand . . . did not wholly neglect the noble savage. To deny that the works of Chateaubriand are literature, or that *Atala* is prior to the *Pioneers* and the *Last of the Mohicans,* appears to be Mr. Matthews's best means of proving his point. . . . Is that a fair hit, O Accuser of the Brethren? *Touché?* ("At the Sign of the Ship," *Longman's Magazine* 15 [Nov. 1889]: 109)

The *Critic* contains no "counter stroke" by BM. BM, however, did continue the discussion with Lang in their personal correspondence. In a letter dated 18 Feb. [1890], Lang remarks that he "lost your note on Chateaubriand &c"; then, after discussing the merits and faults of several British and American critics, he asserts that "our people are not *more* ignorant of [classical literatures] than yours." Lang also suggests that "one can't discuss these personal things in a magazine" (*Friends over the Ocean: Andrew Lang's American Correspondents, 1881–1912,* ed. Marysa Demoor [Riksuniversiteit Gent, 1989], 103–4).

2. Charles Francis Adams's *A Chapter of Erie* (Boston: Fields, Osgood, 1869) details the takeover of the Erie railroad by unscrupulous investors. James Parton's *Topics of the Time* (Boston: Osgood, 1871) is a collection of essays on sundry topics, including "The Government of the City of New York" (350–401), a caustic exposé of the city's spoils system around 1866. TR cites both books in his preface to *New York* (*Works*, 10:359). His preface does not refer to the *Magazine of American History*, but the 1882 volume (vol. 8) contains several articles on New York history that TR would have found useful, including John Franklin Jameson's "The Origin and Development of Municipal Government of New York City" (315–30, 598–611).

3. Thomas Brackett Reed (1839–1919), Republican congressman from Maine and then Speaker of the House. According to BM, Reed did not become a staunch supporter of the copyright cause until reading BM's "The Evolution of Copyright," which TR gave to him (*Years,* 227–28).

4. Reed (who was 6'2" and weighed 300 pounds) was a strong-willed, domineering Speaker; TR refers here to Reed's historic ruling prohibiting congressmen who were on the floor from being counted absent if they did not want to vote on a bill (Morris, *Rise,* 414–15).

To Matthews

Civil Service Commission
April 14th '90

My dear Matthews,

Well hit! I think you touched our friend Lang on the raw. He is a good fellow, evidently; but as you said he is himself a funny illustration of uneasy, sensitive irritation with american criticism.[1] I think the Saturday Review's comment on the "Queen of Sheba" was delicious; I had never seen it before.[2] Langs very list of ten English critics struck my untutored sense as provincial.[3]

But in view of the present temper of Congress towards copyright, a navy, and indeed most things, I do'n't feel inclined to take too high a position.[4] I wish you would write a scathing article in the forum at the proper time holding up *by name* the chief congressional foes of copyright to merited ridicule.[5] You could find rich reading in their speeches.

Remember me to Mrs Matthews
Yours in great haste
Theodore Roosevelt

BMP; 2 pp.; als.; pbd. *LTR,* 1:216.

1. TR refers to BM's "Ignorance and Insularity," first published in *The Independent* on 10 Apr. 1890 and later included in *Americanisms and Briticisms* (103–13). The essay chastises Lang and other British critics for their supercilious attitude toward American critics. At one point in the essay, BM alludes to TR's rebuke of a British general who uttered a "blundering laudation" of Robert E. Lee (*Americanisms and Briticisms,* 105). BM emphasizes Lang's oversensitivity toward American criticism in his 1894 essay "Mr. Andrew Lang" (see TR to BM, 31 Dec. 1893).

2. In "Ignorance and Insularity," BM mentions (but does not identify) a *Saturday Review* review of Thomas Bailey Aldrich's novel *Queen of Sheba* (1877), in which the British reviewer mistakenly refers to the work as a poem. BM cites the incident as being illustrative of British critics' "willingness to con-

demn without knowledge and without any effort to acquire knowledge" (*Americanisms and Briticisms,* 109–10).

3. In "Critics and Criticism," *The Independent,* 27 Mar. 1890, 4–5, Lang cites John Ruskin, Walter Pater, Robert Louis Stevenson, George Saintsbury, Algernon Swinburne, Leslie Stephen, Frederic Harrison, Robertson Smith, Theodore Watts, and John Addington Symonds as examples of astute British literary critics. BM finds fault with Lang's "oddly chosen" list in "Ignorance and Insularity" (*Americanisms and Briticisms,* 111).

4. A staunch advocate of American naval expansion, TR, who would become assistant secretary of the navy in 1897, was disappointed by the naval appropriations bill recently passed by the House of Representatives: the Navy Department had requested eight new battleships and several smaller warships, but the House voted to fund construction of a single cruiser. See "Naval Intelligence," *New York Times,* 1 Apr. 1890, 5, and "The Montana Senators," *New York Times,* 11 Apr. 1890, 1.

5. BM ignored this suggestion from his pugnacious friend, for he never published such an article.

To Matthews

Civil Service Commission
April 28th '90

My dear Matthews,
Of course I had a most pleasant lunch at the Players Club with you; it goes without saying.[1]
I now requite your hospitality by an act of baseness. I send you copies of two speeches I recently made in Cambridge and Chicago; of the one concerning "Americanism" I am really quite proud.[2] I hope Mrs Matthews is all well now

Yours always
Theodore Roosevelt

BMP; 1 p.; als.

1. Founded in 1889 by the great American actor Edwin Booth (1833–93), the Players Club, located at 16 Gramercy Park, New York City, was a favorite meeting place for actors, dramatists, writers, and artists. BM was a member of the club's organizing committee, as was Mark Twain (see *Years,* 367–68).

2. TR delivered an address entitled "True Americanism" at the Marquette Club in Chicago on 25 Mar. 1890. He often lectured on the topic, and he later published a revised version of the fiercely nationalistic and somewhat xenophobic essay in the Apr. 1894 number of the *Forum* (*Works,* 13:13–26). Early in the Chicago address, TR, referring to the notorious Haymarket Square

affair of 1886 that resulted in the unjust executions of four anarchists, praised his audience for dealing severely with the "anarchist dynamite throwers" and expressed his hope that Chicagoans would deal equally severely with any future offenders; he cut this passage, however, for the published essay.

The Cambridge speech in question is probably "Public Life," delivered at Harvard on 11 Mar. 1890. The summary of the speech in the Harvard *Daily Crimson* 17 (12 Mar. 1890): 1, indicates that it was very similar to, if not exactly the same as, TR's "The College Graduate and Public Life," which appeared in the Aug. 1890 number of the *Atlantic Monthly* (rpt. in *Works*, 13:36–46).

To MATTHEWS

Civil Service Commission
May 3d '90

My dear Matthews,

You may be sure I will let you know whenever I get on to New York. I liked your memorial day article immensely by the way.[1]

I feel humiliated as an American citizen over the defeat of the copyright bill and the arguments by which it was brought about: I wish we could have some stinging attack on the congressmen who did it, naming their leaders; and *not* pitching in to those who stood by us.[2] Most of the leaders were for it, except Mills of Texas.[3] Carlisle and McKinley both supported it;[4] Lodge made the best speech in it's favor, quoting your pamphlets, by the way, with proper respect; Tom Reed has stood by us like a trump, and it was only through him that we got the bill up atall.[5]

In great haste.

Yours always
Theodore Roosevelt

BMP; 2 pp.; als.; pbd. *LTR*, 1:218.

1. "A Decoration Day Revery," *Century Magazine* 40 (May 1890):102–5. BM's reflective account of a Decoration Day parade in New York City pays tribute to the honored dead of the Civil War—and takes a swipe at "professional politicians of the baser sort" who exploit the occasion.
2. Supporters of an international copyright bill suffered a frustrating defeat in the House of Representatives on 2 May 1890; the opposition was led by Rep. Lewis R. Payson (1840–1909) of Illinois, who stalled passage by introducing a series of amendments.
3. Roger Quarles Mills (1832–1911), Democratic congressman and chair of the House Ways and Means Committee.
4. John Griffin Carlisle (1835–1910), Democratic Speaker of the House; William

McKinley (1843–1901), whom TR would succeed as president in 1901, was a Republican congressman (Ohio) and majority leader of the House at this time.

5. See TR to BM, 29 Dec. 1889, n. 2.

To Matthews

Civil Service Commission
June 20, 1890.

Dear Matthews:

All right; I will speak in December.[1] I think you had better write O'Reilley at once.[2] How would the editor of the Staats Zeitung do for a German?[3] If that is a poor suggestion could not the Puck people give you a proper idea? You could hold Coudert[4] and Boyeson[5] in reserve.

Present my warm regards to Mrs. Matthews. I shall stay here most of the summer, with occasional visits to my family at Oyster Bay, who are all well.

Yours always,
Theodore Roosevelt

BMP; 1 p.; tls.

1. As the letter of 21 Nov. 1890 below indicates, TR accepted BM's invitation to speak at the Nineteenth Century Club. On the evening of 18 Dec. 1890, TR delivered the lecture (at the Metropolitan Opera House) on the subject of "Americanism in Politics." The *New York Times's* detailed summary of the speech indicates that TR expressed a theme that he would repeat in "True Americanism" (*Works*, 13:13–26) and other writings: namely, that immigrants must abandon allegiance to their ethnic cultures and become 100% American in spirit, character, and patriotism ("But One Kind of American," *New York Times*, 19 Dec. 1890, 5). The *Times* account also notes that TR had been asked (probably by BM) to "invite some typical foreigners in Congress" to be co-speakers, but TR could not oblige because all the congressmen he knew were, despite their ethnic surnames, "straight Americans." TR in this letter is suggesting the names of foreign-born Americans who might join him in addressing the club on the topic of Americanism. In his speech to the club, TR singled out O'Reilly and Boyesen (identified below) as examples of immigrants who had become completely assimilated into the American melting pot; and he remarked that he would prefer either man to the novelist Henry James (1843–1916), whom TR despised for becoming an expatriate. See TR to BM, 1 Jan. 1891.

2. John Boyle O'Reilly (1844–90). Born in Ireland, O'Reilly was imprisoned as a young man for being a Fenian. After escaping, he made his way to the United States (in 1869), where he soon became a popular poet. The patriotic themes of such poems as "The Pilgrim Fathers" (which O'Reilly delivered at

the dedication of the national monument at Plymouth on 1 Aug. 1889) would have appealed to TR. As the next letter indicates, however, O'Reilly rejected the invitation to join the panel because he assumed that TR's speech on 100% Americanism would offend Irish-Americans.

3. See next letter, n. 1.

4. Frederic Rene Coudert (1832–1903), expert in international law and founder of one of New York City's most reputable law firms. When TR addressed the Nineteenth Century Club on the "Spirit of Republicanism" on 11 Nov. 1884, Coudert had been one of the respondents.

5. Professor of German at Columbia University (1880–95), novelist, and critic, Hjalmar Hjorth Boyesen (1848–95), a Norwegian immigrant, was one of the era's staunchest advocates of literary realism, especially of Henrik Ibsen's drama. On 10 Jan. 1890, he had addressed the Nineteenth Century Club on the topic of Russian novelists (*New York Times,* 11 Jan. 1890, 5).

To Matthews

SAGAMORE HILL

July 12th [1890]

Dear Matthews,

How about Ottendorfer?[1] The Hon. Herman Lehlbach of New Jersey, now in Congress, would be a good man.[2] But I am sorry we can't get Boyle O'Reilly. He must be a good fellow and he ought to come. He evidently misunderstands my position—I am going to speak as an *American,* without a prefix, whether that prefix be German, Irish or Native. I am going to single out some of my Irish and German colleagues in the legislature as being the very best types of Americanism. I want to insist only that American politics should be managed on American issues. Can't you write O'Reilly again? Tell him the way I am going to treat it; he may rest assured no good American citizen of Irish birth will have the least cause to feel offended at what I say. Or you can show him this letter.

If he wo'n't come, take a New York congressman—Dunphy is, I understand, a well educated man.[3]

You must have an awfully pleasant set at Onteora.[4] Meanwhile, I am writing Ammon—or *at* Ammon.[5]

Yours always
Theodore Roosevelt

BMP; 4 pp.; als.

1. Moravian immigrant Oswald Ottendorfer (1826–1900) was owner and editor of the New York *Staats-Zeitung,* the largest German-language newspaper in the country. He founded the German-American Reform Union, and was active in New York City reform politics and social organizations.

2. Herman Lehlbach (1845–1904), Republican congressman from New Jersey (1885–91). In his address to the Nineteenth Century Club, TR cited Lelhbach, a German immigrant, as one of the "straight Americans" in Congress.

3. John Edward Dunphy (1856–1926), prominent New York City attorney who served as the state's (Democratic) representative from 1889 to 1895; he was active in Irish-American organizations.

4. The Onteora Club, Tannersville, N.Y., where BM was vacationing.

5. Possibly John Henry Ammon (1840–1904), who headed the publishing department of Harper and Bros. in New York City (1885–1902); but this is conjecture, since the TRP contains no correspondence with any Ammon (or Ammons) during the 1880s or 1890s.

To Matthews

SAGAMORE HILL
Aug 3d '90

My dear Matthews,

It was really kind of you to write me; it showed an interest in my *very* commonplace little book which I need not say I thoroughly appreciate.[1]

I understand fully the force of your suggestion. The trouble is that if I make the chapter dealing with New York in the present—that is, for the past 40 years or there abouts—full in one respect, I must make it full in all, or have it asymetrical. I would much rather write a long, full essay on these forty years than on the two hundred and forty preceeding them; but I do not care to do so unless I write the whole truth, accordingly as I see it; and to do this would make the piece controversial in parts, and in other parts a statement of the reasons why I hold to certain beliefs. For instance, if I go into our development in charities etc I would like also to go a little at length into our political condition; and you can readily perceive the difficulty in the way here.

Again, as to our being a literary centre.[2] To me the clubs are only important by what they produce; and I wish to wait and see what they produce. Is it going to be only Saltus & Fawcett?[3] I would have to go into personalities if I touched on this. For instance I consider yourself and Stedman[4] and Howells[5] and the Century, Scribners & Harpers much more important in determining New Yorks place in letters than the Authors, the Players the Grolier etc.[6]

Nevertheless I think I shall add some pages on the lines you suggest. Again thanking you heartily and with warm regards to Mrs. Matthews, I am

Very cordially yours
Theodore Roosevelt

BMP; 4 pp.; als.; pbd. *LTR*, 1:229–30.

1. As the rest of the letter makes clear, BM had urged TR to expand the discussion of recent history in his "little book" on New York City, but TR was determined to keep the chapter (14) short; in the published *New York*, the chapter titled "Recent History: 1860–1890" runs fewer than 13 pages (*Works*, 10:527–39). In explaining his reasons for not wanting to develop the chapter more fully, TR may not have been entirely candid with BM, for in January he had written George Haven Putnam that the book had been "weighing over me like a nightmare for the past eighteen months," and in April he informed his elder sister Anna that he was hurrying to get the "accursed history of New York city" finished and off his mind (*LTR*, 1:211, 215).

2. In "The Future Literary Capital of the United States" (*Lippincott's Magazine* 37 [Jan.–June 1886]: 104–9) and several other writings, BM insisted that New York City was becoming the nation's literary capital. TR disagreed; in *New York* he emphasizes that, although the city could take pride in its literary culture, there was "no chance for New York to take an unquestioned leadership in all respects" (*Works*, 10:538). See TR to BM, 29 June 1894.

3. Edgar Evertson Saltus (1855–1921) and Edgar Fawcett (1847–1904); New York poets and novelists. BM expresses reserved praise for each writer in *Years* (179–80, 382), and TR lauds one of Fawcett's poems in a letter to Lodge (LTR, 1:185).

4. Edmund Clarence Stedman (1833–1908). One of New York's most respected poets, critics, and scholars, as well as a successful Wall Street stockbroker, Stedman was a close friend of BM and TR. His many books include *Victorian Poets* (1875), *Poets of America* (1885), and his co-edited 11-volume *Library of American Literature* (1888–90).

5. William Dean Howells (1837–1920), novelist, critic, and the era's most influential American champion of literary realism. Though not a New Yorker by birth, as the other writers TR mentions were, Howells recently had taken up residence there, and his novel *A Hazard of New Fortunes* (1890) focuses on the city's social and political problems. BM and Howells were intimate friends and literary allies until the latter's death. TR and Howells were on cordial terms at this point, but later in the decade ideological differences chilled their relationship (see Oliver, *Brander Matthews*, 91–102).

6. In his brief section in chapter 14 highlighting New York's cultural and literary life, TR does not mention any of the writers named in the letter, but he does acknowledge the Players and the Century clubs, as well as *Century*, *Scribner's*, and *Harper's* magazines; he also calls attention to the development of Columbia College into a respected academic institution (*Works*, 10:537). See TR to BM, 21 Nov. 1890.

To Matthews

Civil Service Commission
Oct 21st [1890]

Dear Matthews,

Wednesday at 1.30 you will surely see me. I thought the review of McAllister's book delicious.¹ Did you see, a few days ago, a really very funny editorial in the Tribune on the Brooklyn man who objected to Longfellow as an erotic poet?² It gave some expurgated passages from his poems, adapted to youth, which were very good.

I trust Mrs. M. did not suffer from the Barmecide feast.³

Yours always
Theodore Roosevelt

BMP; 2 pp.; als.

1. Samuel Ward McAllister (1827–1895), New York socialite and self-pro-claimed arbiter of Gilded-Age "high society." Status-minded New Yorkers yearned to be included in his list of the city's elite "Four Hundred" and to be invited to the "Patriarchs' Balls" he originated—lavish events hosted by the heads of the 25 families that formed the city's social aristocracy. His *Society as I Have Found It* (1890) is a mixture of self-aggrandizing reminiscences, rules of etiquette, advice on managing servants, and so on.

   The review that TR found "delicious" was very likely that which appeared, unsigned, in the 1 Nov. 1890 number of the *Critic* (214–15). Its ridiculing of the book is devastating (e.g., "for unconscious revelation of charac-ter, we can recall nothing equal to it since the Autobiography of Benvenuto Cellini") and so subtle that at least one reader completely missed the reviewer's irony (see *Critic*, 22 Nov. 1890, 249). The review's chastisement of McAllister for his slips in French grammar suggests that the piece might have been penned by BM, who reviewed books anonymously for the *Critic* and who may have sent an advance copy of this one to TR.

   In his speech to the Nineteenth Century Club on 18 Dec. 1890 (see TR to BM, 20 June 1890, n. 1), TR similarly disparaged the book, quipping that if McAllister's vision of American high society was accurate, then intelligent people had good reason to embrace radical Socialism (which TR, of course, fiercely opposed). BM cites TR's speech and takes a few shots of his own at McAllister's book in "Of Women's Novels," *Americanisms and Briticisms*, 173–74. TR's disdain for McAllister did not, however, prevent him and his wife Edith from attending several of the Patriarchs' Balls in the 1880s (Sylvia Jukes Morris, *Edith Kermit Roosevelt: Portrait of a First Lady* [1980; reprint ed. New York: Vintage, 1990], 66).

2. On 23 Sept. 1890, the *New-York Daily Tribune* reported (p. 3) that two Brook-lyn school principals, James Cusack and John Gallagher, had demanded that

the city's Board of Education ban Longfellow's "The Building of the Ship" and other of his poems from the classroom, on the grounds that they contained veiled sexual imagery that would corrupt young readers. The attempted censorship of Longfellow—which ultimately failed—stirred much controversy and was denounced not only by the *Tribune* but also by the *New York Times* (24 Sept. 1890, 4) and the *Critic* (27 Sept. 1890, 157). The *Tribune* editorial to which TR refers must be "Is Longfellow a Wicked Poet?" (28 Sept. 1890, 6). The anonymous author facetiously states that a censored edition of Longfellow's works will soon appear. Then follow several "offensive" passages with their expurgated substitutes. Regarding "The Building of the Ship," the central focus of the censorship dispute, the editorialist reports: "This poem as it stands calls the sea the bridegroom of the ship. It also deals with another couple composed of sentient beings, to wit, a young man who is evidently engaged to the shipbuilder's daughter, and that young lady. In the revision, the sea is spoken of as the grandfather of the ship, while the young lady—who is going out in the vessel on its initial voyage as a missionary to the Fiji Islands—is represented as being the elder sister, a good deal freckled but very good, of the young man" (6).

3. In *The Arabian Nights' Entertainment*, Barmecide gives a beggar a pretended feast (no food).

To MATTHEWS

1820 Jefferson Place
Washington [D.C.]
Nov 21st 90

My dear Matthews,

I find I may have to leave New York by the midnight train, on Thursday, the 18th, right after my 19th Century speech.[1] Would it be possible for you to have me to lunch on the 18th instead of the 19th? I am not willing to miss a lunch at your house if by bold suggestion I can avert the catastrophe!

Seriously, I know you will not have the least hesitancy in telling me if you cannot change the date.

I finally re-wrote my preface on the lines laid down in your advice to authors who wish to guide reviewers aright; and made my references to my friends general, but not specific.[2] I kept in what I said about Grant.[3]

Remember me warmly to Mrs. Matthews; Mrs. Roosevelt sends you both her regards.[4]

Yours sincerely
Theodore Roosevelt

Hurrah for Mayor Matthews![5]

BMP; 3 pp.; als.

1. See TR to BM, 20 June 1890, n. 1.
2. In his "The True Theory of the Preface," BM asserts that a preface is perhaps the most important part of a book, because it provides the author the opportunity to "furnish the unwitting critic a syllabus or a skeleton of the criticism" which the author desires (BM, *Pen and Ink* [New York: Longmans, Green, 1888], 50–66).
3. In his brief discussion of literature by New Yorkers in chapter 14 of *New York,* TR praises Ulysses S. Grant's memoirs as the "greatest piece of literary work which has been done in America, or indeed anywhere, of recent years" (*Works,* 10:537). Grant is the only author cited by name.
4. Edith Kermit Roosevelt (1861–1948), whom TR had married in 1886, two years after the death of his first wife, Alice Lee.
5. Nathan Matthews (1858–1927), a Harvard-educated attorney and reform Democrat, recently had received the Democratic nomination for mayor of Boston; he was elected on 9 Dec. 1890. He was respected by many Republicans because of his integrity and commitment to political reform.

To Matthews

1820 Jefferson Place
Washington D.C.
Dec 28th '90

Dear Matthews,

A merry Xmas (in the past) and a happy new year to you and yours! Our children fairly revelled in delight.

I enjoyed my Nineteenth Century experience much; and also, as usual, the lunch at your house. When I next come to New York I am going to have a lunch or dinner of my own, for you and Sturgis (whom I took a fancy to) and one or two others.[1] By the way I wish to have a little friendly sparring with you about French authors—in which I shall have the enormous advantage of not knowing anything of my subject.[2] This always gives one an almost impregnable position.

I'll try to get Lodge to come on; what chance of success I shall have I can not say. I am awaiting with anticipation the Jan. Century.[3]

Yours always
Theodore Roosevelt

BMP; 4 pp.; als.

1. Probably BM's friend Russell Sturgis (1836–1909), architect, critic, writer, and professor at the College of the City of New York. In 1873 TR's father had commissioned him to design the family's new mansion at 6 West 57th Street.

2. TR knew a good deal about contemporary French literature, but he would have been no match for BM, whose *The Theatres of Paris* (1880), *French Dramatists of the Nineteenth Century* (1881), and many essays on French writers had already established him as one of America's foremost experts on French literature. Perhaps TR wanted to spar about Émile Zola and other French naturalist writers, whom he detested; BM held a much more favorable opinion of Zola and his fellow naturalists (see Oliver, *Brander Matthews*, 84–86).

3. See next letter.

1891

To Matthews

1820 Jefferson Place
Washington D.C.
Jan 1st '91

My dear Matthews,

I have just read the editorial in the "Century"; and I need hardly say how much pleased I am with it, and how much I appreciate your kindness.[1] By no possibility could there have been a better introduction for the book—I can only hope it deserves it. The editorial touched on the very points I desired to see emphasized, and it appeared in the magazine which of all others I should have chosen. So I have cause to be greatly obliged to you.

I have been rather astonished at the apparent hit I made in my Nineteenth Century speech.[2] I continue to receive letters and newspapers from all over the country—Texas, Mississippi and California, for instance—commending it.

By the way, have you seen Howell's "Boy's Town"? It seems to me to be very good.[3]

With regards to Mrs Matthews, I am

Cordially yours
Theodore Roosevelt

BMP; 4 pp.; als.

1. BM's "New York as a Historic Town" appeared, unsigned, in *Century Magazine* 41 (Jan. 1891): 476–77. Though ostensibly an essay on New York City, the piece is actually a flattering review of TR's recently published history of New York, which BM had, as earlier noted, commissioned him to write. (For a less enthusiastic review of TR's *New York,* see the *Critic,* 21 Feb. 1891, p. 92.)

2. See TR to BM, 20 June 1890, n. 1. According to the *New York Times,* TR's speech on "Americanism in Politics" was "listened to with close attention by between 300 and 400 ladies and gentlemen" ("But One Kind of American," *New York Times,* 19 Dec. 1890, 5).

3. *A Boy's Town* (1890) is William D. Howells's account of his boyhood days in Ohio.

To Matthews

Civil Service Commission
January 29, 1891.

Dear Matthews:

I was pleased with the editorial you referred to, or perhaps it would be more exact to say, I was pleased that there should be so long an editorial about the book at all.[1] Am glad to hear what you say about the Cosmopolitan. I think that some of the best work you have done has been as a critic, and yet I should be reluctant to see you devote yourself purely to criticism; at least not unless you could so arrange your various critical articles as to make a volume of them at some future time.[2]

Lodge I fear will be entirely unable to debate the Southern problem as you wish. I think Murat Halstead would be your man.[3] In the present ruin of the straight-out Republicans I really do not know who to suggest in his place. How would Senator Hawley do?[4]

Faithfully yours,
Theodore Roosevelt

BMP; 1 p.; tls.
1. Unidentified.
2. BM published a volume of critical essays the following year: *Americanisms and Briticisms* (New York: Harper, 1892).
3. See TR to BM, 13 Jan. 1890, n. 2.
4. Joseph Roswell Hawley (1826–1905), Republican senator from Connecticut.

To Matthews

Civil Service Commission
March 27th 91

Dear Matthews,

I am very sorry to say that on Wednesday I have to dine with a big-game club—the Boone and Crockett.[1] I should much prefer the quartette you mention. Can't you three dine with me on Friday instead? I have been sponging on you very often recently—but it's only the previous engagement prevents my sponging again. If you can't dine on Friday, can you lunch with me that day? and whichever you decide to do, will you tell Gilder and Sturgis, if you see them? I want all three of you. I do'n't know whether any one else would do or not; I think a small party pleasantest.

Yours in haste
Theodore Roosevelt

BMP; 3 pp.; als.

1. Concerned about the destruction of American species of animal life due to wanton hunting, TR in 1887 organized a group of wealthy sportsmen into the (Daniel) Boone and (Davy) Crockett Club. The club's main purpose was to work for the preservation of large game and unspoiled wilderness. TR was the club's first president.

To Matthews

Civil Service Commission
March 31st, 91

Dear Matthews,

How will the Union League Club suit you? I'll see you at the Authors on Thursday evening.[1]

Yours in great haste
Theodore Roosevelt

BMP; 1 p.; als.

1. BM helped establish the Authors Club, New York City's first distinctively literary club, in 1882. In *Years*, he remarks that the (all-male) club provided an opportunity for writers and editors to "rub elbows and to develop a solidarity among men of letters in New York and its immediate vicinity" (224).

To Matthews

Civil Service Commission
April 21st, '91

Dear Matthews,

Good luck to you! May you have a most pleasant summer. I hope that Mrs. Matthews is all right now, and that she will enjoy to the full her trip abroad.

Lodge says the copyright dinner was a great success; I wish I could have been there.[1]

If you see Andrew Lang, give him my regards; and tell him if he'll come over here we'll show him our institutions in all their naked and revolting barbarity. I thought some of his "Essays in Little" very good.[2]

Yours always
Theodore Roosevelt

BMP; 3 pp.; als.

1. A banquet celebrating the eighth anniversary of the founding of the American Copyright League and the passage of the International Copyright Act of 1891 was held on 13 Apr. 1891, at Sherry's restaurant in New York City.

Lodge was one of the featured speakers; BM and his wife attended ("In Honor of the Victory," *New York Times*, 14 Apr. 1891, 5).

2. Lang's *Essays in Little* (New York: Scribner's, 1891) includes pieces on John Bunyan, Charles Dickens, Alexandre Dumas, Homer, Rudyard Kipling, and Sir Walter Scott.

To Matthews

Civil Service Commission
June 23d '91

My dear Matthews,

I am often tempted to write you, to say "bravo" after you have made a particularly good hit in one of your stories or essays; and in this instance I am going to yield to the temptation. Your "Briticisms & Americanisms" is as good piece of work as I have come across in many a long day; I have read it twice already, and shall read it several times again.[1] I shall use it with effect (and ingratitude) at the British Legation, where I dine this evening. And, oh, it preach such a good lesson of Independence and true Americanism to our own people!

How is Mrs. Matthews? I trust well, and that you are both enjoying yourselves. I do'n't know your address abroad, so I send this to your house on spec.

I have been broiling in Washington lately, my family being on Long Island; and my work progresses with it's customary truculent monotony. But I intend to take two months in the west after September 1st; I have a very amusing letter from Tom Reed to show you when you get home.[2]

Yours always
Theodore Roosevelt

BMP; 4 pp.; als.

1. BM, "Briticisms and Americanisms," *Harper's Monthly* 83 (July 1891): 215–22; rpt. in *Americanisms and Briticisms*, 1–31. The essay is a spirited yet scholarly rebuttal of complaints from condescending British writers that "Americanisms"—departures from British diction, spelling, and usage—were "mongrelizing" the sublime English language. BM argues that changes in the language, on both sides of the Atlantic, are signs of linguistic health and vitality, not decadence. In a letter of 26 June 1891 to Henry Cabot Lodge, TR remarks that he plays tennis nearly every day at the British Legation with his good friend Cecil Arthur Spring-Rice (1859–1918), secretary to Britain's Washington Legation; and he recommends BM's "clever little article on Briticisms and Americanisms" to Lodge (*LTR*, 1:254).

2. See Reed to TR, 27 May 1891 (TRP). Writing from Paris, Reed lightheartedly relates his experiences traveling in Europe and comments on American politics.

To Matthews

Washington D.C.
Nov 9th 91

My dear Matthews,
Will you forthwith drop me a line, to 689 Madison Av, telling me the hour at which your lecture begins?[1] It is on Wednsday, is'n't it? You wish me to speak about five minutes? & can I bring my wife and sister, and Cabot Lodge to hear you? Then we'll arrange for a lunch.[2]
I guess my letter hoodoo'd Fassett.[3]
With warm regards to Mrs. Matthews, I am
Yours cordially
Theodore Roosevelt

P.S.
I have just this moment received your book, and open this letter to thank you; it drifted about in the official mail.[4] I already have a copy of the book, which I shall now give to somebody else—and I need not tell you that I like it, because one does not buy a book by an author one knows unless one really wishes to read it.

BMP; 3 pp.; als.

1. TR and Edith often stayed at 689 Madison Ave., the residence of his sister Anna (1855–1931), nicknamed "Bamie," when visiting New York City.

2. BM, in his first semester teaching at Columbia, invited TR to speak briefly to his class in English and American Prose Fiction of the Nineteenth Century (one of the first of its kind in an American university). As reported in the *Critic* (5 Dec. 1891, 322), TR spoke—for much longer than five minutes—on James Fenimore Cooper's fiction and on other literary topics. At the end of TR's lecture, the students exclaimed "'Rah Rah, Rah, C-O-L-U-M-B-I-A! Roosevelt!'"—and BM "knew that his ingenious device of getting another man to deliver his lecture for him had been a great success!"

   Edith and TR's sister Corinne (Mrs. Douglas Robinson, 1861–1933) were lifelong friends, and both were deeply interested in literary matters; TR once remarked that Lodge was among the few people whose knowledge of English literature rivaled Edith's (Sylvia Morris, *Edith Kermit Roosevelt,* 107).

3. Jacob Sloat Fassett (1853–1924); New York state senator (1883–1891) whose investigations in 1890 of New York City political corruption drew national attention. In 1891 he was the Republican nominee for governor, but was opposed by the powerful Republican Sen. Thomas Collier Platt (1833–1910). Fassett drew support from reform-minded Republicans (as well as from mugwumpish Democrats). TR was very fond of Fassett and publicly supported his candidacy in a letter that caused the New York *World* to accuse TR of politicizing the office of Civil Service Commissioner (see TR to Lodge, 29 Oct. 1891, in Henry Cabot Lodge, ed., *Selections from the Corre-*

spondence of Theodore Roosevelt and Henry Cabot Lodge [New York: Scribner's, 1925], 1:119–21). Fassett, however, was defeated by the Democratic nominee, Roswell P. Flower; thus TR's remark that his letter "hoodoo'd" his candidate.

4. Most likely the revised edition of BM's *French Dramatists of the Nineteenth Century* (1881; rev. New York: Scribner's, 1891), the book that helped establish him as one of the foremost scholars on the subject.

To Matthews

Civil Service Commission
December 8, 1891.

Dear Brander:

What are you apologizing for? I can assure you that we all enjoyed the trip to Chinatown greatly, and we enjoyed the previous dinner still more. It was a thoroughly pleasant evening, and I am speaking not only for myself, but for my wife, sister, and friend.

I am going to read to Lodge what you said of his article on colonialism, and shall look forward to the receipt of the Critic.[1] I shall be on, on the 19th of this month, but I fear I shall have to take the 3:20 train back that afternoon. Would it be possible for you to have your lunch a little earlier, say at one, so that I could have at least an hour and a half of time? I never have willingly given up a chance to accept an invitation to lunch with you yet, and I don't intend to now! Therefore I blandly thus ask you to put the hour thirty minutes earlier than you propose. Of course, seriously, don't hesitate to say if this would be inconvenient.

Cordially yours,
Theodore Roosevelt

Thank Heaven we *do* agree on Americanism; I have something to tell you on that point when next we meet.

BMP; 1 p.; tls., with autograph postscript.

1. Henry Cabot Lodge, "Colonialism in the United States," in his *Studies in History* (Boston: Houghton Mifflin, 1884), 330–65. In his essay "The Literary Independence of the United States" (1892), BM showers praise on Lodge's volume, and remarks that "there is no essay more interesting or more stimulating than that on 'Colonialism in the United States'" (*Americanisms and Briticisms*, 62–65).

TR was no doubt awaiting the *Critic* number containing the account of his November visit to BM's American literature class (see TR to BM, 9 Nov. 1891, n. 2).

To Matthews

Civil Service Commission
December 15, 1891.

Dear Brander:

Hurrah!! So long as my invitation to lunch with you is declined, with the distinct understanding that it is only deferred, I shall regretfully accomodate myself to the declination. I shall be on early next month, shall warn you in full time, and shall fast for twenty-four hours beforehand.

Mrs. Roosevelt is very much the worse for wear at the present time, and all my children seem to be suffering under some of the divers ills to which infantile flesh is heir, so you have sympathy in your own indisposition.

Cordially yours,
Theodore Roosevelt

BMP; 1 p.; tls.

1892

To Matthews

Civil Service Commission
Jan 2d '9[2]¹

Dear Brander,

Many thanks for Burk's delicious play.² American literature *has* advanced. But did you see in the last North American the symposium on the best book of the year?³ In it's own way it was as good as Burk. [Miss?] Repplier, whose original essays were no good, is beginning to write like Andrew Lang gone crazy.⁴

A happy new year to you and Mrs Matthews. I hope you are both well now.

Yours
T. R.

BMP; 2 pp.; als.

1. TR wrote "'91," a slip of the pen, as n. 3 below indicates.

2. John Burk, *Bunker-Hill; or, The Death of General Warren: An Historical Tragedy* (1797; reprint ed. New York: Dunlap Society, 1891), with an introduction by BM (1–14). This was one of a dozen American plays published by the Dunlap Society, an organization founded in 1885 by BM and others to promote American drama. In his introduction, BM observes that Burk's patriotic tribute to Gen. Joseph Warren (the American commander at Bunker Hill) was well received by American audiences when first staged in 1797; and he suggests that while its literary merits are debatable, its historical value is great.

3. "The Best Book of the Year," *North American Review* 154 (Jan. 1892): 85–116. Several different writers discuss, in short essays, the most remarkable book they read during 1891. All of the books honored are by British or Continental writers, none by an American.

4. Philadephia essayist Agnes Repplier (1855–1950)—whose last name TR elsewhere mispells as "Replier"—was one of the contributors to the "Best Book of the Year" symposium. She lavishes praise on Oscar Wilde's literary criticism, saying, for example, that his voice is "clear, languid, musical, shaken with laughter, and speaking in strange sweet tones of art and beauty, and of that finer criticism which is one with art and beauty, and claims them forever as its own" (97). A prolific writer, Repplier had published many essays by this point, and her third book, *Essays in Miniature* (1892), was forthcom-

ing. As letters below reveal, TR and BM saw Repplier, who was a great admirer of Andrew Lang, as the epitome of the American "colonial" mind
which worshipped British literature and culture.

TO MATTHEWS

Civil Service Commission
February 25, 1892.

Dear Brander:
    In the first place, I shall be on in New York about March 7th, I shall
let you know the exact date well in advance. I have been intending to
write Howells the article concerning Miss Repplier merely because her
piece on "the praises of war," which I thought a very good piece in many
respects, irritated me savagely by its cringing provincialism and lack of patriotism, especially at the end.[1] I am going to, however, try to prevent it in
any way from being an attack upon her. I shall merely make it a plea for
Americanism (combined with a plea for literature dealing with battle) on
the lines of yours, Higginson's Lodge's and Co's.[2] I shall look for your paper in the May Cosmopolitan with great interest.[3] I have already written
Low that I cannot undertake to deliver a lecture at the Cooper Union, but
that I will see him when I go to New York, on the general subject.[4]
    Heartily thanking you, I am,
                        Cordially yours,
                        Theodore Roosevelt

BMP; 1 p.; tls.
1. The central thesis of Repplier's "The Praises of War" (*Atlantic Monthly* 68
    [Dec. 1891]: 796–805) is that war has inspired great literature throughout the
    ages. In her closing, Repplier argues, however, that the American Civil War
    generated little more than doggerel verse—that view in sharp contrast to
    BM's praise of Civil War songs in his 1888 essay "The Songs of the Civil
    War" (*Pen and Ink,* 140–67). TR was so irritated by Repplier's essay that he
    published a biting response, "A Colonial Survival," in *Cosmopolitan* 13 (Dec.
    1892; rpt. in *Works,* 12:300–16); this was the first number of *Cosmopolitan* ed-
    ited by Howells, who resigned his post only a month later. In the article,
    TR states that he agrees with much of what Repplier says, but he accuses
    her of being in thrall to the English tradition and of ignoring great works of
    battle literature by Fenimore Cooper and other American authors; he fur-
    ther declares that her denigration of Civil War poetry is "colonialism gone
    crazy" (309).
2. TR probably has in mind such works as BM's "Briticisms and American-
    isms" (see TR to BM, 23 June 1891); Lodge's *Studies in History*, particularly
    the article "Colonialism in the United States" (see TR to BM, 8 Dec. 1891,

n. 1); and Thomas Wentworth Higginson's *The New World and the New Book* (1892), the title essay of which was originally presented to the Nineteenth Century Club on 15 Jan. 1891 ("Americanism in Literature," *New York Times,* 16 Jan. 1891, 5). Though known today primarily as the critic who failed to appreciate sufficiently the poems that Emily Dickinson sent to him, Higginson (1823–1911) was a prolific writer and one of the age's most admired essayists and speakers. BM praises Lodge's and Higginson's essays on Americanism in his "Concerning Certain American Essayists" (see next note and TR to BM, 26 April 1892, n. 1).

3. BM, "Concerning Certain American Essayists," *Cosmopolitan* 13 (May 1892): 86–91.

4. Seth Low (1850–1916). President of Columbia College from 1890 to 1901, Low was very active in New York social reform and politics (he was the city's mayor from 1901 to 1903).

Founded by the philanthropist Peter Cooper (1791–1833), the Cooper Union for the Advancement of Science and Art provided free training in the arts and sciences to working-class men and women; many Columbia professors and public figures delivered public lectures there. In *New York,* TR singles out the Union and its founder as exemplifying the city's charitable and public-spirited character (*Works,* 10:535).

TO MATTHEWS

Civil Service Commission
Feb 27th '92

Dear Brander,
Do you want me to come to lunch on either March 9th or 10th?
Yours always
Theodore Roosevelt

P.S.
Mrs. Roosevelt and I have both become as much interested in your St. Nicholas boy's story as in the works really intended for us middle-aged beings.[1] Do'n't you like Laura Richard's reminiscenses, in the same scholarly periodical?[2]

I am glad your vestibule car sketch is in form to be a companion to Howells similiar sketches.[3]

BMP; 2 pp.; als.

1. Before being published as a book, BM's *Tom Paulding: The Story of a Search for Buried Treasure in the Streets of New York* (New York: Century, 1892) was serialized in *St. Nicholas* 19 (Nov. 1891–Oct. 1892). BM gives an account of the story's genesis and plot in *Years,* 378–81. *St. Nicholas* was the foremost children's periodical of the age, and many prominent authors published in it.

2. Laura E. Richards (1850–1943); daughter of Gridley and Julia (Ward) Howe, Richards was a prolific writer of children's literature. Her autobiography *When I Was Your Age* (1893) was serialized in *St. Nicholas* 19 (Jan.–Sept. 1892) before being published as a volume.

3. BM had published, in the Mar. 1891 number of *Harper's Monthly* (572–86), a story entitled "In the Vestibule Limited." The setting of this romantic tale—in which a young man fortuitously encounters, reconciles with, and then marries the young woman to whom he earlier had been engaged—is the vestibule, or parlor, cars on a train traveling from New York to Chicago. Parlor cars are the setting for several of Howells's plays, as well as for many scenes in his novels. TR seems to be referring, however, to BM's revision and expansion of the story into a novella, *In the Vestibule Limited* (New York: Harper, 1892). BM dedicated the volume to "the Author of 'The Parlor Car,' 'The Sleeping Car' and 'The Albany Depot'" (all plays by Howells).

To Matthews

Civil Service Commission
April 8, 1892.

Dear Brander:

Funnily enough, I had bought the "Tales of Soldiers and Civilians" just before your letter was written and took it down south with me on an official trip to New Orleans, from which I have just returned.[1] This must account for my delay in answering your note. The "Tales", with all their defects, are extremely powerful. The man ought to come to something. By the way, I made a peccary hunt down in Texas and killed two peccaries.

I quite agree with you about Davis.[2] It is a pity that a man who can write so very readably should have such desperate shortcomings. As you say, he has his full share of the story-telling faculty, and I have hopes of him yet if he doesn't keep too conceited. I shall look out for the Educational Review.[3]

By the way, can you lunch with me at Delmonico's on Thursday the 21st, and if so at what time? I shall be in New York on that day, and have asked Howells. I think that just we three could have a very pleasant talk. Perhaps I will have Gilder too, although I don't know but that it would be better to have just yourself, Howells and myself.

With warm regards to the Madam, I am, in great haste,

Yours always,
Theodore Roosevelt

BMP; 2 pp.; tls.

1. *Tales of Soldiers and Civilians* (San Francisco: E. L. G. Steele, 1892), a collection of stories by San Francisco's acid-penned critic Ambrose Bierce (1842–

1914?). The volume includes two of Bierce's best stories: "Chickamauga" and "An Occurrence at Owl Creek Bridge." BM reviewed Bierce's book (along with several other collections of stories) in "More American Stories," *Cosmopolitan* 13 (Sept. 1892): 626–30. Though BM faults Bierce's tales for their "unredeemed monotony of insistent horror," his critique is very favorable overall: "The power of these tales is indisputable; their brute-force is beyond question. Mr. Bierce has an astonishing faculty for the selection of the dramatic situation, plucked at the very climax and catastrophe of the drama and presented briefly and boldly and left to speak for itself" (628).

2. Richard Harding Davis (1864–1916); former reporter for the *New York Evening Sun* and at this time managing editor of *Harper's Weekly* (1891 to 1893). Though his fiction is largely ignored today, Davis became an almost instant celebrity with the publication of "Gallegher" (1890). In 1891 he published two collections of stories, *Gallegher and Other Stories* and *Stories for Boys*, and in 1892 a third volume, *Van Bibber and Others*. Contrary to his rather negative assessment of Davis's fiction in this letter, TR elsewhere remarks that he "was among the number who were immediately drawn to [Davis] by the power and originality of 'Gallegher'" (quoted in Gerald Langford, *The Richard Harding Davis Years: A Biography of Mother and Son* [New York: Holt, Rinehart, 1961], 109). Davis would later accompany New York Police Commissioner TR on his excursions into the Bowery and would report on the exploits of TR and the Rough Riders in Cuba, where, according to TR, he "performed valuable service on the fighting line" (TR, *Works*, 20:255). See also TR to BM, 6 Dec. 1892 and 30 Jan. 1894.

3. BM's "Can English Literature Be Taught?" appears in *Educational Review* 3 (Apr. 1892): 337–47. In this cogently argued and astute essay, BM chastises the British for failing to teach English-language literature in their universities and for refusing to acknowledge that the study of literature and that of language are two distinctly different disciplines (i.e., literary criticism and philology). He further scolds the British—Andrew Lang by name—for suggesting that literature cannot be *taught* when they actually mean that it cannot be *examined on*; the British overemphasis on exams, he continues, encourages narrow and rigid thinking. Finally, BM rebukes the British for denigrating American literature, which he argues is, though relatively young, worthy of serious attention.

To Matthews

Civil Service Commission
April 15, 1892.

Dear Brander:

Well, if we can't do any better, lunch with me at 12 at Delmonico's, on the 21st. I will try to get Howells to come, and if I can't we will have a lunch together anyhow. I can't make it 11:30 on account of another engagement.

I have just received the Educational Review, and I am very much pleased with your article. I have not had a chance to look at Draper's.[1]

In great haste,

Yours always,
Theodore Roosevelt

BMP; 1 p.; tls.

1. Andrew S. Draper's "Public School Pioneering in New York and Massachusetts" (3 [Apr. 1892]: 313–36) directly precedes BM's *Educational Review* essay ("Can English Literature Be Taught?") referred to in the above letter. Draper's central thesis, which certainly would have appealed to TR, is that "America is indebted to the Dutch rather than to the English for the essential principles of the great free-school system of the country," and that New York, not Massachusetts, pioneered the development of that system (314). Long active in the New York Republican party, Draper (1848–1913) was state superintendent of public instruction when he wrote the article. President TR would appoint him to the U.S. Board of Indian Commissioners in 1902.

To Matthews

Civil Service Commission
April 26, 1892

Dear Brander:

I have carefully read over your article on Miss Repplier and others, also read it to my wife and to Lodge, and we all agree that it is well worth keeping in permanent form.[1] Do put it with your other essays. You see it is not merely a criticism of Miss Repplier; it is largely an essay on Americanism, using her partly as a peg and partly as an awful object lesson. I am now wrestling with the beginning of my own article on the same subject.[2] I hope you will see Lodge when he is in New York.

With warm regards to Mrs. Matthews, I am,

Cordially yours,
Theodore Roosevelt

BMP; 1 p.; tls.

1. Probably "Concerning Certain American Essayists" (see TR to BM, 25 Feb. 1892, n. 3), which BM did include, in slightly abridged form, in *Americanisms and Briticisms*, 135–50. After extolling collections of essays by Lodge and Higginson for their Americanism, BM turns attention to Repplier. He grants that her collection of essays *Points of View* (1889) is well written and learned, but he ridicules her for idolizing English writers (such as Lang) and

for ignoring American writers. In the closing paragraph, BM sarcastically urges the Philadelphia friends of this American writer who yearns to be a "Poor Islander" to take her to Independence Hall to see the Liberty Bell, and to give her copies of Lodge's and Higginson's books.

2. See TR to BM, 25 Feb. 1892.

To MATTHEWS

Civil Service Commission
May 31st 92

Dear Brander,

I am very sorry you should be having such trouble about the measles. I suppose it does knock our lunch on the head; but at least I shall see you later on. When do you leave New York? I want to see if I can't arrange to meet you.

I have just finished, with sweat and tears, my article for Howells dealing with Repplier and others.[1]

I hope it is true that Kipling is not to be admitted to the Players. There is no earthly reason he should not call New York a pig trough; but there is also no reason why he should be allowed to associate with the pigs. I fear he is at bottom a cad.[2]

Remember me warmly to Mrs. Matthews. I liked both the Page and the Jewett articles you refer to very much.[3]

Yours always
Theodore Roosevelt

BMP; 4 pp.; als.; pbd. *LTR*, 1:286.

1. See TR to BM, 25 Feb. 1892.

2. As later letters will show, TR would develop a much more favorable impression of the British writer Rudyard Kipling (1865–1936), especially after meeting him in person in 1895 (see TR to BM, 9 Mar. 1895). BM and Kipling first made each other's acquaintance in 1891 (at London's Savile Club), and the two became close friends and steady correspondents thereafter. In his travel sketch "Across a Continent" (1892), Kipling described New York City as the product of "shiftless barbarism and reckless extravagance," its streets "long, narrow pig-trough[s]" (*The Writings in Prose and Verse of Rudyard Kipling* [New York: Scribner's, 1920], 28:18). This piece and others disparaging New York and American culture generally, incited howls of protest from Americans, including TR, who targets Kipling in the opening paragraph of "Colonial Survival" (see TR to BM, 6 Dec. 1892, n. 4). BM, however, was not angered by Kipling's criticisms of the United States; in *Years* he suggests that Americans too often have been overly sensitive to Kipling's candid observations (432–33).

3. Probably Sarah Orne Jewett (1849–1909) and Thomas Nelson Page (1853–1922), prominent writers of New England and the South, respectively. The unidentified "articles" (a term that TR often applied to stories) which TR mentions are likely Jewett's "Decoration Day," a story honoring the common men who fought and died to maintain the Union, and Page's sketch (in the "Editor's Drawer" section of *Century Magazine*) of a stereotypical black and his stubborn mule; both pieces had just appeared in the *Century Magazine* (85 [June 1892]: 84–90, 157–58).

To Matthews

June 12th '92

Dear Brander,

I shall be in New York next Thursday. Can't you lunch with me at Delmonicos that day, say at one? or earlier if you wish. Drop me a line to 689 saying if you can, and appointing the hour.

I am glad you drew blood from Repplier.[1] I have'n't heard from Howells and the Cosmopolitan people yet whether they like my article or not.[2]

Delighted you have so nearly suppressed the measles.

Yours

T. R.

BMP; 2 pp.; als.

1. In a letter to BM of 25 May [1892], Andrew Lang remarks that Repplier had sent him "your strictures on her quotations, her unpatriotic quotations" (*Friends over the Ocean*, 117), apparently referring to BM's attack on her in "Concerning Certain American Essayists" (see TR to BM, 26 April 1892, n. 1). BM may have informed TR of Repplier's complaint.

2. See next letter.

To Matthews

Civil Service Commission
June 27th '92

Dear Brander,

I have written to Howells about having you see the article—though I am ashamed of myself for doing so. I have not as yet heard from him; but I expect the article itself to be returned to me for revision soon, as there were a number of small things that needed retouching.[1] What Atlantic article do you mean?

I must look up Hawthorns book; if only to revile it.[2] I do wish you would write a school hand book of American literature; I believe you would do a great service.[3] Who is the bishop of whom Higgenson writes who got out a list of 150 books for American Sunday schools, and not one single American book in the lot?[4] I would like to take *him* for a text. My Parkman article is nearly done; but I am not satisfied with it.[5] I do wish *you* would do it. Reviews are not in my line; I do not seem to be able to get the hang of writing them. I struggle and plunge frightfully, and when written my words do'n't express my thought. I estimate Parkman as high as you do; but I do not seem to be able to put on paper either my belief, or my reasons therefor. I shall send the review, because I have promised it; but I shall send it half heartedly.

I am delighted with your Harper's article on American spelling; it is in your best—and I can truthfully say your usual—vein.[6]

Yours
Theodore Roosevelt

Warm regards to Mrs Matthews.

BMP; 4 pp.; als.; pbd. *LTR*, 1:288.

1. See TR to BM, 25 Feb. 1892, n. 1. Howells's letter to TR regarding his article is not in the TRP.

2. TR refers to Julian Hawthorne's *American Literature: A Text-book for the Use of Schools and Colleges* (Boston: Heath, 1891), co-authored with Leonard Lemmon; it was one of the first such surveys of American literature and a precursor of the textbook that BM would author (see next note). TR and BM would have been displeased by Julian's announcement in the introduction that, "after a few great names [such as Emerson, Nathaniel Hawthorne, and Lowell], we are at the end of our original creative geniuses. All the rest are either reflections of these, or of European models" (ix). BM and TR would not, however, have faulted Hawthorne for asserting, in chapter 9, "Writers of To-day," that BM "is a novelist, poet, essayist and literary and dramatic critic whose productions are never dull, and often possess high literary and artistic merit" (300). Though Julian (1846–1934) never attained the literary stature of his father, Nathaniel, he was a respected and productive author of fiction and nonfiction (Maurice Bassan, *Hawthorne's Son: The Life and Literary Career of Julian Hawthorne* [Columbus: Ohio State Univ. Press, 1970], 164–67). Like BM and TR, Julian was active in New York literary clubs, including the Nineteenth Century, where BM first met him in 1883 (*Years*, 236).

3. BM took TR's advice. The result was *An Introduction to the Study of American Literature* (1896), a survey of American literature from the early Puritans to the 1890s, in 18 chapters, all of which had appeared earlier in *St. Nicholas*. The textbook was influential in shaping the American literary canon of the early twentieth century, and it proved financially lucrative for BM, selling more than a quarter of a million copies within 25 years of its initial publication (see Oliver, *Brander Matthews*, 136–41).

4. The bishop is unidentified.
5. TR, "Francis Parkman's Histories," *The Independent* 45 (24 Nov. 1892); rpt. in *Works*, 12:246–53. The occasion for this review, which originally had been solicited by Howells for *Cosmopolitan* (see TR to BM, 1 Oct. 1892, n. 4), was the publication of *A Half-Century of Conflict* (1892), the final work in Parkman's multivolume history of the French and English in North America, his *magnum opus*. TR praises Parkman (1823–93) as the "greatest historian whom the United States has yet produced" (246). He further states that Parkman "has seen clearly the epochal nature of the long rivalry between France and England in America; and with that eye for the dramatic which no great historian can lack," he has appreciated that rivalry's place in history as "one of the most important in the stages of the conquest of the North American continent" (247). Parkman's influence on TR's historical writings is well known (see, e.g., Morris, *Rise*, 387–88), and BM himself later honored TR as Parkman's successor as the foremost chronicler of the American West (see BM to TR, 8 Jan. 1917, n. 2).
6. BM, "As to 'American Spelling,'" *Harper's Monthly* 85 (July 1892): 277–84; rpt. in *Americanisms and Briticisms*, 32–59. Responding to British charges that American departures from British orthography were corrupting the English language, BM observes that the spelling system is "stupid" overall and in need of the "broom of reform." This essay is the first of many that BM would publish in support of the simplified-spelling movement, in which TR also participated.

To Matthews

Civil Service Commission
July 27th 92

Dear Brander,
 Well done! I like to see the English, and their under-study, Mr. Smalley, wriggle.[1] Evidently the weakling doesn't really know who Lounsbury is; and he actually does not see that he gives away his whole case by his own remarks on seventeenth century spelling.[2] If there was *no* standard of spelling in the seventeenth century, all the "historical" arguments for the present cumbrous system vanish like smoke. Foolish Mr. Smalley does'n't even know enough to state his case. I wish you would write a short but smashing answer, whether for the Tribune or the Critic. Of course Smalley's column against you is a great compliment, and advertisement.
 I hope Mrs. Matthews is all right now. I start west in a few days.
Cordially yours
Theodore Roosevelt

BMP; 4 pp.; als.

1. George Washburn Smalley (1833–1916), *New York Daily Tribune* representative in London from 1865 to 1895, when he became a correspondent for the London *Times*. Outspoken and often belligerent, Smalley was one of the most prominent journalists of his age; his pompous attitude and conservative ideology earned him the label "America's Tory Squire." Though TR disdained Smalley at this point, he would seek his support after becoming U.S. president in 1901, initiating an uneasy friendship between the two. See Joseph J. Mathews, *George W. Smalley: Forty Years a Foreign Correspondent* (Chapel Hill: Univ. of North Carolina Press, 1973), 3–4, 102–3, 215–18, and *passim*.

In "Notes from London," *New York Daily Tribune*, 27 July 1892, 6–7, Smalley attempts, in sarcastic tones, to rebut BM's "As to 'American Spelling'" (see preceding letter, n. 6).

2. Thomas Raynesford Lounsbury (1838–1915); professor of English at Yale (1870–1906) and an internationally respected philologist and literary scholar. Like BM, Lounsbury was an advocate of simplified spelling, as well as of literary Americanism, and he was the first elected president of the Simplified Spelling Board (1907). In *Studies in Chaucer* (1892), Lounsbury employs his erudition in philology to counter British criticisms of American spelling practices. He argues, for example, that *center* is not, as some British critics claimed, an Americanized variant of *centre*, because sixteenth- and seventeenth-century British writers—including Shakespeare—actually used the termination *er* more often than *re*. BM (who dedicated *Americanisms and Briticisms* to Lounsbury) quotes Lounsbury's passage on this point in "As to 'American Spelling'" (*Americanisms and Briticisms*, 45–46).

In his attack on BM's essay, Smalley contends that Lounsbury's argument demonstrates astounding "unacquaintance with the history of English printing and of English spelling," because no seventeenth-century book "could properly be quoted as an authority for spelling; . . . There was no scientific basis of orthography; there was no settled practice" ("Notes from London," 6).

To Matthews

Washington D.C.

Oct 1st 92

Dear Brander,

Yesterday morning Mrs. Roosevelt walked down with me to the office, and on the way posted a letter to you; on reaching the office I found your letter! I delayed answering until today, hoping to receive the Quarterly; it will doubtless turn up in due time.[1] Did you receive one or two letters I wrote you this summer, anent various matters? I did not try to see you last Saturday in New York, for I was too much hurried to have time for anything but mere business—and I want to see you at leisure, with nobody, not even Gilder or Howells or Bunner at the table with us, and with *ample* time to discuss the twenty seven different subjects I have stored up. What are your free days for luncheon this year? I shall be in N.Y. on the 12th; can you lunch with me at Delmonico's on that day? Fiske's book is excellent; Campbells is a deep and very important work, though too extreme in it's conclusions.² Still it is *very* useful, for it upsets a theory which has become stereotyped, and which has cramped our intellectual developement at times. I have already been chaffing Lodge about it. I thought his Homeric article admirable.³ I am told that my Repplier article will probably appear in the December Cosmopolitan. I sent Howells my Parkman article; he wrote me he liked it; but I have just received a letter from Walker, very polite, but explaining that they do not want the article, as it is not a subject in which their readers would be interested.⁴ I shall look out for your Trent & Page article;⁵ also, and especially, for the publication in book form of your more than admirable "Briticisms and Americanisms" essays.⁶ Warm regards to Mrs Matthews

Yours

Theodore Roosevelt

BMP; 4 pp.; als.

1. Probably the *Quarterly Review* 175 (Oct. 1892), which includes Andrew Lang's "Homer and Recent Discoveries," a review essay on several books about archeology, Greek history, and Homer (372–93). (The review is unsigned, but the *Wellesley Index to Victorian Periodicals, 1724–1900,* 1:773, lists Lang as the author.) An admirer of Homer and Greek civilization, TR would have been interested in the essay by Lang, who was a respected scholar of Homer.

2. Almost certainly John Fiske's *The Discovery of America* (New York: Houghton Mifflin, 1892) and Douglas Campbell's *The Puritan in Holland, England, and America: An Introduction to American History* (New York: Harper, 1892). One of the era's most influential historians, Fiske (1842–1901) helped popularize the evolutionary paradigm of historical studies; the central thesis of his *Discovery* is that the "discovery" of America was not a single event but a gradual evolution. TR was less impressed with Fiske's political views, for he called him a "demented mugwump" in an earlier letter to Lodge (LTR, 1:175).

In *Puritan,* Campbell (1839–93) argues that, since the Dutch influence on sixteenth- and seventeenth-century England was immense, the Netherlands, not England, is the true source of origins of American culture. In a review titled "The Dutch Influence in America," *Atlantic Monthly* 70 [Nov. 1892]: 698–704, the anonymous author praises Campbell for helping liberate the study of American history from its obsessive concern with Anglo-Saxon influences.

3. Lodge, "As to Certain Accepted Heroes," *Cosmopolitan* 13 (Oct. 1892): 713–19; rpt. in *Certain Accepted Heroes and Other Essays in Literature and Politics* (New York: Harper, 1897). Lodge stresses that Homer's heroes must be judged by their, and not modern, cultural values, and he defends the classical tradition in general.

4. John Brisben Walker (1847–1931), owner of *Cosmopolitan* from 1889 to 1905. Walker, whose domineering personality impelled Howells to resign as *Cosmopolitan*'s editor in June 1892, printed TR's essay on Repplier in the Dec. 1892 number of the magazine (see TR to BM, 25 Feb. 1892; and Howells, *Selected Letters of W. D. Howells*, ed. Thomas Wortham et al. [Boston: Twayne, 1981], 4:21). Howells also had accepted TR's essay on Parkman (see TR to BM, 27 June 1892, n. 6), but Walker refused to publish it. In a letter to Lodge dated 11 Oct. 1892 (LTR, 1:292), TR expresses his frustration with Walker, adding that he would never again write for *Cosmopolitan*.

5. "Two Studies of the South," *Cosmopolitan* 14 (Nov. 1892): 124–28; rpt. in BM, *Aspects of Fiction*, 25–39. In this favorable review of William P. Trent's *William Gilmore Simms* (New York: Houghton Mifflin, 1892) and Thomas Nelson Page's *The Old South* (New York: Scribner's, 1892), BM suggests that the two writers exemplify the progressive literary movement underway in the New South; such progress, he emphasizes, could not occur under slavery, which prevented southern authors from writing truthfully about their culture. Trent (1862–1939) was a professor of English at the University of the South, where he founded the *Sewanee Review* in 1892; he later joined the English Department at Columbia, thanks to the influence of BM and TR (see TR to BM, 7 Mar. 1894, n. 1).

6. See TR to BM, 23 June 1891, n. 1. *Americanisms and Briticisms* (1892) includes the title essay and several other previously published articles, all directly or indirectly addressing the topic of literary Americanism.

To Matthews

Civil Service Commission
Oct 3d '92

Dear Brander,

All three articles interested me much; I do'nt know Thompson's address; if you do, will you forward the enclosed to him, after reading it?[1] I send it to you for the latter purpose. Morses article on the Republican party is excellent.[2]

I ill requite your kindness by enclosing you an article of mine on the foreign policy of the administration; but I do it, nevertheless.[3]

In great haste

Yours

T. R.

BMP; 2 pp.; als.
1. TR and BM knew several Thompsons, but the one referred to here is most likely Daniel Greenleaf Thompson (1850–97); lawyer, teacher, and author, he was president of the Nineteenth Century Club at the time (see *Years*, 237). BM later sent TR a copy of Thompson's *Politics in a Democracy* (TR to BM, 24 Oct. 1893).
   The articles in question have not been identified.
2. Anson Daniel Morse, "Our Two Great Parties: Their Origin and Tasks. II. The Republican Party," *Political Science Quarterly* 7 (Sept. 1892): 522–35. Distinguished professor of history and political science at Amherst College, Morse (1846–1916) was one of America's most important political theorists. In this article, he argues that the Republican party must cross class and regional boundaries to become the nation's "conservative party," defending American culture against the "alien, the monopolist, the inflationist, the repudiator, the anarchist and many another who would overturn and destroy" it (532). Republicans, he further contends, must attempt to reconcile North and South by abandoning the campaign, begun during Reconstruction, to "make the negro the ruler of the South" (535). Blacks, he suggests, are not yet ready to wield political power: "Their attitude toward the liquor and lottery questions confirms this view" (535).
3. TR, "The Foreign Policy of President Harrison," *The Independent* 11 Aug. 1892, 1–3; rpt. in *Works*, 14:140–55. TR defends the administration's foreign policy, esp. its handling of the so-called "Chilean affair." After two American sailors were killed by a Chilean mob in October 1891, the Harrison administration responded with threats of war; the Chilean government's apologies and indemnities, however, averted the armed conflict that American jingoes desired.

To Matthews

Civil Service Commission
Oct 20th 92

Dear Brander,
   The Lang skit is very amusing.[1] I was so much pleased with your Trent article; you touched the very points worth touching.[2] I have one or two Mohunk incidents to relate when we meet.[3] In a day or two I'll send you the "politician" fragment; also the preface.[4]
   In great haste
                    Yours always
                    Theodore Roosevelt

BMP; 2 pp.; als.
1. Unidentified.

2. See TR to BM, 1 Oct. 1892, n. 5. In a letter dated 25 Oct. 1892 (BMP), Trent thanked BM for his *Cosmopolitan* review of *William Gilmore Simms*, remarking that BM was the only reviewer to perceive that he (Trent) aimed to "make a thorough study of the conditions that controlled the production of literature in the antebellum South." TR had favorably reviewed Trent's book in the June 1892 issue of *Atlantic Monthly* (*Works*, 12:287–91). In his reply to Trent (28 Oct. 1892, BMP), BM states that TR had recommended Trent's biography of Simms to him, adding: "Like myself, Roosevelt is a Southerner on his mother's side."

3. After visiting a Sioux reservation in Washington state, TR had attended the annual conference on Indian affairs at Lake Mohonk, N.Y., on 12, 13, and 14 Oct. (The conferences were held annually between 1883 and 1916.) TR spoke in favor of applying Civil Service hiring and firing policies to all Indian reservation agents and inspectors ("The Lake Mohonk Indian Mission Conference," *The Independent*, 20 Oct. 1892, 13).

4. Possibly a draft of TR's preface to his *The Wilderness Hunter* (New York: Putnam's, 1893), xxix–xxx, but impossible to verify.

To Matthews

Washington
Oct 23d '92

Dear Brander,
I enclose you the preface (if it do'nt bother you, please send it back) and the other scrawl, simply as a skeleton; I do'nt know whether it will be of any use.
Yours in wild haste
Theodore Roosevelt

BMP; 1 p.; als.

To Matthews

Washington
1215 19th St
Monday [Oct. or Nov. 1892?][1]

Dear Brander,
Unfortunately I shall probably only be in N.Y. on the 18th, arriving some time the day before & leaving the day after; so I fear I must defer the lunch. We called on your mother yesterday; she was out, but we saw your sister.[2] Remember to tell us the exact date you are coming as early as possible; I wish to arrange to have you both here a couple of times to dinner, and then one or two politics-literary lunches [outside?].

I have seen Field's book[3] and shall look up Bunner. My Mohonk colleagues were—bar Lieutenant Wotherspoon[4]—quite abnormal idiots. I am hoping the Bookbuyer will arrive today. I wish I could have seen Remington's pictures.[5]

Yours

T. R.

BMP; 4 pp.; als.

1. The contents of this letter, esp. the reference to the Mohonk conference (see TR to BM, 20 Oct. 1892), suggest that it was written during late Oct. or Nov. 1892.

2. BM's mother was Virginia Brander Matthews (1814–87); he had two sisters, both of whom rest in complete obscurity.

3. Eugene Field (1850–95), newspaper reporter and editor, and poet. In the 1918 edition of *An Introduction to the Study of American Literature,* BM praises Field's lyric verse, and mentions his *Second Book of Verse* (1892), probably the book referred to in this letter. See BM to TR, 20 Sept. 1918.

4. William Wallace Wotherspoon (1850–1921); he attended the 1892 Mohonk conference ("The Lake Mohonk Indian Mission Conference," *The Independent,* 20 Oct. 1892, 13). The army lieutenant was to have a long and distinguished career in the military; before retiring from the service in 1914, he attained the rank of major general, headed the army's War College, and served as chief of staff.

5. Frederic Remington (1861–1909), American painter and writer. TR greatly admired Remington's art, particularly his paintings of the American West.

To Matthews

Civil Service Commission
December 6, 1892.

Dear Brander:

I consider it a trifle soul-harrowing to get worked up about two heroes and then have them left on the top of a burning hotel in the midst of a sentence describing their escape.[1] I have but two suggestions to make in reference to the cowpuncher. Don't make him praise the fried pork. The good cook with the hash knife outfit on would doubtless have taken care that the boys had beef as often as was possible, with, at certain times, rice, prunes, corn, potatoes, tomatoes, etc. The cowpuncher who had been over the trail and spent a winter near Miles City would not be apt to think very much of fried pork. In the next place, as to the dance. It is absolutely true to nature to paint him as not understanding Patience (I had a very similar experience with one of my own cowpunchers in New York); but a man who had been up the trail would have been almost certain to see some kind of variety shows, in Deadwood, Denver, Cheyenne, Miles City, or elsewhere. The skirt dance would doubtless appeal to him as something better than he had yet seen; but he would have compared it with these and other variety shows, and not with a cowboy dance at the Mexican's home at Sagebrush Crossing. Another small point is that the onlooker would probably at first be a little uncertain whether the man were a cowboy, which, strictly interpreted, means merely a cow hand, or some ranchman or other person connected with the cattle business. I don't know, however, that this point is worth notice.

I was so driven to death that I didn't have a chance to get into the Century, and I am very sorry to have caused you the trouble of stopping in.[2] I have written to propose Thompson's name, and asked if the paper can be sent to me for my signature; in which case I shall forward it to you.

Richard Harding Davis was here yesterday and I met him at a dinner given by two of the British Legation. He was of course stirred up to much wrath by my Cosmopolitan article, and was so entirely unintelligent that it was a little difficult to argue with him, as he apparently considered it a triumphant answer to my position to inquire if I believed in the American custom of chewing tobacco and spitting all over the floor.[3] To this I deemed it wisest to respond that I did; and that in consequence the British Minister, who otherwise liked me, felt very badly about having me at the house, especially because I sat with my legs on the table during dinner. The man has the gift of [narration?]; but when it comes to breeding, upon my word it is hardly too much to say that even Kipling could give him points. I am glad I hit Kipling in the jaw, by the way; he needed it.[4] There was in my article, however, one joke on myself, for the final poem I quoted, the name of whose author I had forgotten, was by Oliver Wendell Holmes.[5] Funnily enough neither Howells nor Lodge remembered this author, although both were much struck by the poem.

Yours always,
Theodore Roosevelt

P.S.

I'll do the 500 words about Harts book as soon as I get a little time.[6]

BMP; 3 pp.; tls. with handwritten postscript; pbd. *LTR*, 1:298–99.

1. BM apparently tried his hand at writing a cowboy story, but I have found no published or unpublished story that fits the description rendered in this letter.

2. Founded in 1847 primarily as an organization for writers and artists, the Century Club by this time had become a bastion of New York elite culture; TR had become a member in 1884, BM in 1886. TR may have nominated Daniel

Greenleaf Thompson (see TR to BM, 3 Oct. 1892), who became a member of the club in 1892 (Century Association, *The Century, 1747–1946* [New York: Century Association, 1957], 407). However, both BM and TR knew other Thompsons whom they may have nominated.

3. Davis apparently objected to TR's castigations of "colonial"-minded Americans and of condescending British critics of American culture in "A Colonial Survival" (see TR to BM, 25 Feb. 1892, n. 1).

4. The opening paragraph of "A Colonial Survival" rebukes Kipling for his criticisms of New York, which TR believed were distorted and biased (see TR to BM, 31 May 1892, n. 2). Davis admired and was influenced by Kipling's fiction. But even he took umbrage at Kipling's sneering comments about "vulgar" American culture (Langford, *Richard Harding Davis Years*, 114–15).

5. Toward the end of "Colonial Survival," TR quotes (supposedly from memory) several lines of verse by a "nameless author" (*Works*, 12:312). The lines are from Holmes's "To Canaan: A Puritan War-Song," which he published anonymously in the Boston *Evening Transcript* in 1862 (*The Poetical Works of Oliver Wendell Holmes*, ed. Eleanor M. Tilton [Boston: Houghton Mifflin, 1975], 191–92).

6. Albert Bushnell Hart's *Formation of the Union, 1750–1729* (New York: Longmans, Green 1892). TR probably wrote the favorable review of the book in the *Nation* 56 (16 Mar. 1893): 203. The review is unsigned, but its contents and style mark it as TR's, and his letter to BM of 17 Feb. 1893 provides further evidence that it came from his hand. As earlier noted, BM was an advisory editor to Longmans, Green; and he was on the book-reviewing staff of *The Nation* from 1875 to 1895 (*Years*, 171).

To Matthews

Washington
Dec 13th 92

Dear Brander,

I stopped in at the Century, on Dec 7th, and posted Thompson's name; whenever you happen to be passing, forgive my past iniquity, and second the name.

My sister in law's death was very sad; poor girl; and so really beautiful, too.[1]

Lodge made almost exactly the same comment on the Repplier article about humour that you did.[2]

Yours
Theodore Roosevelt

You may rest assured that, for your sins, you'll know whenever I get to N.Y.

BMP; 3 pp.; als.

1. Anna (Hall) Roosevelt, wife of TR's brother Elliot, died of diptheria on 7 Dec. 1892, at the age of 29.

2. Repplier, "Wit and Humor," *Atlantic Monthly* 70 (Dec. 1892): 801–8. Repplier attempts to distinguish between humor and wit, and to account for the higher status generally accorded the latter. In his later essay "The Penalty of Humor" (1896), BM takes issue with those who exhibit, as Repplier does in her essay, a "kindly condescension" toward humor; using Mark Twain's fiction as his prime example, he argues that "true humor" can be superior to mere wit (see TR to BM, 4 May 1896, n. 2).

1893

To Matthews

Washington
Jan 4th '93

Dear Brander,

1. I liked your piece about New York poets very much—but I wish you had given some hint of your own poem.[1] By the way, many people have spoken to me of your Carmencita pastel.[2]

2. Did you send me Lang's editorial on my Cosmopolitan article?[3] If not I'll forward it to you. It is very bright and amusing, and, of course, very petulant, with much insisting that I said exactly what I did'n't say.

Any chance of your getting on here this winter? Warm regards to Mrs. Matthews.

Yours
Theodore Roosevelt

P.S.
Your letter has just come. We have "blooded up" Lang himself, I think![4] Walker *is* impossible.[5] The "Picturesque New York" was excellent.[6] What is the address of your mother, here? Mrs. R wishes to call. I shall be here myself in early February, and shall promptly engage you for a couple of nights, at the least—aside from lunches etc. Must consult Mrs. R. first

Yours
TR

BMP; 4 pp.; als.

1. "The Muses of Manhattan," *Cosmopolitan* 14 (Jan. 1893): 324–32. BM surveys poetry celebrating New York City; poets cited include H. C. Bunner, Richard Watson Gilder, Clarence Stedman, and Walt Whitman. Introducing Whitman's "The City of Ships," BM remarks: "The city discovered by a sailor is above all things a city of ships; and it is so that the self-styled poet of democracy sang her in his strange rhythmic chant, musical despite its roughness, poetic perhaps by sheer force of moderness" (325). Considering that many of BM's "genteel" contemporaries considered Whitman unpoetic and/or obscene, BM's compliment to Whitman is significant.

   BM's New York poem has not been identified.

2. "A Cameo and a Pastel," *Harper's Monthly* 86 (Dec. 1892): 130–35, rpt. in BM, *The Story of a Story*, 53–75. In the "Cameo," two dancing slave girls enthrall Vergil and Horace. Set in New York City in 1892, the "Pastel" links

past to present, as the voluptuous Spanish dancer Carmencita stirs the "barbarian" emotions of a modern poet. The pastel is based on Carmencita's performance at a private party BM attended (*Years,* 256). TR had seen her dance in 1891 and thought her very good (*Letters from Theodore Roosevelt to Anna Roosevelt Cowles* 1870–1918 [New York: Scribner's, 1924], 115).

3. Lang's witty response to TR's "Colonial Survival" appears in the *London Daily News,* 21 Dec. 1892. In a letter to BM dated 18 Jan. [1893], Lang explains that he rushed to Repplier's defense because she was a friend, even though he himself was put off by her "twittering about contemporary twitterers" (*Friends over the Ocean,* 120).

4. TR probably refers to BM's "Ignorance and Insularity," *Americanisms and Briticisms* (103–13). In his forthcoming review of BM's book in the *Illustrated London News* 102 (21 Jan. 1893): 90, Lang—whose letters to BM often contain statements and ideas that later appeared in a published review or article—expressed mild irritation at BM's accusation that he and other British critics were largely ignorant of American literature (see TR to BM, 30 Mar. 1893, n. 3).

5. See TR to BM, 1 Oct. 1892, n. 4. BM may have been having troubles of his own with *Cosmopolitan*'s strong-willed owner, for he soon ceased writing for the magazine.

6. "Picturesque New York," an illustrated essay by M. G. Van Rensselaer celebrating the beauty of New York City, had recently appeared in the *Century* 45 (Dec. 1892): 164–75.

To Matthews

Civil Service Commission
February 8, 1893.

Dear Brander:

Picking up the Critic, my attention was caught by a bit of colonialism so flagrant, so snobbish, and in such bad taste that I really wish you would call the attention of the Critic people to it. It is in the review of the Life of Allston.[1] The reviewer begins by calling him the American Raphael, a piece of silly vulgarity which is bad enough in itself; but he caps the climax by saying that he made the great mistake of his life, the irreparable blunder, when he left England, where, perhaps, he could have succeeded West[2] as president of the London Academy, and returned to America. He goes on to say that had he remained in England he might have had more of his pictures hanging in the English "manors." It might be pointed out to him that you can't hang pictures in manors, at least not with due regard for the pictures. The writer mentions that Congress offered to give Allston two of the panels in the rotunda to paint historical scenes, but actually hasn't got the sense to see that this gave him a chance such as he could not have had if he had remained in England a century, and that it was because he got tangled up in attempting to do a piece of work which was beyond him that he was unable to take advantage of the Congressional offer.[3] He also fails to see that undoubtedly one of the reasons why Allston was a much greater painter than West was his possessing those traits of character which made him remain an American instead of becoming an Englishman, as West did. I can stand with complete indifference an article by Andrew Lang, but I must say I get ravingly angry at so thoroughly snobbish an[d] unAmerican an article as this, and no less angry with the Critic people for publishing it. I wish you would show those of them who are my friends this letter.[4] I only write it because I am so anxious to see the Critic do well.

I have written to the Atlantic to ask permission to review Lodge's book and yours.[5] I do not know whether it will be granted. I do wish that you would go even more into the work of literary reviewing, and I also wish that you would write what might be called a history of American literature,—that is, a series of reviews, written in your characteristic style, of our different American authors and schools of literature.[6] If you would only do this, taking your time about it, you would make a book of the utmost permanent value and interest.

Remember me warmly to Mrs. Matthews. We enjoyed so much seeing you here.

Cordially yours,
Theodore Roosevelt

BMP; 2 pp.; tls.; pbd. *LTR*, 1:306–7.

1. Unsigned review of Jared Bradley Flagg's *The Life and Letters of Washington Allston* (New York: Scribner's, 1892), *Critic* 22 (28 Jan. 1893):41–42. TR's summary of the review is accurate.

2. Benjamin West (1738–1820); the expatriate American painter was very popular in his adopted country of England. He helped establish the Royal Academy of Arts in London in 1769, and succeeded Sir Joshua Reynolds as the academy's president in 1792. Allston (1779–1843) studied under West at the Royal Academy during his first stay in England (1801–8); he returned to England in 1811 and probably would have succeeded West as the academy's president had he not decided to move back to the United States permanently in 1818.

3. In 1817, Allston began his *Belshazzar's Feast,* the painting that would virtually obsess him for the rest of his life, but which he never finished. In 1830 and again in 1835–36, he declined offers by Congress to paint scenes from American history on two of the Rotunda panels of the Capitol. His letters explaining the reasons for his refusal—which included but were not limited to his desire to complete *Belshazzar's Feast*—are printed in Flagg, *Life and Letters,* 228–39, 287–91.

4. The *Critic,* a review of literature and the arts, was founded by Joseph B. Gilder (1858–1936) and Jeanette Gilder (1849–1916), brother and sister of Richard Watson Gilder, influential editor of the *Century.* BM reviewed books regularly for the magazine during its 35-year existence (1881–1906), and he was an intimate friend of the editors (see *Years,* 243–45).

5. Probably Lodge's *Historical and Political Essays* (1892) and BM's *Americanisms and Briticisms* (1892). As next letter indicates, the *Atlantic* rejected the proposal.

6. See TR to BM, 27 June 1892, n. 3.

To Matthews

Civil Service Commission
February 14, 1893.

Dear Brander:

New York *is* a pretty good place. I wish Miss Repplier could be chained up there until she got civilized.

The Atlantic has declined to take my essay, or review, concerning yours and Lodge's books. Do you think that Gilder would let me work it into the Century, under some such title as "American Essayists?" I wish he would, but I don't know, because the Century seems to have a rooted aversion to anything literary.[1]

I enclose you a copy of the part of my letter in answer to my English friend which dealt with his request to keep his own spelling.[2]

It may be that Lodge and I will be on in New York on the 22d or 23d; if so, would there be a chance of meeting you on that date?

Cordially yours,
Theodore Roosevelt

P.S.

Who should I send my "Winning of the West" to, to try for the Loubat prize?[3] I think your examination paper *excellent.*[4]

BMP; 1 p.; tls. with handwritten postscript; pbd. *LTR,* 1:309.

1. TR never published the review in the *Century Magazine.*
2. Unidentified.
3. In 1893, Joseph Florimond Loubat (1831–1927) established at Columbia College a $1,000 prize for the best work of original research on North America, open to any scholar whose book had been published after 1 Jan. 1888. The circular (bearing the signature of Seth Low, Columbia's president) for the prize was reprinted in the *Critic* 22 (11 Feb. 1893): 81. TR's *The Winning of the West* (1889) lost out to a worthy competitor: Henry Adams's 9-volume *The History of the United States in the Administrations of Jefferson and Madison* (1889–91).

4. BM several times sent to TR copies of examinations given in Columbia literature courses (see TR to BM, 21 May 1894). Several of the exams are in the BMP (Box 47), including one dated 11 Feb. 1893. BM's 10-question exam on American literature opens with the question: "What is Americanism in literature?"

To Matthews

Civil Service Commission
February 17, 1893.

Dear Brander:

Many thanks for the Loubat circulars.[1]

Lodge and I accept with pleasure for a lunch on the 22d. If you could have Howells and Gilder I know that Lodge would be especially pleased as he much wants to meet both, and so do I; and it would be a first class idea to have Bunner too, and any one else you wish—but those mentionned would be a host in themselves, and we would have great fun alone with them.[2]

I think Trent the very man to write the Motley.[3]

I will consult with you in reference to the letter about yours and Lodge's books for the Century when we meet.[4]

All four of my children are on the road to recovery now, so I leave with a clear heart.[5]

I wish I could get hold of the Nation's double review of Mahan,[6] and as soon as I get back here I will give you the Hart.[7] Address me at 689 Madison Ave., where I shall arrive for breakfast on the 22d; and tell me where we are to meet you at lunch and when.

Yours in great haste,
Theodore Roosevelt

BMP; 1 p.; tls.

1. See preceding letter, n. 3.
2. TR's use here of the word "meet" should not be interpreted to mean that he and Lodge had not yet made the personal acquaintance of Howells and (Richard Watson) Gilder: TR first met Howells at a dinner at Lodge's in 1884 (Morrison, *Rise*, 290); and he mentions having lunch with Lodge, BM, and Gilder in a letter dated 9 Mar. 1891 to his sister Anna (*Letters from Theodore Roosevelt to Anna Roosevelt Cowles*, 115).
3. John Lothrop Motley (1814–77), whose studies of Dutch history included *The Rise of the Dutch Republic* (1856) and the 4-volume *The History of the United Netherlands* (1860, 1867). TR greatly respected Motley, often linking his name with Francis Parkman's (see, e.g., *LTR*, 3:72). I find no record of Trent having written a book or separate essay on Motley, but Trent accords him a

brief section in chapter 19 of his *A History of American Literature, 1607–1865* (1903; reprint ed. New York: Appleton, 1920), 549–53, in which he emphasizes the historian's eloquence.

4. See preceding letter, n. 1.

5. TR's children were recovering from the measles as he was preparing to visit New York City (Cowles, *Letters from Theodore Roosevelt to Anna Roosevelt Cowles*, 125–26).

6. Alfred Thayer Mahan's 2-volume *The Influence of Sea Power upon the French Revolution, 1793–1812* (London: S. Low, Marston, 1892) was favorably reviewed (anonymously) in the *Nation* 56 (9 Feb. and 16 Feb. 1893): 108–10, 126–27. Historian and naval officer, Mahan (1840–1914) was president of the War College at the time. His arguments in favor of naval expansionism greatly influenced TR. TR, who had declared Mahan's earlier book *The Influence of Sea Power upon History* (London: S. Low, Marston, 1890) to be the "best and most important" naval history to appear in America or Europe (*Works*, 12:264), extolled the new work in a review published in *Atlantic Monthly* (Apr. 1893; rpt. in *Works*, 12:273–79). Mahan, he asserted, had managed to produce yet another historical study of "marked excellence and originality" (12:274).

7. See TR to BM, 6 Dec. 1892, n. 6.

To Matthews

Washington D.C.
March 16th [1893]

Dear Brander,

Would it bother you to send the enclosed to the Critic? I do'n't care whether they put it in with, or without, my signature; but the little volume referred to is worth noticing—and it is in our line of non-chauvinistic Americanism.[1] Who ought I to write to, on the Critic, if I ever wish to send them anything else? I may want to lend a hand to Trent's "Sewanee Review," which is a really good publication, by calling attention to it somewhere.

I shall probably be in New York some time towards the end of April; then we must meet. I hope the Critic has taken Bunners delicious Repplier [paragraph?].[2]

Regards to Mrs. M.

Yours
Theodore Roosevelt

BMP; 3 pp.; als.

1. See next letter, n. 2.

2. See next letter, n. 4.

To Matthews

Civil Service Commission
March 30th 93

Dear Brander,

What are the dates next week when your play is to be acted?[1] If we have no previous engagements I shall *get* tickets (*not* accept them from you—I have a few rays of propriety left) and go.

The Critic made me speak of the wild geese as "howling" instead of "honking" which was a trifle distressing.[2]

Bro. Lang was miffed; it hardly seems worth while for Lodge to answer him.[3] What a jack the Critic is not to have put in Bunner's delightful snapper on the Lang-Repplier combination.[4] I fear it comes in the category of feeble folk, with subdued anglo-maniac tendencies.

Lodge wishes to be remembered.

Yours in haste
Theodore Roosevelt

BMP; 3 pp.; als.

1. *The Decision of the Court: A Comedy* (New York: Harper, 1893); see next letter, n. 1.

2. TR's signed letter, dated 17 Mar. 1893, praising Ernest McGaffey's *Poems of Gun and Rod* (1892), appears in the *Critic* 22 (25 Mar. 1893): 182; the misprint of "honking" occurs in the sentence: "The howling of the wild geese smote his ear."

3. In his aforementioned review of *Americanisms and Briticisms* (TR to BM, 4 Jan. 1893, n. 4), Lang attempted to rebut BM's charge, in "Ignorance and Insularity," that a *Saturday Review* piece on Aldrich's *The Queen of Sheba* exemplified British ignorance of American literature (see TR to BM, 14 Apr. 1890, n. 2). Lodge entered the debate with a letter to the editors of the *Critic* 20 (18 Feb. 1893), 97–98, wryly observing that Lang displayed his own ignorance by suggesting that Aldrich's prose *novel* was a *poem*. Lang retaliated with "Insular and Continental Ignorance," *Critic* 22 (25 Mar. 1893): 182. He acknowledged his mistake, but continued his argument that British critics are no more provincial than their American and Continental counterparts.

4. In a signed letter, dated 1 Mar. 1893, to the editors of the *Critic* 22 (1 Apr. 1893): 205, Bunner chastised Lang for misspelling, in a review of Repplier's poetry, the last name of the American Revolutionary War general Francis Marion as "Marian." Bunner also took a swipe at Repplier for being an Anglophile, imaging her "standing anxiously a-tiptoe, waiting for the Ghost of Sydney Smith to ask 'Who reads an Amerian book?,' to reply with eager, feminine enthusiasm, 'Twasn't I, sir!'" The *Critic* editors apparently rejected the "snapper" initially, but then decided to print it, followed by a note explaining that the misspelling "Marian" was the printer's, not Lang's, error.

To Matthews

Civil Service Commission
April 6th [1893]

Dear Brander,

Last night Lodge and Mrs. Roosevelt and I saw your piece acted; we all agreed that it was very clever and amusing, the dialogue being bright, in delightful English, the [bits?] being first rate, and there being no flagging; and we thought Mrs. Booth acted the part well.[1] But we did not like the Squirrel Inn.[2]

As for the enclosed, take no notice of it. Nobody ever heard of Van Horne; and such a preposterous ass is simply incapable of seeing the truth underlying the wit of your statement; he is a mere colonial fool, of rebel proclivities, the latter making him welcome any tribute to Lee, even if silly, and his colonialism endearing to him a tribute by an Englishman.[3]

The Critic review of Edwin Arnold's poem was really good.[4]

Yours
Theodore Roosevelt

BMP; 4 pp.; als.

1. BM's one-act comedy *The Decision of the Court* was staged by the Theatre of Arts and Letters (at a playhouse on the corner of Broadway and 29th Street). During its brief existence (1892–93), the Theatre sponsored several one-act plays by fiction writers. Agnes Booth (1846–1910), sister-in-law of the famous actor Edwin Booth (1833–93), played the heroine of BM's farce; BM considered her "brilliant" in the part (*Years*, 337–38). A *New York Times* review (24 Mar. 1893, p. 4) also lauded Booth, and mildly praised the play overall.

2. *Squirrel Inn*, a play by fiction writer Francis R. Stockton (1834–1902), was also a Theatre of Arts and Letters production. A review of *Squirrel Inn* in the *New York Times*, 23 Apr. 1893, 13, notes that Stockton's play was not well received by audiences.

3. The BMP (Box 51) contains a clipping of a letter to the editor of the London *Times* signed by John D. Van Horne and dated 23 Feb. Van Horne attacks BM's assertion in "Americanisms and Briticisms" that Lord Wolseley insulted the memory of Robert E. Lee with "ignorant praise"; he also challenges TR's similar accusation quoted in BM's "Ignorance and Insularity" (See TR to BM, 14 Apr. 1890, n. 1). Van Horne later published two works on the South: *Jefferson Davis and Repudiation in Mississippi* (1915) and *Concerning a Full Understanding of the Southern Attitude Toward Slavery* (1921).

4. Sir Edwin Arnold (1832–1904), whose favorite poetic subject was the Orient, enjoyed a large audience on both sides of the Atlantic at the time. His verse play *Adzuma; or, The Japanese Wife* is the subject of a wittily sarcastic review in the *Critic* 22 (1 Apr. 1893): 196; the anonymous author may have been BM.

To Matthews

Civil Service Commission
May 7th '93

Dear Brander,

I reenclose Lang's letter; it is bright, as everything he writes is, and I wish somebody would write such a book as he describes.¹ There is a wealth of picturesque incident which has never been utilized in the fighting between Tarleton's red dragoons, Ferguson's riflemen, Cornwallis's admirable grenadiers of the line, and the stolid, well drilled, valiant Hessian infantry on the one side, and on the other the Continental line troops of Greene and Wayne, the light-horse of Harry Lee, the homespun minute-men, and the wild riflemen of the backwoods, with their wolfskin caps, and their hunting tunics, girded in with beadworked belts; while the painted Indian tribes add yet another element.² It ought to be written up purely from the military side, by someone able to appreciate brave deeds by whomever done, and the equal valor displayed by friend and foe.

I guess Lang is a good fellow; I wish he would come to this side sometime; we would give him a chance to see every side of our barbarous character!

Is'nt Bunner bright!³

Yours always
Theodore Roosevelt

BMP; 4 pp.; als.

1. In Feb., Lang had sent BM a letter which opens with the question: "Why does not a patriot like you write a short *picturesque* history of your war of Independence? A deal more interesting than those interminable accounts of the skirmish of 1863, or thereabouts" (*Friends over the Ocean*, 121).

2. TR had in fact already painted several of the "picturesque" Revolutionary War figures and incidents he mentions, and he would soon do so again in *Hero Tales from American History* (1895), co-authored with Lodge (see TR to BM, 25 Aug. 1894, n. 4). The first volume of *The Winning of the West* (1889), for example, devotes an entire chapter (21) to the defeat of British commander Patrick Ferguson (1744–80) by American backwoodsmen at the battle of King's Mountain (*Works*, 8:467–509); vol. 2 (also 1889) opens with "What the Westerners Had Done during the Revolution" (*Works*, 9:3–23), and chapter 11 of the same volume focuses on "Mad Anthony" Wayne's defeat of hostile Indians (*Works*, 9:312–48). Chapter 10 of *New York* (*Works*, 10:464–79) outlines the history of the Revolutionary War in that city. TR's contributions to *Hero Tales* include essays on Ferguson's defeat at the battle of King's Mountain and Wayne's victory at Stony Point (*Works*, 10:35–45).

3. Impossible to identify which of Bunner's many "bright" comments or writings TR refers to.

To Matthews

Washington D.C.
June [8?]th '93

Dear Brander,

I am really pleased that you liked my Century article, for I felt very doubtful over it; and the Wholly Innocent Man had to have all the snap taken out of his speech.[1]

I saw Kipling's article and thought it quite good;[2] I certainly can not hazard any guess concerning your Trombone-Frog.[3] By the way, without altogether agreeing with all of Boyeson's positions, I most emphatically do agree with what he said about your reviewing; we have hardly any good reviewers, and I do hope you will keep up your work of this sort.[4] And the Essays too! It will be long before I read other essays as good as those in Americanisms and Briticisms.

Indeed Chicago *was* worth while.[5] The buildings make, I verily believe, the most beautiful architectural exhibit the world has ever seen. If they were only permanent! That south lagoon, with the peristyle cutting it off from the lake, the great terraces, the grandeur and beauty of the huge white buildings, the statue, the fine fountains, the dome of the administration building, the bridges guarded by the colossal animals— well, there is simply nothing to say about it. And the landscape effects are so wonderful. In the fine-arts building, by the way, did you not like the "Death arresting the hand of the sculptor," and the "Peace Sign," the quiet pose of the naked warrior on the naked horse?[6]

In a week or so you will receive my "Wilderness Hunter." Just glance at the fourth chapter, because I know you like out-of-doors things, and at the last, for the sake of the allusions to Washington.[7]

Warm regards to Mrs. M.

Yours
Theodore Roosevelt

BMP; 7 pp.; als; pbd. *LTR*, 1:320.

1. "In Cow-boy Land," *Century Magazine* 46 (June 1893): 276–84. The essay is composed of sketches of and tales by several real-life characters whom TR met during his ranching days in Dakota, including a "true backwoods Donatello" who had no sense of right and wrong. TR strives to capture the earthy dialect of the characters, but apparently omitted, or was forced to delete, "snappy" language that might offend the *Century*'s genteel readers. See TR to BM, 16 Oct. 1893.

2. It is uncertain which Kipling article or story TR has in mind.

3. BM's "The Frog that Played the Trombone" appeared later in *Harper's Monthly* 87 (Nov. 1893): 911–17. The essay is a touching reminiscence about a deceased friend who, 20 years earlier, had given BM an ashtray in the shape of a frog

with a trombone. Before he died, the friend broke off his engagement to the woman he loved and married a wealthy socialite, an act that caused him feelings of guilt.

4. H. H. Boyesen, "American Literary Criticism and Its Value," *Forum* 15 (June 1893): 459–66. In this essay, BM's Columbia colleague argues that the quality and importance of book reviewing are in decline. But he knows of "no wielder of the critical lance in the United States . . . who in point of scholarship, perspicacity, and hospitality of mind rivals Mr. Brander Matthews" (466).

5. TR had recently visited the Chicago World's Fair, or Columbian Exposition; the rest of the paragraph describes the exposition's famous White City. See *The Chicago World's Fair of 1893: A Photographic Record*, ed. Stanley Appelbaum (New York: Dover, 1980).

6. Almost certainly *The Signal of Peace*, a bronze statue by Cyrus E. Dallin (1861–1944), and *The Angel of Death and the Sculptor*, a bas-relief by Daniel C. French (1850–1931). Both pieces were part of the United States sculpture exhibition in the fair's Palace of Fine Arts (*World's Columbian Exposition: Revised Catalogue with Index of Exhibitors*, ed. Department of Fine Arts [Chicago: W. B. Conkey, 1893], 25 and 31). Dallin's statue of a mounted warrior won a medal at the fair (see William Howe Downes, "Cyrus E. Dallin, Sculptor," *New England Magazine* 21 [Oct. 1899]: 196–209). French's figure of an angel arresting the hand of a sculptor was a memorial to the sculptor Martin Milmore (1844–83) (see Michael Richman, *Daniel Chester French: An American Sculptor* [Washington, D.C.: Preservation Press, 1976], 71–78).

7. The fourth chapter of TR's *The Wilderness Hunter* is titled "On the Cattle-Ranges; the Pronghorn Antelope." The last chapter, "Hunting Lore," devotes several pages to George Washington's love of hunting, and suggests that his hunting experiences helped develop the "manly virtues" that later would make him a great military and political leader (*Works*, 2:361–66).

To Matthews

Washington DC.
June 2[9?]th [1893]

Dear Brander,

I think the "Slang" piece is in your best style; it is *very* good.[1] As you know I have a peculiar affection for your essays. Did you see how Trent, in the Sewanee Review, alluded to your "Briticisms & Americanisms"?[2] You did him a real service, too; he greatly admires you, and your writings hit just at the moment to prevent his excellent and successful effort to de-provincialize himself from turning into a process of de-nationalizing himself. Warm regards to Madame. I am here alone—grappling with politics, and a *very* dull and truculent colleague.[3]

Yours
Theodore Roosevelt

BMP; 3 pp.; als.

1. "The Function of Slang," *Harper's Monthly* 87 (July 1893): 304–12; rpt. in BM's *Parts of Speech: Essays on English* (New York: Scribner's, 1901), 187–213. The essay is an enlightened analysis of the important linguistic functions performed by the different types of slang

2. Trent, "The Teaching of English Literature," *Sewanee Review* 1 (May 1893): 257–72. Contending that the study of "literature as literature," as opposed to philological analyses of literary texts, deserves a place in the college curriculum, Trent cites BM's "The Whole Duty of Critics," *Americanisms and Briticisms*, 114–34 (267). Trent also argues that students must study the "critical masters," and states that he divides his own literature course into sections on English and American literature.

3. Probably Gen. George D. Johnston (1832–1910), TR's fellow Civil Service Commissioner during 1892–93; TR and Johnston (who always wore a pistol!) continuously feuded until President Cleveland removed Johnston from the commission (in Nov. 1893). See Morris, *Rise*, 472; and *LTR*, 1:342.

To Matthews

Civil Service Commission
Aug 26th '93

Dear Brander,

Did you ever see anything more ingrainedly snobbish than Davis' description of his English electoral experiences in the last Harpers?[1] Incidentally he knows nothing whatever of American politics, of course. I think at the end, where his emotions at seeing the conservative candidate (liberals of course are vulgar) elected, and he gazes in tears at the portrait "of the sixth counters" (no common people for *him*), there is a touching resemblance to Mark Twain weeping at the tomb of Adam.[2]

I have a rather good story for you. Recently a sister of Winty Chanler[3] (whom you must know) was at a dinner in London, where there was also that somewhat heavy British wit Comyns Carr?[4] He began inveighing against the "higher education of women" and stated that he was going to introduce a society to promote their lower education. She sweetly asked what women he meant—English, French or American? He fixed her with an eye of cold disapproval, and, prancing into the trap, responded "I should begin with American women"; to which she, with a merely explanatory air "Oh, but you know Mr Carr, American *women* are not atall too highly educated for American *men*!"

Yours
T. R.

I am now off for thirty days on my ranch.

BMP; 4 pp.; als.
1. Richard Harding Davis, "A General Election in England," *Harper's Monthly*
87 (Sept. 1893): 489–506. Davis recounts the two weeks he spent with a Conservative candidate running for Parliament; he suggests that British elections
are more exciting than American ones, and admits that he was pulling for
the Conservative, who defeated his Radical opponent. The essay ends with
a maudlin description of the Conservative's return to his manor, where he is
greeted by his wife and servants.
2. Describing his visit to the Holy Sepulchre in Jerusalem, in *Innocents Abroad*
(chap. 53), Twain, having been told that he is standing over Adam's tomb,
wryly exclaims: "How touching it was, here in a land of strangers, far away
from home and friends and all who cared for me, thus to discover the grave
of a blood relation. . . . I leaned upon a pillar and burst into tears."
3. Winthrop Astor Chanler (1863–1926); descendant of Governor John Winthrop
and of John Jacob Astor, Winty belonged to the Players and other social clubs
of which TR and BM were members. He shared TR's love of outdoor sports
and the strenuous life.
4. Joseph W. Comyns Carr (1849–1916), English playwright and critic of art as
well as drama.

To Matthews

Civil Service Commission
Oct 16th 93

Dear Brander,
Archer¹ has just turned up; he seems a very good fellow; I've asked
him to dine with Lodge & myself this evening, and will take him round
to see the Sec'y of State² in the morning.
You're dead right about Van Allen,³ (aside; what the Senate really
needs is Tom Reed and his [rules?]).
I will surely remember to ask you for the unreconstructed rebel story;⁴
and remind me to tell you the Tale of the Lunatic and Sheriff Hell-
Roaring Bill Jones, and his deputy Snyder, who was plumb stuck on
his running, and the humourist Bixby, and what befell him.⁵
I will gladly lunch with you on the 28th; on the 21st I am already en-
gaged, but can I not see you just to shake hands? When do your lectures
begin & end?
Warm regards to Madame.
Yours
Theodore Roosevelt

BMP; 3 pp.; als.
1. William Archer (1856–1924); theater critic for the London *World* from 1884
to 1905 and a close friend of BM.

2. Walter Q. Gresham (1833–95), who had been the Republican presidential nominee in 1888, jumped parties and became Grover Cleveland's secretary of state in 1893. TR was on friendly terms with Gresham at this point, but he soon criticized him for being a weak secretary (see *LTR*, 1:335, 423; and Lodge, *Selections from the Correspondence of Theodore Roosevelt and Henry Cabot Lodge*, 1:140).

3. President Cleveland's appointment of James J. Van Alen (d. 1923) as minister to Italy, a reward for the latter's large campaign contributions to the Democratic party, enraged not only Republicans but also reform-minded independents like BM. Van Alen was confirmed by the Senate, but the public outcry led him to resign (see *LTR*, 1:341).

4. Possibly BM's "The Speech of the Evening," which later appeared in *Harper's Weekly* 38 (14 July 1894): 653–54; one of the main characters is an unreconstructed former Confederate.

5. TR relates the incident involving Sheriff "Hell Roaring" Bill Jones, the Lunatic, and the other personages mentioned—all of whom were part of the "Wild West" culture that TR encountered at his Dakota ranch—in the "In Cowboy Land" chapter of his autobiography (*Works*, 20:118–20).

To MATTHEWS

Civil Service Commission
Oct 24th 93

Dear Brander,

I will gladly burden you by accepting all three invitations; but will you let me get you to put off one until a little later than my lecture-course? and then will you let me bring on Cabot Lodge?[1] You see I am not modest!

Meanwhile, besides lunching with you next Saturday, I greedily name Nov 25th as the second day; on the 4th, 11th & 18th I have engagements. I am anticipating the receipt of "Politics in a Democracy".[2] I thought the "Frog that played the Trombone" excellent; so much so that I much wish to learn the after-fate of the girl.[3]

Lodge grimly remarks that he could never believe, unless it were proved, that you and Madame actually did come up to hear me lecture.

Yours,
Theodore Roosevelt

BMP; 3 pp.; als.

1. Beginning on 21 Oct. 1893 and continuing weekly through 25 Nov. 1893, TR delivered a series of Saturday morning lectures on the topic "The Westward Growth of the United States during the Revolution" at Columbia College. The initial lecture was titled "The Backwoodsmen of the Western Border and Their Foes"; the second (28 Oct. 1893) was on "The West in the Revolution."

The lectures were open to students and nonstudents, and they drew large audiences ("Lectures by Theodore Roosevelt" and "Theodore Roosevelt's Second Lecture," *New York Daily Tribune*, 22 Oct. 1893, 12; and 29 Oct. 1893, 24).

2. Daniel Greenleaf Thompson, *Politics in a Democracy* (New York: Longmans, Green, 1893). Thompson contends that selfish individualism and a decline in moral values threaten American democracy; he proposes less government and better education as cures. The most controversial chapters (9–12) argue that the Tammany Hall machine—which Progressives like TR and BM of course deplored—actually did more good than evil.

3. See TR to BM, [8?] June 1893, n. 3. BM does not relate what happens to the jilted girl in the piece.

To Matthews

Civil Service Commission
Nov 1st '93

Dear Brander,
The genial Lodge shall be invited.
What is a century between friends? however, if you have any feeling in the matter, I'll get my dates a hundred years closer next time.
I am looking forward to the arrival of the Figaro book.[1]
Yours
TR

BMP; 2 pp.; als.
1. Unidentified.

To Matthews

Sagamore Hill,
Nov 5th 93

Dear Brander,
You would have been crazy to have come to the lecture yesterday; you have given the last proof of friendship by coming to the first two![1] As for myself, being in for a lamb, I took the sheep also by going to see the Harvard-Cornell football game in the afternoon.[2]
Mrs Roosevelt says that she is really sorry she is not going to be in town and so cannot go to the Booth celebration, which she would particularly like to do.[3]
I hope this "Sun" story about Bartlett is one of the Sun falsehoods; at any rate the thing to do now is to beat Maynard.[4]
Yours
T. R.

BMP; 3 pp.; als.

1. On 4 Nov. 1893, TR delivered the third lecture in his series of lectures at Columbia (see TR to BM, 24 Oct. 1893, n. 1); the topic was "The Foundation of the Trans-Allegheny Commonwealth."

2. Harvard played Cornell in New York at Manhattan Field on 4 Nov. 1893, and won by a score of 34 to 0 in cold, rainy weather.

3. The great American actor Edwin Booth died on 8 June 1893. In 1889 he had established the Players, a New York club for persons associated with or interested in the theater; BM was among the original organizers (*Years*, 367–69). On 13 Nov. 1893, the Players sponsored a lavish memorial tribute to the deceased Booth at the Madison Square Garden Concert Hall, attended by about 1300 people ("In Memory of Edwin Booth," *New York Times*, 14 Nov. 1893, 8).

4. Edward T. Bartlett (1841–1910) was the Republican nominee for associate judge of the New York State Court of Appeals; his opponent was Isaac H. Maynard, an ally of Democratic boss and TR adversary David Bennet Hill (1843–1910). A front-page article ("This Bartlett Did") in the New York *Sun* on 5 Nov. 1893 denounced Bartlett for his "venomous and wholly unjustifiable" attacks on Maynard, and also accused Bartlett of fraud and deceit. Bartlett, however, won by a landslide, and his victory was hailed as a defeat for "bossism" ("Dragged down by Maynard," *New York Times*, 8 Nov. 1893, 1).

To MATTHEWS

Civil Service Commission
Dec 18th '93[1]

Dear Brander,

The perpetual wonder both to myself and the hard-featured Lodge is that you should come to *any* of my lectures.

I was really pleased that you should have liked my Boston address; when it comes to Americanism I guess we are both of us usually on deck.[2]

Mrs. Roosevelt will probably be at my lecture next Saturday, and afterwards I am to take her to a toyshop to get the childrens' Xmas presents; I'll have time to before lunch, will I not?

Regards to Mrs. Brander.

Yours

T. R.

BMP; 2 pp.; als.

1. Apparently, TR, who misdated several letters to BM, misdated this one, writing "December" when he meant "November." The evidence for my conjecture is as follows:

The last paragraph of the letter indicates that TR will give a lecture in New York "next Saturday" and then meet BM for lunch; since Dec. 18 was a

Monday, the next Saturday would have been Dec. 23. But I find no record of a TR lecture in New York on that date or at any time during late December; moreover, a letter dated 24 Dec. 1893 from TR to his sister Anna bears a Washington, D.C., return address and speaks of his pleasant week in that city (Cowles, *Letters from Theodore Roosevelt to Anna Roosevelt Cowles*, 132). Finally, some of TR's remarks in the next letter (21 Dec. 1893) are inexplicable if they were written just *three days* after the present letter. For example, without any mention of cancelling the Saturday lecture and lunch, TR states that he feels "rather dismally about [his] chances of seeing you soon"—no sooner than January 9, in fact.

    As noted earlier (TR to BM, 24 Oct. 1893, n. 1), TR delivered the last of his Columbia lectures on 25 Nov. 1893; it was probably the Saturday lecture referred to in the letter's closing paragraph.

2. On 15 Nov. 1893, TR delivered an address on "Our Common Schools: The Importance of Enlisting in Their Support Citizens of Every Religious Faith and of All Political Parties," to a large audience at Boston's Huntington Hall. In addition to arguing for equal educational opportunity and against intolerance, TR made a strong pitch for Americanism, so much so that the *New York Times* report on the address (19 Nov. 1893, 22) appears under the title "The True American Spirit."

To Matthews

Civil Service Commission
Dec 21st '93

Dear Brander,

    Funnily enough Lodge & I *did* drink your health at dinner last evening; and, by a more odd coincidence our host, one Captain Davis U.S.N.[1] (it was a nonpartisan dinner to secretary Herbert)[2] in speaking of my article took precisely your ground about French literature—Lodge & I holding the contrary, and incidentally quoting Lowell's article in support.[3] I'll discuss the matter with you when next we meet. Also intercollegiate games; the trouble here is that we wish enough competition to arouse healthy rivalry, without which the games are pretty sure to languish, but not so much as to excite *un*healthy rivalry; I sometimes think that intercollegiate contests arouse too much enthusiasm, but I am afraid that inclass contests merely would arouse too little.[4]

    At present I feel rather dismally about my chances of seeing you soon. I have to go on to New York about Jan 10th, to present my accounts for audit to the Boone & Crockett; & also to go out to my Long Island place and prepare for the stringent measures of reform within the party which the Hard Times Call For![5] But that is in the middle of the week, so there is no chance for a lunch. Could'n't you dine with me at the

Union League club on the evening of the 9th? I'll ask Bunner; and try to get Lodge, too, as he will then be returning from Boston.

> Yours
> TR

BMP; 4 pp.; als.; pbd. *LTR*, 1:343–44.

1. The dinner was probably hosted by naval officer Charles Henry Davis, Jr. (1845–1921), TR's friend and Lodge's brother-in-law.
2. Hilary A. Herbert (1834–1919) was appointed secretary of the navy by Grover Cleveland in 1893, serving until 1897.
3. I have not located an article by TR on French writers, but he clearly did not share BM's high regard for French literature (see TR to BM, 28 Dec. 1890, n. 2). TR and Lodge may have quoted from Lowell's "Rousseau and the Sentimentalists" (in Lowells's *Among My Books* [Boston: Osgood, 1870], 458–62); Lowell suggests that Rousseau, Hugo, and other French writers lack the sincerity and conviction of their Anglo-Teutonic peers.
4. Because of many and sometimes severe injuries resulting from athletic contests (and from the brawling that often accompanied them), many educators and journalists wanted to curtail or even abolish some intercollegiate sports, especially football. TR publicly entered the debate with his "Value of an Athletic Training," *Harper's Weekly* 37 (23 Dec. 1893): 1236. TR strongly defended college athletics, particularly football, arguing that the benefits to the individual athlete and to society in general outweighed the risks. BM probably read the essay, and TR's comments in this letter suggest BM did not entirely concur with the views expressed. See also TR's "'Professionalism' in Sports," *North American Review* (Aug. 1890); rpt. in *Works*, 13:583–88.
5. Democrat Grover Cleveland was in the White House, and the country was in the throes of the Panic of 1893.

To Matthews

Civil Service Commission
Dec 27th 93

Dear Brander,

I liked the cowboy article, though I rather objected to the cowboy's demise;[1] and I also liked your Harper's Weekly vignette.[2]

I had already heard that the dinner was a great success. Lodge and I were really very sorry we were kept here.[3] Now Lodge has again backed out, and can't get on; but *I* accept with Dutch stolidity your substitute, and will dine with you on Thursday at the Players at 7.30; and very glad I shall be to see you.[4]

> Yours
> Theodore Roosevelt

BMP; 2 pp.; als.
1. This appears to be the same "cowboy" story alluded to in TR's letter to BM of 6 Dec. 1892.
2. "In the Midst of Life," *Harper's Weekly* 37 (16 Dec. 1893): 1206. Set in New York City on Christmas Eve, the story dramatizes the thesis that those who ask for charity probably do not deserve it, whereas others would rather die than beg. This is the closing story in BM's *Vignettes of Manhattan* (see TR to BM, 3 Apr. 1894, n. 3).
3. TR and Lodge were unable to attend a testimonial dinner given to BM on 20 Dec. 1893 at Sherry's restaurant in New York City. The speakers included Mark Twain, who delivered a hilarious—but very affectionate—speech. The affair was reported in the *Critic* 20 (30 Dec. 1893): 432; see also Oliver, *Brander Matthews*, xii–xiii.
4. TR mentions the Thursday evening dinner with BM at the Players Club in a letter to Anna Roosevelt (14 Jan. 1893, LTR, 1:305).

To Matthews

Washington D.C.
Dec 31st '93

Dear Brander,
Your article on Lang is simply delightful; but I am not atall sure he will altogether relish it. And the best of it is that you have been *so* complimentary—justly complimentary—that he can't very well object. I hardly know which he will find most offensive; to be defended and excused for being sensitive to American criticism, or praised upon the absence of Briticisms in his style. By the way, I had forgotten his deliciously inept remark about Poe's being a gentleman among canaille. Altogether I think that your article is admirable, in tone, in temper, in everything.[1]
Regards to Madame.
Yours
Theodore Roosevelt

BMP; 4 pp; als.; pbd. *LTR*, 1:345.
1. BM, "Andrew Lang," *Century Magazine* 47 (Jan. 1894): 375–81; rpt. in BM's *Books and Play-Books*, 138–60. BM praises Lang's abilities as a critic and scholar, but mildly chides him for being overly sensitive to "darts of transatlantic criticism" and for describing Poe as a "gentleman among *canaille.*" Lang makes that remark in "Edgar Allan Poe," one of the essays in his *Letters to Dead Authors* (New York: Scribner's, 1886), 151. In a personal letter, Lang thanked BM for the essay but did not respond to any of the compliments or criticisms (*Friends over the Ocean*, 123).

1894

To Matthews

Civil Service Commission
January 2, 1894.

Dear Brander:

Lodge won't be with me, I am sorry to say. Next to dining with yourself alone I should most like to dine with yourself and Bunner. I will look at the last paragraph in the Critic, but I don't need to be told anything about the colonialism of the Dial.[1] I will also see the chump paper in the Forum and discuss it with you later on. (I have seen it; the man is an idiot; would it be worth while answering him?).[2] I was much pleased with the calendar.

Yours,
Theodore Roosevelt

BMP; 1 p.; tls.

1. The last paragraph of the 30 Dec. 1893 number of the *Critic* is an unsigned letter from a self-described "good New Yorker" denouncing the *Dial* for its acute "colonialism" (433); the letter's inclusion in BM's collected periodical writings in the BMP (Contributions to Periodicals, 5:264) suggests that it was written by BM. The letter notes that a recent issue of the *Dial* gave three times more space to two minor British writers than to Francis Parkman. The *Dial* was genteel and often Anglophilic in its literary taste. See TR to BM, 14 Feb. 1894, n. 3.

2. The "chump paper" is most likely "Has Immigration Dried up Our Literature?" *The Forum* 16 (Jan. 1894): 560–67, by the historian Sydney G. Fisher (1856–1927). Fisher's xenophobic argument is that unrestricted immigration of non-Anglos was directly responsible for a supposed decline of American literature during the second half of the nineteenth century.

To Matthews

Civil Service Commission
Jan 15th 94

Dear Brander,

Herewith I send you back the Sexual Morality, Prince Prigio, and Snob Circular; each is delightful in its own way, and all have been much admired by Lodge, who sends you his regards.[1]

I can not get over the silliness of the Evening Post in publishing that female idiot's answer to your article.[2] The sporadic she-fool who writes I can comprehend; but not the attitude of the colonnial editor.[3] I enjoyed greatly my dinner with you. Next time I come on I wish you to dine with me to meet Winty Chanler; then I'll try to get Dan Wister,[4] and I'll ask Bunner too. Is there any chance atall of your getting on here this winter?

Alice and Ted love Prince Prigio.

Warm regards to Mrs. B.

> Yours ever
> Theodore Roosevelt

BMP; 4 pp.; als.; pbd. *LTR*, 1:351–52.

1. *Prince Prigio* (Bristol: J. W. Arrowsmith, 1889) is an original fairy tale by Andrew Lang, set in the mythical kingdom of Pantouflia; Lang drew on his scholarly knowledge of mythology and folklore when writing the tale.

   The "Sexual Morality" and "Snob Circular" are unidentified; the latter probably was one of the numerous American or English guides on etiquette available at the time, which were often attacked for promoting snobbery. For example, in an anonymous review titled "The Snob's Guide," *Spectator* 70 (1 Apr. 1893), 417–18—a periodical that BM regularly read—Lucie Heaton Armstrong's handbook *The Etiquette of Party Giving* (1893) is disparaged as a set of rules for the "aspiring but ignorant snob."

2. Probably "A Phase of Literary Criticism," *New York Evening Post*, 9 Jan. 1894, 6. The letter to the editor defends Andrew Lang against BM's "patronizing" criticisms in his recent article on the Scotsman (see TR to BM, 31 Dec. 1893). Since the letter is signed "America," it is unclear how BM could have determined the gender of the author, but he apparently believed that it was written by Lang's foremost American admirer, Agnes Repplier. See TR to BM, 1 Feb. 1894, n. 3.

3. The *New York Evening Post's* chief editor was Edwin Lawrence Godkin (1831–1902), former editor of the *Nation* (1865–1881). The influential and outspoken mugwump had in 1884 blasted TR for refusing to join the revolt against the Republican party (see TR to BM, 31 July 1889, n. 1), and the two remained bitter enemies thereafter. Though Scotch-Irish by birth, Godkin was a lifelong Anglophile. BM, who was a reviewer for the *Nation* during Godkin's tenure as editor, admired his intelligence and integrity but found him cranky and intolerant (*Years*, 173–74).

4. The novelist Owen "Dan" Wister (1860–1938) had met TR at Harvard; they remained close friends for the rest of their lives. Wister dedicated (and in 1911 rededicated) his bestselling novel *The Virginian* (1902) to TR; he also published *Roosevelt: The Story of a Friendship* (New York: Macmillan, 1930). After being introduced to Wister by TR, BM became the novelist's friend and correspondent, and frequently praised his writings in reviews and essays.

To Matthews

Civil Service Commission
Jan 30th '94

Dear Brander,

I am going to look up the Academy article; but Lodge lost all interest as soon as he found who the author was, as he says he is "an antiquarian animalcule", of much philological learning and pedantry, who has always lived in England, and is quite abnormally colonnial in [turn?] of mind.[1] Very characteristically, congressman Everett, who is a silly anglomaniac, spoke to me of the article with a snigger of approval.[2] I am curious to see it. My friend, you have drawn blood.

I am so sorry you have had the grip; I am just getting over a slight attack myself. I will read your St. Nicholas paper on Franklin at once, and write you about it.[3]

Of course the lunch you propose will be delightful. I *think* I can get on for it—it is needless to say I shall try my utmost to—the only thing that may by any chance prevent me is Mrs. Roosevelt's health.

Let me know when you get the day fixed, and just as far in advance as possible, so that I may make every effort to be present. A lunch at your house, with such guests, would be worth travelling a much longer distance than from Washington to New York.

What an everlasting cad R. H. Davis is![4]

Warm regards to Mrs. M.

Yours ever
Theodore Roosevelt

BMP; 4 pp.; als.; pbd. *LTR*, 1:358.

1. F[itzeward] H[all], "The American Dialect," *The Academy* 44 (30 Dec. 1893): 587–88. The American-born Hall (1825–1901) received his D.C.L. at Oxford Univ. and then became a professor at King's College in London, living his adult life in England. Contrary to Lodge's snide description of him, Hall was a widely published and respected philologist, whose special interests were American idioms and Sanskrit (he was the first American to translate a Sanskrit text into English). In "American Dialect" he purports to elucidate the "deterioration, more or less deliberate, which the English language is undergoing at the hands of [his] fellow countrymen." The fellow countryman who is the central target of the essay's sarcasm is BM. After announcing that "no one has dissertated in a loftier tone, or with more cathedral complacency" about the American language and literature than BM—who is described as an influential representative of the "cock-a-doodle-doo school"—Hall launches a diatribe against *Americanisms and Briticisms.*

2. William Everett (1839–1910), son of the famous orator and educator Edward Everett (1794–1865), was a Democratic congressman (1893–95) from Massachusetts; he was educated at Trinity College, Cambridge, as well as at Harvard, where he taught classics during the 1870s. A former Republican and a committed mugwump, he ran against Lodge for a congressional seat in 1890, losing by a slim margin. TR once called him a "very un-venerable mountebank" (quoted in John A. Garraty, *Henry Cabot Lodge: A Biography* [New York: Knopf, 1965], 122).

3. BM, "Benjamin Franklin," *St. Nicholas* 21 (Feb. 1894): 316–23; rpt. in *An Introduction to the Study of American Literature* (1896), 21–39. BM honors Franklin as the "first great American," whose attitude toward Europe was never "colonial." He also lauds Franklin's spirit of public service, pragmatic temperament, and scientific habit of mind, and he emphasizes that Franklin was as gifted a writer as he was a statesman. See TR to BM, 4 and 7 Feb. 1894, for TR's comments on the essay.

4. TR may have been provoked by Richard Harding Davis's opinions on American women expressed in his recent essay "The West and East Ends of London," *Harper's Monthly* 88 (Jan. 1894): 279–92, which compares and contrasts London's high and low cultures to those of New York City.

To Matthews

Civil Service Commission
Feb 1st 94

Dear Brander,

I read the Academy article, & it *did* make me bound with wrath; I think I shall have to give that muddy-minded ass a dressing somehow—though I suppose he is really of no special importance.[1] See also the present Atlantic for an article on Essayists which shows a similiar crawling servility in the writer.[2]

Now, a question; did the person who wrote about your Lang article have her letter published in the Evening Post or Nation, or both?[3]

Yours
Theodore Roosevelt

BMP; 2 pp.; als.

1. See n. 1, preceding letter.

2. "Contemporary Essays," *Atlantic Monthly* 73 (1894): 262–69. The anonymous author praises Agnes Repplier, whom TR despised, and asserts that American writers have produced no great literature.

3. See TR to BM, 15 Jan. 1894, n. 2. There is no article in the *Nation* attacking BM's essay on Lang.

To MATTHEWS

Washington D.C
Feb 4th '94

Dear Brander,
Your "Franklin" is really admirable; I felt a little needless anxiety as to how you would do it; but I can say quite sincerely that it could not have been done better.[1]

Envy is a mean trait; so I do not envy you the permanency of the success of Briticisms and Americanisms; it has drawn *such* quantities of blood! I think it has been one of the few essays which have a real effect on our thought. Of course you have seen Birrells article on it; which I esteem another compliment to it, of a very marked kind.[2] Birrell's own attitude towards all English literature is good; but he fails to understand the contemptible mental position of the Repplier type of individual; and of course it is rather a shock to him to have the truth borne in on him that the best English, the highest standard of our own language, may be in America quite as well as in England.

Yours
T. R.

BMP; 4 pp.; als.
1. See TR to BM, 30 Jan. 1894, n. 3.
2. Augustine Birrell (1850–1937), English author and political figure whom TR much respected (see Cowles, *Letters from Theodore Roosevelt to Anna Roosevelt Cowles*, 141, 204). Birrell's review essay on BM's *Americanisms and Briticisms* appears in Birrell's *Essays about Men, Women and Books* (New York: Scribner's, 1894), 200–210. Birrell declares that BM's essays stem from a "diseased patriotism" that overvalues American and degrades British literature, and he defends Repplier against BM's charge in *Americanisms and Briticisms* that she is Anglophilic (see TR to BM, 26 Apr. 1892, n. 1).

To MATTHEWS

Civil Service Commission
Feb 7th 94

Dear Brander,
The clippings merely amused me; I had recovered from my anger.[1] But what a servile spawn we have here! Luckily they are not very influential and they are diminishing in number.

Lodge's paper in Harpers will be out soon; he has corrected the proof.[2]

I had nothing to correct in your Franklin; you hinted at his fault with just the right mixture of delicacy and emphasis.[3]

I shall read the "Fur & Feathers" with interest.[4] It is hard to say whether [similar?] volumes would succeed here or not. They *might*. But (this is of course not for general circulation) they would be poor stuff if Sandys edited and wrote them.[5] He admits into Outing just the cheap, sensational clap trap of which he complains; and most of the sporting papers put out therein are as ill-written as can be. A far better man with whom to get in touch is George Bird Grinnell, the editor of Forest and Stream.[6] *Possibly*, but only possibly, the Boone and Crockett Club might be willing to go into editing such a series.

Yours

Theodore Roosevelt

BMP; 4 pp.; als.

1. Unidentified, but probably more "colonial-minded" essays, perhaps by Repplier or Fitzeward Hall.

2. Henry Cabot Lodge, "The Opportunity of the Republican Party," *Harper's Weekly* 38 (17 Feb. 1894): 150–51.

3. In "Benjamin Franklin" (see TR to BM, 30 Jan. 1894, n. 3), BM suggests that Franklin "lacked the spirituality, the faith in the ideal, which was at the core of [Abraham] Lincoln's character. And here was Franklin's limitation: what lay outside of the bounds of common sense he did not see—probably did not greatly care to see" (321). BM's later essays praising President TR often portray him as a "practical idealist" who combined in his character the best traits of Franklin and Lincoln.

4. In 1893, Longmans, Green published the first of a 14-volume *Fur and Feather* series of sporting and naturalist works, under the general editorship of Alfred Edward Thomas. As the next letter indicates, BM, as advisory editor of the American branch of Longmans, Green, solicited TR's opinion about a similar series for the American market.

5. Edwyn Sandys (1860–1909) wrote on hunting and fishing for *Outing*, a gentleman's outdoor magazine established in Albany, N.Y., in 1882. Despite TR's low opinion of *Outing*, it enjoyed great success during the 1890s and attracted articles by many prominent writers, including TR. See Frank Luther Mott, *History of American Magazines* 1885–1905 (Cambridge, Mass.: Harvard Univ. Press, 1957), 4:633–38.

6. In addition to being owner and chief editor (1880–1911) of the very popular *Forest and Stream*, George Bird Grinnell (1849–1938) helped TR organize the Boone and Crockett Club (see TR to BM, 27 Mar. 1891, n. 1) and was one of America's leading naturalists (see Paul Russell Cutright, *Theodore Roosevelt: The Making of a Conservationist* [Urbana: Univ. of Illinois Press, 1985], 171–77). Neither Grinnell nor the Boone and Crockett Club accepted BM's offer, if he extended one, to undertake the project.

To Matthews

Civil Service Commission
Feb 8th '94

Dear Brander,
 The enclosed explains itself; I send it merely that you may know the exact situation. Later I'll write Gilman again.[1]
 The (Fur & Feathers) book has come; it seems a good one. To whom shall I return it? I think such a series for the United States would be a good one, *if, and only if,* edited and written by exactly the right people. Sandys would botch it hopelessly. Even Grinnell could hardly do the scientific part. The Boone & Crockett club *might* take hold; but one or two men should have the real control. I have no idea as to the chances of a good sale, but I think the series would be a success.
 Different men would have to write the different volumes and parts of volumes.

Yours
T. R.

BMP; 3 pp.; als.
1. Unidentified; perhaps a letter from or concerning Dr. Daniel Coit Gilman (1831–1908), president of Johns Hopkins Univ. (1875–1901) and later (1901–1904) first president of the Carnegie Institution.

To Matthews

Civil Service Commission
February 14, 1894.

Dear Brander:
 The Sewanee Professor turned up all right, and I gave him your letter.[1] I was of course interested in your examination paper, and I thought it admirable. I had already seen Whitcomb's paper that you referred to, and have written him a letter about it; I don't know whether he ever got it or not.[2] I thought it a very good article. I am amused that the English papers should have taken up Birrell's piece in reference to you with such glee.[3] As Lounsbury said, they are *very* sensitive whenever they know about any one's criticising them. Of course no one is sensitive when he doesn't know that any one has criticised him. In great haste

Very cordially yours,
Theodore Roosevelt

BMP; 1 p.; tls.
1. William P. Trent; see next letter.

2. Seldon Lincoln Whitcomb (1866–1930) published an article titled "Nature in Early American Literature" in the *Sewanee Review* 2 (Feb. 1894): 159–79. Whitcomb received his A.M. in English from Columbia in 1893 and was a fellow in literature there in 1894. He joined the English Department at Grinnell College in 1895. (There is no letter to or from Whitcomb in the TRP.)

3. See TR to BM, 4 Feb. 1894. The newspaper pieces are unidentified. The *Dial* review of Birrell's book (16 [1 Mar. 1894]: 149) quotes approvingly the British critic's disparaging remarks about BM, thus providing further evidence to TR and BM of that American magazine's "colonialism" (TR to BM, 2 Jan. 1894).

To Matthews

Civil Service Commission
March 7, 1894.

Dear Brander:

Trent has just written me in the very warmest terms of how much he owes to you for the pleasure of his visit in New York. He is emphatically a deserving fellow and a man of promise, and you have done real good by the kindnesses you have in so many different ways shown him. He thoroughly appreciates them, and his estimate of you personally is sufficiently appreciative to merit even the endorsement of Lodge and myself![1]

Now, I have got to come on to New York this month, and so I write you to know if you have yet made up your mind as to any day it would be convenient for me to come to lunch with you. Do remember however that the man I want to lunch with is *you*, and that, pleasant though the people you speak of having to meet me are, I really do not care at all whether you have them or not; but I *do* care to see you to talk over various things. I am also going to try to see Bunner.

Regards to Mrs. Matthews.

Very cordially yours,
Theodore Roosevelt

BMP; 1 p.; tls.

1. Trent's letter is not in the TRP. In addition to the flattering review of Trent's *William Gilmore Simms* in 1892 (see TR to BM, 1 Oct. 1892, n. 5), BM's kindnesses included a strong recommendation to Thomas Lounsbury in 1893 supporting Trent's application for a faculty position at Yale. (Trent did not get the job, however). In 1900, BM successfully lobbied—with support from Governor TR—for Trent's appointment to the Columbia English Department, where Trent remained until the end of his career. However,

Trent's pro-German sympathies during World War I ignited a long and bitter feud between him and BM (see Oliver, *Brander Matthews*, 141–42, 226n).

To Matthews

Civil Service Commission
March 20, 1894.

Dear Brander:

My sister wrote me in a rather nervous mood about her presentation at court.[1] As she was there as a member of the ambassadorial household, and was acting as such, I told her I would alter my severe republican notions sufficiently to acquiesce in her presentation. (Not that it mattered whether I did or not.) I shall write her forthwith your views as to the demoralizing effect of reading Littell's Living Age.[2]

Since writing you last I succumbed to an attack of bronchitis and was forced to give up my intended holiday and take a trip to South Carolina, where I recovered my health fox hunting; so that for the present, I am very sorry to say, I am unable to go to New York. But will not your duties as Professor keep you there till about June 1st? By that time I shall be on and will claim my lunch. I was much interested in your Dial piece.[3]

Yours ever,
Theodore Roosevelt

BMP; 1 p.; tls.

1. TR's sister Anna, who had spent the entire winter in London, was to be presented at the royal court there (see *LTR*, 1:363–64).
2. Founded by Eliakim Littell (1797–1870) in 1844, the *Living Age*, published in Boston, was composed mainly of material reprinted from British periodicals. As a major channel for British comments on American affairs, it thus helped promote the Anglophilic spirit that BM and TR disdained.
3. "English at Columbia College," *Dial* 16 (16 Feb. 1894): 101–2; BM describes his department's faculty and course offerings.

To Matthews

Civil Service Commission
April 3, 1894.

Dear Brander:

I don't usually write that I am sorry to get your letters, but I was to get this one. In the first place I am sorry about your cough. I sympathize with you on this point keenly, as I have had a cough myself for two months past, and it was because of this that I was not able to get on to New York. Now, I can't tell whether I will be able to get on before the first of June or not, but I shall make every effort, so as to get a glimpse of you before you leave. I do hope you will have a pleasant trip. It certainly sounds attractive.

Did you notice Miss Replier's allusion to your carmencita piece in her article on pastels?[1] Do you know I think you have had a decidely chastening effect on that young lady?

When I see you I want to tell you of a row I have had with the Atlantic Monthly people over yourself and Lodge.[2] It is an epistolary battle, which has raged at intervals of a few weeks all winter. I want you to make one or two cheerful vignettes of New York. I like your vignettes very much, and if I liked them less I wouldn't feel so melancholy about it.[3]

> Yours,
> Theodore Roosevelt

P.S.

I enclose a sheet from a letter of Trent's, just to show you how he appreciates what you have done; indeed you did render him a service.[4] The letter was confidential; so do'n't speak of it.

When, or if, you see Lang, give him my love & tell him I like *all* his writing, and especially his reviews and his assaults on the U.S. Do'n't you like Kipling's "Rhyme of the Three Sealers"?[5]

BMP; 2 pp.; tls. with handwritten postscript; pbd. *LTR*, 1:370–71.

1. Repplier, "Pastels—A Query," *Cosmopolitan* 16 (Apr. 1894): 762–64. Attempting (futilely, she concludes) to define what a literary pastel is, Repplier briefly discusses a variety of writings titled or labeled as pastels, including BM's "A Cameo and a Pastel" (TR to BM, 4 Jan. 1893, n. 2), which she describes as a "vivid description of Carmencita dancing in a New York studio" (763). It is unclear where TR detected a "chastening effect," however.

2. The *Atlantic Monthly* was then edited by Horace E. Scudder (1838–1902). TR often corresponded with Scudder about literary matters and the *Atlantic* (see, e.g., *LTR*, 1:229, 420, 472), but the letters about Lodge and BM to which TR refers apparently have been lost, so the reason for the "row" is unknown.

3. BM had been publishing in *Harper's Monthly* a series of vignettes of New York City, which he intended to be realistic "snap-shots" of life in the great metropolis (see *Years*, 381–86). Though several of the tales focus on social problems and deal with suffering and/or death—as, for example, does "In the Midst of Life," which TR praises in his letter of 27 Dec. 1893—they are not, overall, as depressing as TR suggests. BM seems to have responded to TR's plea for a more "cheerful" story; see TR to BM, 29 June 1894.

4. See TR to BM, 7 Mar. 1894, n. 1.

5. *The Rhyme of the Three Sealers* (New York: Macmillan, 1893; rpt. in Kipling's *The Seven Seas* [London: Methuen, 1896]) is a verse tale of a bloody battle

among rival sealing vessels off the coast of Russia near Japan. TR later used several lines from the poem as the epigraph to his essay "The Fur Seal Fisheries," *Metropolitan Magazine* 25 (Mar. 1907): 687–701.

To MATTHEWS

Civil Service Commission
May 5, 1894.

Dear Brander:

I am awfully afraid I am not going to be able to get on to New York before you leave. I am very sorry, as there were some things I particularly wished to talk over with you. Lodge regretted so much failing to find you while in New York.

Yes, we have a small boy.[1] I begin to think that this particular branch of the Roosevelt family is getting to be numerous enough. Mrs. Roosevelt is very well. She was out for a two hours' drive with me yesterday through this beautiful country. Are you so fond of New York that you don't care for the country? If not, I do wish you could come on to Washington sometime in the spring that I may show you Rock Creek when the trees are budding and the flowers are out. Do you know I don't believe our people half appreciate how picturesque and beautiful our landscapes are.

I decidedly envy you your reputation as being the champion of American methods and ways in literature, in spelling, and in all other directions.

I reinclose your cowboy article.[2] I like it. I began to be a little doubtful about my own dialect accuracy. The things I have been trained to observe I can observe all right, but it is astonishing how difficult it is to record even what one is familiar with if one is not accustomed to recording it.

If on the other side you see Andrew Lang give him my love.

Faithfully yours,

Theodore Roosevelt

P.S.

Apropos of your article on bookbinding[3] I have just seen a very beautiful specimen from Philadelphia; a book written by Henry Adams on Samoa, but not yet published.[4] Warm regards to the Madam.

I am glad the Harvard boys did so well; I have been supplying them with some arguments.[5]

BMP; 2 pp.; tls. with handwritten postscript; pbd. *LTR*, 1:376.
1. Edith Roosevelt gave birth to Archibald Bullock Roosevelt, her fourth child (third son), on 9 Apr. 1894.
2. See TR to BM, 27 Dec. 1893.

3. BM, "Bookbindings of the Past," *Century* 48 (May 1894): 60–73. BM describes the article as a "voyage in retrospection in search of the masters and masterpieces of the bibliopegic art" (61).

4. Henry Adams (1838–1918), American historian, writer, and cultural critic. TR must be referring to *Memoirs of Marua Taaroa, Last Queen of Tahiti*, Adams's account of his South Seas travels with the American artist John La Farge (1835–1910) during 1890–91. The book was privately printed (about ten copies) in 1893; a revised edition was published, also privately, in 1901 under a different title. For discussion of the *Memoirs'* contents and background, see William Merrill Decker, *The Literary Vocation of Henry Adams* (Chapel Hill: Univ. of North Carolina Press, 1990), 70–71, 226–32. TR's friendship with Adams dated back to the late 1870s, when TR was a student and Adams a professor at Harvard; during TR's years as Civil Service Commissioner, he dined frequently with the Adamses in Washington (see *LTR*, 1:22, 277, 304).

5. The 7th Harvard-Yale debate was held at the Hyperion Theatre in New York City on 27 Apr. 1894, with BM serving as one of the three judges. The Harvard team argued against and the Yale team for the proposition that members of the Cabinet be given full membership in the House of Representatives. Harvard won the debate on a 2-to-1 vote ("Among the Undergraduates," *New York Times*, 23 Apr. 1894, 9; "Harvard Wins Debate," *New York Times*, 28 Apr. 1894, 1).

To Matthews

Civil Service Commission
May 10, 1894.

Dear Brander:

You are a trump to dedicate the Vignettes of Manhattan to me, and I am very much touched and very much pleased that you should.[1] I greatly appreciate the compliment, old fellow. I am glad that Harpers have asked you for a new series.[2]

By the way, about Flashlights.[3] While I thought it very clever, I do wish that our people would not always proceed upon the assumption that all American gentlemen bow down to a lord and toady to him, and that all American girls are anxious to marry him. The instances where the girl marries the foreign adventurer are of course blazoned about with full details of the wedding, etc., but nothing is said of the multitude of times where she refuses. I could give a dozen such instances out of my own personal experiences during the last five years. There is an immense amount of snobbishness and bowing down to foreigners, and I see some lamentable instances of it here in Washington in connection with the diplomatic service; but there is also a very considerable section, even of our people in good social position, where the foreigner, whether duke or commoner, is treated simply on his merits, where the men are courteous to him but not over anxious to be on an intimate footing with him, and where the girls are distinctly more reluctant to marry him than to marry an American. Do some time if you can, incidentally, do justice in some vignette or elsewhere to this forgotten section of our community. I should think it could be brought in not isolated, but by contrast with the snobs, who take the other tack.

Mrs. Roosevelt and the Lodges were delighted with the extracts from the issue of the Review Encyclopedique.[4]

Faithfully yours,
Theodore Roosevelt

BMP; 2 pp.; tls.

1. BM, *Vignettes of Manhattan* (New York: Harper, 1894). See TR to BM, 3 Apr. 1894, n. 3. BM's dedication is quoted in TR to BM, 13 Oct. 1894, n. 1.

2. Harper and Bros. later published a second collection of BM's New York vignettes, *Outlines in Local Color* (1898).

3. Lester Raynor, "Flash-lights," *Century* 48 (May 1894): 145–51. The story conerns a young American heiress who is attracted to a duplicitous, debt-ridden English lord. Raynor seems to have been influenced by Henry James's *Portrait of a Lady*. TR despised James (see TR to BM, 29 June 1894).

4. *Revue Encyclopédique*; a bimonthly published by the Libraire Larousse in Paris. The issue in question was most likely vol. 80 (1 Apr. 1894), which opens with "La Littérature contemporaine aux États-Unis" (37–45). The author, B. H. Gausseron, surveys and assesses the works of a large group of contemporary American writers, "minor" as well as "major," including BM and TR. He cites BM as one of the two foremost authorities on the theater, and praises TR's *Winning of the West* and *Hunting Trips of a Ranchman* (145). Gausseron's closing paragraph would have pleased TR, BM, and Lodge, for it contends that the writers discussed were developing a national literature, influenced by but distinctive from British literature. BM may also have sent TR the issue's second essay, "Les Indiens dans la poésie américaine" (145–47), by Eugene Asse.

To Matthews

Civil Service Commission
May 21, 1894.

Dear Brander:

I cannot say how much I like your examination papers, and I think, on the whole, this is the best one you have had yet.[1] It is great comfort to be engaged on a piece of work well worth doing, and I think you ought to feel heartily satisfied with the effect you have produced and are producing upon the very class of young men who need it most.

By the way, I saw a review in the Tribune of Hamlin Garland's new book of Essays.[2] He is a man with some power and with half an idea, but he is such a hopeless crank that nothing can be done with him, I fear. He is one of the very men who give us most trouble in producing a spirit of sane Americanism, because his excessive foolishness creates a reaction against us. Do you know I think you have had a decidedly chastening effect upon Miss Agnes Replier?[3]

If you ever come on here again I want you to meet Senator Cushman Davis of Minnesota.[4] He is a remarkable man, and gifted with great capacity for apt quotation. He is on this new investigating committee of the Senate, and when the committee met he remarked that its evident intent reminded him of Byron's description of Mitford, who, "had every characteristic of a historian,—violent partiality, and abundant wrath."[5]

Give my warm regards to Mrs. Matthews. I do hope you have a most pleasant trip.

Faithfully yours,

Theodore Roosevelt

BMP; 2 pp.; tls.; pbd. *LTR*, 1:379.

1. See TR to BM, 14 Feb. 1893, n. 4.
2. Hamlin Garland (1860–1940); fiction writer, critic, and lecturer, best known for his realistic stories of midwestern rural life and for his theory of literary "veritism" (the artistic expression of life's verities). Garland expounds the theory in *Crumbling Idols* (1894), a central argument of which is that American writers must cease worshipping such literary idols as Shakespeare and Milton and develop a uniquely American literature (see next letter).

   Crumbling Idols was anonymously reviewed in the *New York Tribune*, 20 May 1894, 14, the author poking fun at the "comic earnestness" with which Garland develops his "amusing" theory. Garland later moved away from realism toward the romanticism that TR embraced. He was a staunch ally of TR and BM in their campaign for literary Americanism during the 1890s and beyond, and he eulogized both men after their deaths (see Oliver, *Brander Matthews*, 112–13, 177–80).
3. The evidence for the alleged "chastening effect" might be Repplier's "Opinions," which appeared in the Apr. 1894 number of the *Atlantic* (545–49). Repplier expresses surprise at the "vigorous reproaches" her critical essays have sometimes generated, and she asks her fellow critics to be more open to different points of view.
4. Cushman Kellogg Davis (1838–1900); the Republican senator (1887–1900) was an influential advocate of American expansionism later in the decade.

5. English historian William Mitford (1744–1827). Byron refers to him in Canto 12.19.7 of *Don Juan*; in his note to that reference, Byron calls Mitford the "best of all modern historians," whose virtues were "learning, labour, research, wrath, and partiality" (*Byron's* Don Juan: *Notes on the Variorum Edition,* ed. Willis W. Pratt [Austin: Univ. of Texas Press, 2d ed. 1971], 4:237).

To Matthews

Civil Service Commission
June 29, 1894.

Dear Brander:

I think the cutting about Mahan's book was one of the most delicious things I have ever read.[1] It circulated freely throughout Washington, from Lodge on. Some time or other I shall write an article on James Stuart, the Hanoverian Pretender, or on the Duke of Cumberland, the well-known Jacobin leader who fell at Colloden.[2]

I am very glad the immigration has come to a standstill for the last year.[3] We are getting some very undesirable elements now, and I wish that a check could be put to it.

I shall be ranching in September. Up to that time I shall alternate between Sagamore Hill and this hot city. I shall get back from the West early in October and report at 121 promptly.[4]

After receiving your letter I got Hamlin Garland's book and read it.[5] I think you are right about Garland, excepting that I should lay a little more stress upon the extreme wrong-headedness of his reasoning. For instance, he is entirely wrong in thinking that Shakspeare, Homer and Milton are not permanent. Of course they are; and he is entirely in error in thinking that Shakspeare is not read, in the aggregate, during a term of years, more than any ephemeral author of the day. Of course every year there are dozens of novels each one of which will have many more readers than Shakspeare will have in the year; but the readers only stay for about a year or two, whereas in Shakspeare's case they have lasted, and will last quite a time! I think that his ignorance, crudity, and utter lack of cultivation make him entirely unfit to understand the effect of the great masters of thought upon the language and upon literature. Nevertheless, in his main thought, as you say, he is entirely right. We must strike out for ourselves; we must work according to our own ideas, and must free ourselves from the shackles of conventionality, before we can do anything. As for the literary center of the country being New York, I personally never had any patience with the talk of a literary center.[6] I don't care a rap whether it is New York, Chicago, or any place else, so long as the work is done. I like or dislike pieces in the Atlantic Monthly and the Overland Monthly because of what they contain, not because of one's being published in San Francisco or the other in Boston.[7] I don't like Edgar Fawcett[8] any more because he lives in New York, nor Joel Chandler Harris[9] any the less because he lives at Atlanta; and I read Mark Twain with just as much delight, but with no more, whether he resides in Connecticut or in Missouri. Garland is to me a rather irritating man, because I can't help thinking he has the possibility of so much, and he seems just to fail to realize this possibility. He has seen and drawn certain phases of the western prairie life with astonishing truth and force; but he now seems inclined to let certain crude theories warp his mind out of all proper proportion, and I think his creative work is suffering much in consequence. I hate to see this, because he ought to be a force on the right side.

By the way, have you seen that London "Yellow Book?"[10] I think it represents the last stage of degradation. What a miserable little snob Henry James is. His polished, pointless, uninteresting stories about the upper social classes of England make one blush to think that he was once an American. The rest of the book is simply diseased. I turned to a story of Kipling's with the feeling of getting into fresh, healthy, out-of-doors life.

I think your vignettes are really admirable, and I am much pleased that in your last you allowed a more cheerful ending than you sometimes do, and that when the bullet struck the young lady it should have only made a flesh wound in her arm.[11] There is more than one particular in which that vignette struck a high note. I think that Dan Wister has been doing some very good work.[12]

Give my warm regards to Mrs. Matthews.

Faithfully yours,

Theodore Roosevelt

BMP; 4 pp.; tls.; pbd. *LTR*, 1:389–90.

1. Mahan's *The Influence of Sea Power upon History* was enthusiastically received in England, where his visit in spring 1894 generated a flood of news articles and reviews. BM, who spent the summer of 1894 in England, apparently sent TR several of the English news clippings, but they have not been identified (see next note).

2. TR is being facetious here, for as he certainly knew, James Francis Stuart, the "Old Pretender" (1688–1766), was of the house of Stuart, not Hanover; and the Duke of Cumberland (1721–65) *defeated* the Jacobite forces at the battle of Culloden in 1746, ending Prince Charles Edward's (the "Young Pretender") attempt to wrest power from the Hanoverian George II. (The duke was not killed at the battle.) The unidentified cuttings on Mahan that BM had sent probably displayed an ignorance of American history—as British writings on American history often did, to BM's and TR's great amusement.

3. Immigration had slowed, but not ceased; census figures indicate that the number of immigrants dropped from about 439,000 in 1893 to 285,000 in

1894. Like millions of their countrymen during the so-called "new immigrant era," TR and BM were somewhat xenophobic and favored restrictive immigration laws (such as the literacy-test law that Lodge sponsored in 1896, but that President Cleveland vetoed). See Oliver, *Brander Matthews*, 33–81.

4. BM's residence was 121 East 18th Street, New York.

5. See preceding letter, n. 2.

6. Garland declares that New York has become the nation's literary center (*Crumbling Idols*, 116). TR had demonstrated his impatience with BM on the issue of literary centers 4 years earlier (TR to BM, 3 Aug. 1890).

7. Founded in 1868, the *Overland Monthly*, of San Francisco, was the West Coast's most important literary magazine. The *Atlantic Monthly* was, of course, published out of Boston.

8. See TR to BM, 3 Aug. 1890, n. 3.

9. Joel Chandler Harris (1848–1908); the author of the immensely popular Uncle Remus stories was considered by BM as well as TR to be one of the best southern writers of the day.

10. The first number of *The Yellow Book: An Illustrated Quarterly* appeared in Apr. 1894; it opens with Henry James's story "The Death of the Lion" (7–52). With illustrations by Aubrey Beardsley, the magazine aimed to be daring and rebellious; but contemporary readers may find it difficult to understand why TR found the contents "diseased."

11. BM, "Before the Break of Day," *Harper's Monthly* 89 (July 1894): 222–26. Perhaps in response to TR's plea for a "cheerful" vignette (TR to BM, 3 Apr. 1894), BM produced this melodramatic tale of heroism, with its pronounced theme of Americanism. The story is in fact a romantic re-visioning of Stephen Crane's tragic novella, *Maggie: A Girl of the Streets* (1893); see Oliver, "Brander Matthews' Re-visioning of Crane's *Maggie*," *American Literature* 60 (1988): 654–58.

12. In a letter to Wister dated 26 May 1894, TR wrote that he "greedily" read all of Wister's western stories and that he thought "your June Harper article the best" (quoted in Wister, *Roosevelt: The Story of a Friendship 1880–1919* [New York: Macmillan, 1930], 37). The "article" was Wister's story "Little Big Horn Medicine," *Harper's Monthly* 89 (June 1894): 118–32, which Wister later placed as the lead piece in his first book of western stories, *Red Men and White* (1895).

To Matthews

Civil Service Commission
August 25, 1894.

Dear Brander:

Last evening I read through the opening of your story about a "Narragansett Idyl", and am very much pleased with it.[1] Today comes your interview in the "Daily Chronicle".[2] It is most interesting. There was a delightful frankness about some of your statements, over which I chuckled. It must be rather a novel thing for the British public to have an American in the frankest and kindest way tell them about the decrease in the percentage of English books on the American reading table, and to speak of the immensely greater reading public which we have over here. I was very glad that you emphasized as you did that literary independence did not in the least mean dialectical differences. By the way, did you see a short piece on "Washington" in the last Harpers or Scribners by Marion Crawford?[3] It was very well done, and I was touched by his declaration of his intense Americanism. I think he really believes it and feels it.

I have not been doing much of anything this Summer. In July I was home. I have been back here working over civil service business in August. Next month I shall be out on my ranch, and will not be here to greet you when you come back, and so send this letter instead. I have just started to do something for St. Nicholas by giving them a series of short stories of incidents in our fights against the English, Mexicans, French, etc. I do not suppose they want all my stories, if they want any, but I feel much interested, and think I may get out a volume called "Hero Stories for Young Americans"; and I am going to put in between each pair of stories one or two stanzas from some of our poems of warfare.[4] I do not know that I can work out the idea, but I think the idea is a good one.

Give my best love to Mrs. Matthews.

Faithfully yours,

Theodore Roosevelt

BMP; 2 pp.; tls.

1. BM, "Royal Marine: An Idyl of Narragansett Pier," *Harper's Monthly* 89 (Sept.–Oct. 1894): 577–92, 680–94; a romantic tale of a young musician's courtship of a southern belle, with detailed description of leisure-class life at the Narragansett resort where BM often vacationed. See TR to BM, 7 Dec. 1894.

2. I was unable to secure the *Daily Chronicle* interview, but TR's comments suggest that BM voiced the major arguments of *Americanisms and Briticisms.*

3. Francis Marion Crawford, "Washington as a Spectacle," *Century* 48 (Aug. 1894): 482–95. Born in Italy of American parents, Crawford (1854–1909), a successful novelist, maintained his permanent residence in Italy but visited the U.S. regularly. This essay, a response to criticisms of the nation's capital by certain foreigners and "Europeanized Americans," celebrates Washington's buildings, monuments, and people.

4. TR published 6 sketches of famous historical figures and battles in *St. Nicholas* between May and Oct. 1895. He then asked Henry Cabot Lodge to join

him in producing additional sketches for a volume, which the two men published as *Hero Tales from American History* (New York: Century, 1895); reprinted in TR's *Works*, vol. 10, with an introduction by Lodge (xiii–xxi).

To Matthews

Civil Service Commission
October 13, 1894.

Dear Brander:

I have just got back from the West, and coming on here from New York I bought a copy of the Vignettes. You could not have put into your introduction anything that would have pleased me more than what you said.[1]

By the way, I am so glad that you spoke of the sky line of the city when seen from one side. It is a perpetual delight to me when I come in on the ferryboat on my trip from Washington, and I don't believe there is anywhere to be seen a more beautiful sight than on the night train to Boston, which, as you know is ferried around from the Pennsylvania depot down the North River and up the East River into the Harlem, where the sleepers are put on the Boston train. On a clear night the view of the city with all its lights is as beautiful as anything can be.

As for the Vignettes, you know what I think of them already.[2] There is but one that I had not already read. I am greatly touched, and greatly pleased, old fellow, at reading the preface. My acquaintance and growing friendship with you has been one of the pleasantest things of recent years to me. I shall be in New York in November, and shall look you up as soon as I come, although I haven't got any new ranch stories to tell you.

Did you find a letter of mine waiting for you when you got home? I am very anxious to hear of your European trip.

Remember me warmly to Mrs. Matthews.

Faithfully yours,
Theodore Roosevelt

P.S.

I have but one complaint about the Vignettes; there are two or three that should have had sequels; among them, I should like much to have known the future of the fairhaired woman at the young actor's funeral; and something about the big specular, and how he happened to marry the artist's fiancée, and how the tragedy came about.[3]

BMP; 2 pp.; tls. with handwritten postscript.

1. The dedication (what TR calls the "introduction" in the opening paragraph and the "preface" in the third paragraph) to *Vignettes of Manhattan* reads:

My dear Theodore,—You know—for we have talked it over often enough—that I do not hold you to be a typical New-Yorker, since you come of Dutch stock, and first saw the light here on Manhattan Island, whereas the typical New-Yorker is born of New England parents, perhaps somewhere west of the Alleghanies. You know, also, that often the typical New-Yorker is not proud of the city of his choice, and not so loyal to it as we could wish. He has no abiding concern for this maligned and misunderstood town of ours; he does not thrill with pride at the sight of its powerful and irregular profile as he comes back to it across the broad rivers; nor is his heart lifted up with joy at the sound of its increasing roar, so suggestive and so stimulating. But we have a firm affection for New York, you and I, and a few besides; we like it for what it is; and we love it for what we hope to see it.

It is because of this common regard for our strange and many-sided city that I am giving myself the pleasure of proffering to you this little volume of vignettes. They are not stories really, I am afraid—not sketches, nor studies; they are, I think, just what I have called them—vignettes. And there are a dozen of them, one for every month in the year, an urban calendar of times and seasons. Such as they are, I beg that you will accept them in token of my friendship and esteem; and that you will believe me, always,

> Yours truly,
> Brander Matthews

2. See TR to BM, 3 Apr. and 29 June 1894.
3. "In the Little Church down the Street" and "At a Private View," the first and third chapters of *Vignettes*. In the first vignette, a young actress (whose hair is dark and not, as TR states, fair) attends the funeral of a promising actor who onstage was her Romeo and offstage the father of her unborn child. "At a Private View" centers on a portrait (the "specular") that projects the cruel, sinister essence of a business tycoon; he has crushed the spirit of his beautiful wife, to whom the portrait's painter had once been engaged. TR's responses to these two vignettes suggest his dislike of ambiguity in fiction.

To Matthews

Civil Service Commission
October 24, 1894.

Dear Brander:

I was much amused at the failure of Miss Replier with "Mollie of Monmouth." I will bet she never heard of the lady until she saw her mentioned as your favorite heroine.[1]

I will look up Whitcomb's "Outlines."[2] I haven't seen the book yet.

I will surely let you know the date of my arrival well in advance, but can tell you now that it will be about the 23d or 24th of November.

I didn't see Jim Ford's story; I wish I had.[3]
By the way, did you see in Gilder's poems the poem on the City
and on the Bay?[4] I thought them good, and they both have the feeling
for New York of which we have so often spoken.
Always yours,
Theodore Roosevelt

BMP; 1 p.; tls.

1. Molly Ludwig (1754–1832), better known by her nickname "Molly Pitcher,"
earned a place in the annals of the American Revolution by her heroic actions at the battle of Monmouth, N.J., on 28 June 1778. BM's *Poems of American Patriotism* includes a ballad about Molly by the Irish-American poet
William Collins (1838–90). Lang's correspondence with Repplier indicates
that she sent him a story about Molly of Monmouth (Lang to Repplier, 17
Jan. and 16 Feb. [1894], Van Pelt Library, Univ. of Pennsylvania); but I found
no record of its publication, nor do Repplier's unpublished papers at the Univ.
of Pennsylvania contain a manuscript on Molly. Since TR refers to Repplier's
"failure," it may be that Repplier's piece was rejected by an English magazine,
and that BM learned of the rejection from Lang or some other source.
   In "Some Personal Preferences," *Book Buyer* 9 (Jan. 1893): 657–61, BM,
Repplier, and other writers list their favorite authors, books, historical figures,
and so on. BM cites Mollie of Monmouth as his favorite real-life heroine (658).

2. Selden L. Whitcomb, *Chronological Outlines of American Literature* (New
York: Macmillan, 1894); a literary history for classroom use, it is a precursor
of BM's *An Introduction to the Study of American Literature* (1896).

3. James Lauren Ford (1854–1928); the Long Island fiction writer was a mutual
friend of TR and BM; the latter's personal library includes an inscribed copy of
Ford's *Dolly Dillenback* (1895). The story to which TR alludes is unidentified.

4. Richard Watson Gilder, "On the Bay" and "The City," in Gilder's *Five Books
of Song* (New York: Century, 1894).

TO MATTHEWS

Civil Service Commission
December 7, 1894.

Dear Brander:
   Being laid up in the house with a slight attack of bronchitis I have
just got your book. I feel a little ashamed of having you send it to me;
but there is one comfort when I receive books from you, and that is that I
have always read them before, and have always liked them. I feel about
your books like the traditional Kentuckian about whisky; some of them
are better than others, but they are all good. I think "Royal Marine,"
however, one of the best of your stories.[1]

By the way did you see Hamlin Garland's piece in the last Harper's Weekly?[2] It is very good, and is much less morbid than his pieces have grown to be. It looks to me as though he were going to, in a somewhat different way, suffer as Howells has done, by taking a jaundiced view of life.[3] This is not an uncommon development of the reform spirit, unfortunately. Even in this piece I am amused at one thing. He often predicates the unhappiness of people accustomed to entirely different surroundings from his because he, or because cultivated men brought up in ease, would mind such surroundings.[4] I really doubt whether he has seen from the inside the life he describes nearly as much as I have, and he certainly must mind it far more. For instance, I have been a great deal in logging camps such as the one he describes in this last article in Harper's, and I know that the men in them regard a good logging camp as a first-rate place, very comfortable, very warm, with an abundance of good food, and often pleasant company. I have thoroughly enjoyed such camps myself. He speaks of the greasy quilts, etc. Well, they are distressing to an over-civilized man; but for my own pleasure this year when I was out on the antelope plains I got into a country where I didn't take my clothes off for ten days. I had two cowpunchers along, and the quilts and bedding, including the pillows which they had, were quite as bad as those Garland describes in his logging camp; yet they both felt they were off on a holiday and having a lovely time. Our food on this ten days' trip was precisely like that he describes in the logging camp, except that we had venison instead of beef, and we ate it under less comfortable surroundings as a whole, or at least under what my men regarded as less comfortable surroundings. I have worked hard in cow camps for weeks at a time, doing precisely such work as the cow punchers, and I know what I am talking about. I did'n't play; I *worked*, while on my ranch. There is a great deal of toil and hardship about the out of door life of lumbermen & cowboys; and especially about some phases which he doesn't touch, such as driving logs in the springtime and handling cattle from a line camp in bitter winter weather; but the life as a whole is a decidedly healthy and attractive one to men who do not feel the need of mental recreation and stimulus—and few of them do.

However, this story of Garland's is a good one, and I am glad that he should go back to writing good stories, and not try to evolve some little school of literary philosophy, where the propriety of his purpose is marred by the utter crudity of his half-baked ideas, and where he is not tempted to group himself and one or two friends under some such absurd heading as "veritists".

I shall see you in mid January when I come on to New York. Meanwhile I wish you would come on here.

Theodore Roosevelt

BMP; 3 pp.; tls.; pbd. LTR, 1:410–11.

1. BM, *The Royal Marine: An Idyl of Narragansett Pier* (New York: Harper, 1894); separate publication of BM's *Harper's Monthly* story praised by TR in his letter of 25 Aug. 1894.

2. "Only a Lumber Jack," *Harper's Weekly* 38 (8 Dec. 1894): 1158–59. Garland's local-color story of Wisconsin logging-camp life centers on an alcoholic lumberjack who decides to give up the bottle and return to the wife he left behind.

3. This marks a turn in TR's opinion of Howells, who is referred to positively in previous letters. TR probably has in mind Howells's *A Hazard of New Fortunes* (1890), which TR would have condemned on two counts: it ends tragically and is sympathetic towards labor. Howells and his theory of realism were under fierce attack during the early 1890s. Though he remained a staunch ally of Howells and the realists, BM too came to feel that the elder writer had become "jaundiced" (see Oliver, *Brander Matthews*, 145–57).

4. Though a member of the eastern literary establishment at this time, Garland had not been brought up in ease (as TR and BM had been). His parents were poor farmers, so he knew firsthand the hardships of midwestern farm life, if not of logging camps. See next letter, n. 6.

To Matthews

Washington D.C.
Dec 9th '94

Dear Brander,

When you see your friend Kipling again tell him that the "Walking Delegate" has been used as a tract in the Senate.[1] Manderson, of Nebraska, first saw it's possibilities.[2] Do you know him? He has a most gallant record in the Civil War, where he was badly wounded; and now has at last overthrown the populists in his state, in a square knock-down-and-drag-out fight, and is going to leave the Senate, as he finds he can't afford to stay in politics. He tried the article on Peffer, who is a well-meaning, pin-headed, anarchistic crank, of hirsute and slabsided aspect; it did'nt do Peffer any good—he is'nt that kind—but it irritated him, and so it pleased Manderson.[3] Wolcott of Colorado,[4] whom you met here, is now going to try it on Kyle of South Dakota.[5] Lodge would like to use it, but he is anathema to the populists anyhow, as he comes from Massachusetts and is a Harvard man—a record that would taint anything.

I liked the article as in a way an anti-septic to Hamlin Garland's stories,[6] though it is no more fair than the latter; the truth lies between. I know the populists and the laboring-men well, and their faults; I like to see a mob handled by the regulars, or by good State guards, not over-

scrupulous about bloodshed; but I know the banker, merchant and rail-road king well too, and *they* also need education and sound chastisement.
Hastily yours
Theodore Roosevelt

BMP; 4 pp.; als.; pbd. *LTR*, 1:411–12.

1. Kipling, "The Walking Delegate," *Century* 49 (Dec. 1894): 289–97. Set on a Vermont farm and narrated by a horse, the tale is a contemptuous satire of reformers. A ragged "yellow" horse visits the farm, determined to enlighten the herd about the social injustices they suffer and to foment revolt. Kipling takes clear aim at the Populists when he has one horse exclaim: "What the horses o' Kansas think to-day, the horses of America will think to-morrow; an' I tell you that when the horses of America rise in their might, the day o' the Oppression is ended" (291). But the farm horses do not feel oppressed and therefore kick out the outside agitator.

2. Charles Frederick Manderson (1837–1911); the aristocratic and conservative Republican senator from Nebraska (1889–95) was the ideal audience for Kipling's satire.

3. William Alfred Peffer (1831–1912), Populist senator from Kansas (1891–97), noted for his earnest and humorless manner.

4. Edward Oliver Wolcott (1848–1905); Republican senator from Colorado (1889–1901).

5. James Henderson Kyle (1854–1901); Populist senator from South Dakota (1891–1901), who during his first term in office usually sided with the Democrats.

6. Garland was an outspoken advocate of agrarian reform and Populism. His collection of stories *Main-Travelled Roads* (1891) aimed, as he remarks in the preface to the 1922 edition of the book, to expose the "ugliness, the endless drudgery, and the loneliness of the farmer's lot."

To Matthews

Civil Service Commission
December 22, 1894.

Dear Brander:

I thought your philological piece admirable, and chuckled over your plea for a disinterested and purely scientific attitude.[1] What fearful Briticisms some of them were, and to think of Walter Pater[2] and Coventry Patmore[3] being among the offenders! I don't care for either myself; but language was supposed to be what we would call out West their "hold."

At this moment I am in a great quandary over a matter concerning which I will speak to you when we meet. I also have a brief correspondence which I think you will like. Lodge was as much pleased with your piece as I was.

Ever yours,
Theodore Roosevelt

BMP; 1 p.; tls.

1. BM, "A Note on Recent Briticisms," *Modern Language Notes* 9 (Dec. 1894): 225–27. Using examples from the writings of several British writers, including the two TR mentions, BM contends that "Briticisms" (British variations from standard English) are as common as "Americanisms"; and he advises any American who might want to undertake a study of Briticisms to do so with an "attitude of scientific calmness" (227).

2. Walter Pater (1839–94), English essayist, critic, and novelist. His "fearful Briticism" was *evanescing.*

3. Coventry Patmore (1823–96), English poet, guilty of using the Briticism *essayettes.*

1895

To Matthews

Civil Service Commission
January 2, 1895.

Dear Brander:
I like your Emerson in the St. Nicholas very much.[1] I also like your appreciative little review of Stephenson, which I thought particularly happy.[2]

On the 17th, 18th, and possibly the 19th, of this month I shall be in New York, and one day I want to have you lunch with me. I shall try to get a young Kentuckian, named John Fox, Jr.,[3] who has written one or two pieces about feuds, and the like, to lunch with us. Would either the 17th or the 18th do?

Faithfully yours,
Theodore Roosevelt

BMP; 1 p.; tls.

1. "Ralph Waldo Emerson," *St. Nicholas* 22 (Jan. 1895): 199–206. With a few minor revisions and updating, BM's admiring sketch of Emerson's life and writings could be read with profit by students today. BM declares Emerson the "foremost representative of that New England influence on American life and American literature which has been very powerful," and observes that the Brahmin was more a "poet with moments of insight than a systematic philosopher," his essays composed of loosely linked ideas that lay "side by side like unset gems in a box" (202). Contrasting Emerson's idealism with Franklin's pragmatism, BM contends that "taken together they give us the two sides of the American character" (206).

2. BM, "Robert Louis Stevenson," *Harper's Weekly* 38 (29 Dec. 1894): 1248–49. Stevenson, whom BM knew personally, had died recently; the essay honors the man as well as his fiction.

3. John Fox , Jr. (1862–1919); Harvard graduate, adventurer, journalist, and fiction writer. His first two novels, *Mountain Europa* (1894) and *A Cumberland Vendetta* (1894), portray the harsh conditions of life in backwoods Kentucky, where Fox had mined during the 1880s. *Cumberland Vendetta*, serialized in the *Century* (June–Aug. 1894) before publication as a novel, is a violent tale of feuding Kentucky clans. TR greatly admired the work of Fox, with whom he often corresponded (*LTR*, 1:384–85, 407–8). Fox later served in the Rough Riders.

To Matthews

Civil Service Commission
February 11, 1895.

Dear Brander:

I am sure it is needless for me to say how glad I should be to write an article such as you describe about yourself. I shall only make one stipulation, and that is that I be allowed to lay proper stress upon your Americanisms and Briticisms.¹ That was published by Harpers, was it not? I mean when the essays were put out in book form. Do read my article in the Forum.² I have a touch there about Edward Atkinson, at the very end, which I want you to see.³

I am very sorry you are suffering from a cold.

Some day I will draw up with you an examination sheet for candidates to fill Ward McAllister's place.⁴

Yours always,
Theodore Roosevelt

P.S.
What is Trent's address abroad? I wish to send him a letter.

BMP; 1 p.; tls. with handwritten postscript.

1. TR never published an essay specifically on BM or on *Americanisms and Briticisms*, but he later reviewed BM's *An Introduction to the Study of American Literature*, at BM's request (see TR to BM, 6 Dec. 1895); in it, he recommends "Americanisms and Briticisms" as being "by far the most noteworthy critical or literary essay which has been published by any American writer for a score of years" (*Works*, 12:294).

2. TR, "True American Ideals," *Forum* 18 (Feb. 1895): 743–50; rpt. in *Works*, 13:3–12.

3. Edward Atkinson (1827–1905); economist, industrialist, and author, his essay "Present Industrial Problems in the Light of History" had appeared in the *Forum* 28 (Sept. 1894): 42–53. In the essay, Atkinson, who was a pacifist and free-trade advocate, calls for elimination of trade barriers and contends that the armed services, especially the navy, are useless and a drain on the national economy. TR denounces Atkinson's essay in the closing pages of "True American Ideals" (*Works*, 13:10–11), calling him a "quack" and suggesting that the "purely commercial" values he promotes threaten to undermine the heroic ideals exemplified by such great Americans as Washington and Lincoln.

4. Ward McAllister, New York's leading snob, died on 31 Jan. 1895 (see TR to BM, 21 Oct. [1890]).

To Matthews

Civil Service Commission
February 23, 1895.

Dear Brander:
 I won't say peccavi, merely because it would be trite. I shall simply enclose the copy of your article, the letter from Gillette,[1] and a copy of my correspondence with the immortal Lord Aberdeen.[2] By the way, the latter came to the ears of the British Ambassador[3] here, and his family were hugely delighted with it, as the Aberdeens have victimized them and they can't resent it on account of their official position. I am greatly interested and amused with Gillette's letter. I remember the piece very well, and I think Gillette's unconscious compliment to it is one of the most striking things I have ever come across.
                    Always yours,
                    Theodore Roosevelt
P.S.
I enclose also copies of the two St. Paul Dispatches containing a story by a man, now a railway mail clerk on the Northern Pacific, who was a small ranchman and cow puncher when I was on the Little Missouri.[4] I have often worked with him on the roundup, but I had no idea he had any literary taste. He certainly has the local color down fine, and he catches the exact tone of a cow puncher conversation in a way that I have never known any one else. I wish you would read this through carefully, and tell me candidly what you think of it and whether there is any promise in the stuff.

   BMP; 2 pp.; tls.
   1. William H. Gillette (1853–1937), American playwright and actor. In 1881 he co-wrote, with Mrs. Frances Burnett (1849–1924), the play *Esmerelda*, one of the most successful hits of the day. In his "The Dramatization of Novels," an 1889 essay that BM included in his *Studies of the Stage* (New York: Harper, 1894), BM cites the play as one of the rare examples of a successful dramatization of a narrative fiction. The reason for TR's "peccavi" is unknown, and the letter and article mentioned remain unidentified.
   2. Lord Aberdeen, John Campbell Hamilton Gordon (1847–1934), was at this time governor general of Canada. The correspondence to which TR refers is not in the TRP or BMP.
   3. Sir Julian Pauncefote (1828–1902), British ambassador to the United States from 1893 until his death; TR was "quite devoted" to him and his family (LTR, 1:344).
   4. The Little Missouri was the river near TR's ranch in Dakota; he describes his ranching adventures and his fellow cowboys there in "In Cowboy Land,"

a chapter of his *Autobiography* (*Works*, 20:96–132). The cowpuncher and his story remain a mystery.

To Matthews

Civil Service Commission
March 9, 1895.

Dear Brander:

I am more sorry than I can say to hear about your daughter.[1] I had supposed she was now well. Indeed I know just how you feel, with all your eggs in one basket. Even with my eggs in five I can imagine nothing so terrible as the sickness of a child one loves, unless it is the sickness of the child's mother. I am awfully sorry, old fellow.

Yes, I met Kipling last night at dinner.[2] He was very pleasant, and we shall have Mrs. Kipling and himself to dinner before he goes away, if he seems to want to come. I am a little bit chary about asking him, merely because I do not know whether he is or is not the type of Englishman who misunderstands courtesy.

With best wishes, old man,

Faithfully yours,
Theodore Roosevelt

BMP; 1 p.; tls.

1. Edith Brander Matthews (1875–1922), BM's only child.
2. Noting that there has been much confusion regarding the day—even the year—in which TR and Kipling first met, Morris sets the date at 7 Mar. 1895 (*Rise*, 819–20n.); but if this letter is dated correctly, then TR first met Kipling on 8 Mar. 1895. In a letter to his sister Anna, TR remarks that Kipling struck him as a "pleasant little man, bright, nervous, voluble, rather underbred," adding that he could not help "sparring with him a little" (*LTR*, 1:433). Though they would often spar over literary and political issues in years to come, the two men began developing a lasting friendship at this point.

To Matthews

Civil Service Commission
March 19, 1895.

Dear Brander:

I am delighted to hear that your daughter is all well again. I was sure nothing had happened, because I hadn't heard. Mrs. Roosevelt will be as pleased as I am.

Kipling's last story was first-rate, as indeed all of his animal stories are.[1] I don't myself think he is much of a success when he deals with city life, whether in London or elsewhere. I haven't had a chance to see much of him here. Every now and then he can't resist making a raid on things American. When I get to know him better I shan't mind this, but at present I can not resist the temptation to take a fall out of him.[2] I think we would probably have gotten along better if I had met him first under your auspicies.

Lodge and I have nearly finished our Hero Tales from American History. I think that your Poems of American Patriotism ought to be issued copy for copy with our book as a missionary tract.[3]

Yours faithfully,
Theodore Roosevelt

BMP; 1 p.; tls.; pbd. *LTR*, 1:436.

1. Kipling's most recent story was "The King's Ankus," *St. Nicholas* 22 (Mar. 1895): 362–73; this tale about Mowgli the jungle boy and his talking animal friends is an allegory of human violence and greed. Kipling's very popular *The Jungle Book* had been published in 1894; he included "The King's Ankus" in *The Second Jungle Book* (1895).

2. For Kipling's (very amusing) first impressions of TR, see his *Something of Myself for My Friends Known and Unknown* (New York: Doubleday, 1937), 131–34.

3. BM, *Poems of American Patriotism* (New York: Scribner's, 1882); an anthology of such patriotic poems as "Paul Revere's Ride," "Old Ironsides," and "The Star-Spangled Banner." (BM dedicated the 1922 edition to TR.)

To Matthews

Civil Service Commission
April 6, 1895.

Dear Brander:

I have come round to your way of looking at Kipling. When one knows him it seems preposterous to mind anything he says about the United States. He is both parochial and sensitive himself, and as there is plenty that is parochial and sensitive about us he of course hits at it; but his small peculiarities do not interfere with his being a very pleasant companion as well as a writer of genius. It has been a great pleasure meeting him. Last night he dined at my house, and I had Owen Wister, Rockhill[1] and John Hay, and a few others, to meet him.

By the way, I think Owen Wister's last piece, "The Second Missouri Compromise," is capital.[2]

Give my warm regards to your wife and to your daughter, who I hope is now entirely recovered.

I shall be on about the middle of May, and shall then look you up

of course. One of the things that I especially like about Kipling is that he seems almost as fond of you as I am.
Yours,
Theodore Roosevelt

BMP; 1 p.; tls.; pbd. *LTR*, 1:439.
1. William Woodville Rockhill (1854–1914); Orientalist, diplomat, and explorer. At this time he was third assistant secretary of state. Rockhill would later sign the protocols ending the Boxer Rebellion and would assist John Hay in constructing the Open Door policy toward China.
2. Owen Wister, "The Second Missouri Compromise," *Harper's Monthly* 90 (Mar. 1895): 534–45. Set in the untamed Idaho Territory in 1867, the story concerns a political conflict between the governor, who came from the North, and the "unsurrendered rebels" (540) in the legislature. A "second Missouri Compromise," made possible by the clever action of Wister's soldier-hero Specimen Jones, avoids a violent showdown.

To Matthews

Police Department[1]
New York, May 13th. 1895.
Dear Brander:—
Can you make the lunch on Saturday next at two o'clock? if so, I will come, bar a cataclysm.
Yes, I saw the most important article in the Sewanee Review before it was in type; and wrote Trent that he had done you *bare* justice.[2]
Yours,
Theodore Roosevelt

BMP; 1 p.; tls.
1. TR's appointment by Mayor William L. Strong (1827–1900) to the New York City Police Commission was confirmed on 17 Apr. 1895; he was sworn in on 6 May. TR had been a supporter of Strong, whose victory in the 1894 mayoral election was a triumph for the city's reform movement (see Morris, *Rise*, 477–82).
2. Trent, "Mr. Brander Matthews as a Critic," *Sewanee Review* 3 (May 1895): 373–84. The "bare justice" remark is facetious, for Trent extols BM's critical writings. As earlier noted, BM had been, and would continue to be, instrumental in advancing Trent's academic career (TR to BM, 7 Mar. 1894, n. 1).

To Matthews

Police Department
Oct. 18th. 1895.

Dear Brander:—

I thank you very much for the book. I should rather review the two books together as you request.[1] I will make the Forum this proposition. I won't put that quotation in Latin; I am weak on Latin. I am pressed to death, and have not time for another line.

Yours,
Theodore Roosevelt

BMP; 1 p.; tls.

1. BM published three books in 1895. Two were collections of essays: *Book-bindings Old and New: Notes of a Booklover, with an Account of the Grolier Club of New York* (New York: Macmillan) and *Books and Play-books: Essays on Literature and Drama* (London: Osgood, McIlvane). The third was a novel, *His Father's Son: A Novel of New York* (New York: Harper). BM may have asked TR to review one or two of these, along with *Americanisms and Briticisms* (see TR to BM, 11 Feb. 1895). TR's letter to BM of 6 Dec. 1895 below makes BM's soon-to-be-published *An Introduction to the Study of American Literature* yet another possibility. However, as the next letter indicates, the *Forum*, and then the *Atlantic*, rejected the review proposal.

To Matthews

Police Department
Nov. 11th. 1895.

Dear Brander:—

The Forum, after waiting until after the election,[1] rejected my proposition to review your books; so did the Atlantic; at least it would not let me review them on the scale I desired, or with a signed name. I am rather at a loss to know what to do.

Faithfully yours,
Theodore Roosevelt

BMP; 1 p.; tls.

1. Police Commissioner TR's campaign against corruption brought him considerable press attention during the state and local elections of 1895, much of it negative. Republicans swept the state, but Tammany Hall Democrats won by a landslide in New York City, in part because of a backlash vote against TR (see Morris, Rise, 511–13).

To Matthews

Police Department
Dec. 6th. 1895.

Dear Brander:—
Do you know the novels of Brockden Brown?[1] They were the first real novels published in America. One or two of them are worth reproduction.

Of course I will gladly review your "Introduction of the Study of American Literature" in the February number.[2] I suppose they will write me about it. I will have to get them to send me a stenographer.

I thought Kipling's poem excellent; but I did not like the comment of the paper on it at all.[3] Kipling properly rules us out as aliens; and I should not much respect him if he didn't; but I can't pardon the cringing attitude of the Editor in writing about it, as if we were colonists ourselves. A couple of centuries hence we *may* all be in one great federation; but just at present the Englishman is a foreigner and nothing else.

Faithfully yours,
Theodore Roosevelt

BMP; 1 p.; tls.; pbd. *LTR*, 1:499.

1. Charles Brockden Brown (1771–1810). Many contemporary scholars of early American literature concur with TR's opinion that Brown was the first important American novelist. He has received much critical attention, and his novels *Wieland* (1798), *Edgar Huntly* (1799), and *Arthur Mervyn* (1799, 1800) continue to enjoy a wide readership.

2. TR reviewed BM's *An Introduction to the Study of American Literature* in the Feb. 1896 number of the *Bookman*, 519–21 (rpt. in *Works*, 12:292–95). (See next letter.) TR showered the book with praise, declaring it to be "a piece of work as good of its kind as any American scholar has ever had in his hands" (519).

3. Kipling, "The Native-Born"; the poem is a paean to the British empire, the "native born" being those who, like Kipling himself, were loyal Englishmen even though born far from England's shores. Americans are implicitly excluded from the poem, since they are no longer part of the Empire. The poem was first published in the *London Times* on 18 Oct. 1895, but TR is referring to its reprinting in H[arry] T[hurston] P[eck]'s "The Question of the Laureate," *Bookman* 2 (Dec. 1895): 292–97. Professor of Latin at Columbia College and editor-in-chief of the *Bookman*, Peck (1856–1914) argues that Kipling should be England's new poet laureate, because he "represents not only in his verse, but in his own person, at once the extension and the unity of the [Anglo-Saxon] race" (294).

1896–1897

To Matthews

Police Department
Jan. 3rd. 189[6].[1]

Dear Brander:—

A happy New Year to you and yours. The Madam and the children are on their way in town.

All of the men I asked to meet Lounsbury went back on me, so I will have to have him to a merely family entertainment.[2]

This morning I got a letter from the Bookman telling me that they wanted 1500 words right away, and would send me a copy of the proof and a stenographer to-morrow afternoon. Is this satisfactory?[3]

I have set the detectives at work at once on the clues you gave me about the Burden robbery.[4]

Faithfully yours,
Theodore Roosevelt

BMP; 1 p.; tls.
1. TR typed "1895," but the contents make clear that this letter was written in 1896.
2. In a note dated 26 Dec. 1895 (BMP), TR invited BM to dine on 4 Jan. with him, Lounsbury, and others.
3. See preceding letter, n. 2.
4. On 28 Dec. 1895, thieves stole $75,000 in jewels from I. Townsend Burden of 5 East 27th Street. The culprits were later caught in London, but not as the result of clues provided by BM ("A $75,000 Diamond Robbery," *New York Times,* 28 Dec. 1895, 1; "Burden Robbers Caught," *New York Times,* 18 Apr. 1896, 1).

To Matthews

Police Department
May 4th. 1896.

Dear Brander:—

The appearance of the story of the unhappy veteran (which you remember I saw and liked so well before it was in print) reminds me that you have never seen one of my trial days.[1] One occurs next Thursday and one the following Thursday. If you could be present at either any time between ten, and five or six, o'clock you would get more insight into the police side of New York life than in any other way.

I was particularly delighted with what you said of Mark Twain in your recent article on humorists.[2]

Faithfully yours,

Theodore Roosevelt

BMP; 1 p.; tls.

1. BM, "A Letter of Farewell," *Scribner's Monthly* 19 (May 1896): 644–48, a story about an Irish-American veteran of the Civil War whose efforts to secure a patronage job with the New York City government are stymied by Civil Service rules. In despair, the veteran decides on suicide and writes his farewell letter. Thus, rather than celebrating the merits of the Civil Service Commission, BM's story suggests that the Civil Service reforms had a negative impact on many ethnic immigrants. It is curious that TR, who indicates that he read the story in draft form, should have liked it, since it implicitly challenges the Civil Service reforms he championed.

2. BM, "The Penalty of Humor," *Harper's Monthly* 92 (May 1896): 897–900; rpt. in BM, *Aspects of Fiction*, 43–56. In this astute essay, BM attacks the critical prejudice against humorous literature in general and defends Twain against the unjust criticism that his novels are merely "funny." Twain "is one of the foremost story-tellers of the world, with the gift of swift narrative, with the certain grasp of human nature, with a rare power of presenting character at a passionate crisis" (*Aspects*, 55).

To Matthews

Police Department

July 1st. 1896.

Dear Brander:—

Besides thanking Trent I feel I must thank you most heartily for his article about me in the Forum; it touched and pleased me greatly, for it said of me just what I like to have said, but what I never hoped would be said.[1] I thank you most warmly as well as Trent for it.

I called at your house the other day and was awfully sorry to have missed you.

Faithfully yours,

Theodore Roosevelt

BMP; 1 p.; tls.

1. Trent, "Theodore Roosevelt as a Historian," *Forum* 21 (July 1896): 566–76. Trent seeks to redress the lack of attention given TR's achievements as a historian. Surveying TR's historical works to date, he proclaims TR to be

one of the "most thoughtful, conscientious, and illuminating historians of our national career" (566). He also lauds TR's Americanism and his "friendly feeling toward Southerners of a different way of thinking" (571).

To Matthews

Police Department
November 2, 1896.

Dear Brander:—

Until January first Saturday is an impossible day for me. I am awfully sorry.

Garland is a good fellow, and he can do first rate work as a story writer, but he is daft whenever he comes to put his theories on paper in the shape of essays, and he is just the sort of half baked man who can be taken in by utterly cheap social reformers of the Henry George type.[1] He has never tried to *do* reform work, anymore than George; they only discuss it. I wish I could meet him and Howells together. I am very sorry I cannot accept.

Faithfully yours,
Theodore Roosevelt

BMP; 1 p.; tls.

1. Henry George (1839–97); the economist and social philosopher was one of the era's most trenchant critics of American capitalism. His proposed cure for the nation's economic problems was the "single tax" on real estate, which he argued would allow members of the underclass to participate fully in the nation's material progress. His book *Progress and Poverty* (1879), which spells out his single-tax theory, won him many admirers, among them Garland, whose early fiction dramatizes George's social and economic principles. George resided in New York City at this time, and, although he was derided as a crank by his political opponents, he had made a strong run for mayor of New York in 1886.

To Matthews

Police Department
Jan. 28, 1897.

Dear Brander:—

I know you don't go out now, but can't you come up and dine with me alone simply to meet two men, one James Lane Allen,[1] whom you know, and another, a friend of mine here at Police Headquarters, who is on the Evening Post[2]—absit omen[3]—who seems to have in him the promise of doing some excellent work in fiction about the real New York of to-day, and who is taking advantage of very unusual opportunities in seeing into the life of important New York, that is, New York, outside the four hundred.[4]

Faithfully yours,
Theodore Roosevelt

BMP; 1 p.; tls.

1. James Lane Allen (1849–1925); literary critic and fiction writer. He authored *Flute and Violin and Other Kentucky Tales and Romances* (1891) and several novels representing life in his native Kentucky.
2. As TR's next letter, below, indicates, the unnamed *Evening Post* reporter is (Joseph) Lincoln Steffens (1866–1936), who began supporting—and admiring—TR on the day he was sworn in as Police Commissioner (see *The Autobiography of Lincoln Steffens* [New York: Harcourt, Brace, 1931], 257–65).
3. Latin expression for "may it bear no ill omen"; TR had a longstanding grudge against the *Evening Post* and its editor E. L. Godkin, though the paper in fact supported TR's crusade against corruption (see Morris, *Rise,* 504).
4. That is to say, outside the New York elite, or members of the "Four Hundred." Steffens had published only one short story by this time ("Sweet Punch," *Harper's Monthly* 88 [Dec. 1893]: 126–29), and he would not shift his energies from journalism to fiction in any major way until many years later. But when he became city editor of the *New York Commercial Advertiser* in 1897, he sought out young writers intent on producing the same kind of "human-interest stories" of New York ghetto life that he had written for the *Evening Post.*

To Matthews

Police Department
Feby. 11, 1897.

Dear Brander:—

All right! I will come to lunch with you on the 20th. at 1.30; but that won't help me to have you meet my friend Mr. J. A. Steffens[1] of the Post, whom I really do want to have you meet, so I shall have to make an arrangement with you later on.

Very truly yours,
Theodore Roosevelt

BMP; 1 p.; tls.

1. Steffens's middle initial was "L," not "A," as TR typed.

To Matthews

Police Department
March 6, 1897.
Dear Brander:—
Can you dine with me next Wednesday at 689 Madison Avenue at half past seven? Do come, if you possibly can, for Steffens is coming, and I want to have him meet you, and I am very anxious to see you myself. I'll try to get Trent.
Yours very sincerely,
Theodore Roosevelt

BMP; 1 p.; tls.

To Matthews

NAVY DEPARTMENT[1]
June 10, 1897.
Dear Brander:
I don't know whether this will catch you at home or not. You spoke to me once about publishing a volume of essays. I fear I am bound to Putnams', but I will frankly say I would much rather publish them in your series than anywhere else.[2] I don't think I ought to get out of my arrangement with Putnams', although this arrangement was merely implied; but it is possible they will not wish to publish them in the shape I should prefer, and so I should like to know whether in such event you would care to have a volume from me or not. By the way, will you tell me what are the money arrangements in publishing these volumes.
I have been heartily enjoying myself here, and really like the work. Remember me warmly to Mrs. Matthews and Miss Matthews.
Faithfully yours,
Theodore Roosevelt

BMP; 2 pp.; tls.; pbd. *LTR*, 1:624.
1. TR assumed his duties as assistant secretary of the navy on 19 Apr. 1897.
2. As the next letter indicates, TR is referring to the collection of essays *American Ideals, and Other Essays, Social and Political,* which G. P. Putnam's Sons would publish in 1897 (rpt. in *Works,* vol. 13). BM was soliciting the volume for his publisher, Harper and Brothers, to whom he was advisory editor. Though TR states in this letter that he would prefer to publish with Harper, his letter to G. P. Putnam's Sons of 1 July 1897 makes clear that he was playing one publisher off against the other in an attempt to secure the best terms for himself: "I would of course rather have [the volume] go out by your firm than any other," he wrote Putnam's, adding that if Putnam's did not want

the volume "it might be that Harpers' would care for it in the series of volumes of essays by Brander Matthews, Cabot Lodge and others . . . Also please tell me the terms upon which you think they should be published" (*LTR*, 1:635).

To Matthews

June 14, 1897.
Dear Brander:
I shall never get entirely used to your new address even if the factory *has* shifted quarters.[1]
You have given me just the information I wished. I shall have to hear from the Putnams before writing you definitely. My book will be called "American Ideals; and Other Essays in Applied Politics and Sociology"; at least this would be the title unless we thought it well to change it.[2] The theses would run about as follows:

American Ideals,
True Americanism,
The Manly Virtues and Practical Politics,
The College Graduate and Public Life,
Phases of State Legislation,
New York Machine Politics,
Six Years of Civil Service Reform,
Administering the New York Police Force,
The Vice-Presidency in the Campaign of 1897,
President Harrison's Foreign Policy,
The Monroe Doctrine,
Washington's Forgotten Maxim,
The Law of Civilization and Decay,
Social Evolution,
National Life and Character.

I could have them ready for you within a month, but I have got to hear from Putnam first. He has the call; but it may be possible he will not want to publish them as he has a great theory of having me put in only the six or eight purely political essays—which as a matter of fact I could not differentiate from the others, for they all dove-tail into one another.
Where do you go after the 22d?
Faithfully yours,
Theodore Roosevelt

TRP; 2 pp; ccs.

1. In 1897, Columbia College, which BM sometimes referred to as the "factory" where he worked, relocated its campus from 49th Street to its present site at Morningside Heights. BM subsequently changed his residence, from 121 East 18th Street to 681 West End Avenue.

2. See preceding letter. Putnam's consented to TR's request; the first edition of *American Ideals* includes all the essays on TR's list (with several minor title changes), excepting "President Harrison's Foreign Policy," which was replaced with "How Not to Help Our Poorer Brother" (*Works*, 13:157–67).

To Matthews

NAVY DEPARTMENT
September 4, 1897.

Dear Brander:

I send this to your city address because I am not sure how long a "few days" really is. No, I hadn't seen that in the NATION. I am glad you wrote it; and that you touched them on the raw was evident from their attempted retort.[1] I shall try to get ahold of your AMERICAN-ISM piece; I never saw it.[2]

I have directed Putnam's Sons to send you my fourth volume of the WINNING OF THE WEST, and the AMERICAN IDEALS just as soon as the latter comes out.

I am very glad you liked Mahan's article.[3] To me it seemed very strong. What an awful pity it is that the people who are so right on civic matters should so often be hopelessly wrong on every question of national or international significance![4]

Give my warm regards to Mrs. Matthews and Miss Matthews. I should be very glad to receive your "Outlines"; but I guess I have read almost all of them already![5] I read "after" you, as we say in the south.

Faithfully yours,
Theodore Roosevelt

I am very anxious to have a really satisfactory talk with you on many matters.

BMP; 2 pp.; tls. with handwritten postscript.

1. BM, letter to the editor, *Nation* 65 (26 Aug. 1897): 167. The letter responds to an unsigned editorial column in the *Nation* (65 [12 Aug. 1897]: 131) complaining that a recent story by Wister ("Sharon's Choice," *Harper's Monthly* 95 [Aug. 1897], 447–57) manifests the "pseudo-patriotic virus" that poisons literature. BM defends Wister by observing that the "virus" has infected eminent American writers from Washington Irving onward. "Perhaps the *Nation*," he sarcastically suggests, "could issue a call for a meeting to form a

society to combat the evil—an active organization on the model of the Anti-Vaccination League." The *Nation* editor(s) replied (directly below BM's letter): "We are more fearful that we have been derelict in Professor Matthews's own case, though he modestly forebears to press it."

2. BM, "Americanism," *Harper's Round Table,* 6 July 1897, 873–74. The primary meaning of the slippery term "Americanism," BM maintains, is "a love for this country of ours, an appreciation of the institutions of this nation, a pride in the history of this people to which we belong. . . . But it means also . . . a frank acceptance of the principles which underlie our government . . . [and] a faith in our fellow-man, a belief in liberty and in equality" (873). Though he condemns "hysteric" jingoism, BM nonetheless vigorously endorses American expansionism.

3. Mahan's "Twentieth-Century Outlook," *Harper's Monthly* 95 (Sept. 1897): 521–33, focuses on international relations at the *fin-de-siècle*. He urges the United States and the European colonial powers to continue their Providential task of spreading Christian civilization throughout the globe. The essay ends with a plea for Americans to resist isolationism and pacifism and to preserve the "warrior" spirit.

4. Unknown to BM, TR believed that BM had been somewhat influenced by the "hopelessly wrong" ideas of his New York friends. In a letter dated 5 Nov. 1897 to newspaper editor Curtis Guild, Jr. (1827–1911), TR remarked that he was very fond of BM, but that BM mixed with certain people who "look down on patriotism"; the result was that BM sometimes appealed to the "false gods of the men by whom he is surrounded" (*LTR,* 1:710). TR probably had such anti-imperialists as Howells and Garland in mind.

5. *Outlines in Local Color* (New York: Harper, 1897), BM's second collection of sketches of New York City life; most of the stories had been previously published in *Harper's Monthly.*

To Matthews

NAVY DEPARTMENT
September 27, 1897.

Dear Brander:

May I keep that piece on "Americanism?"[1] It is admirable; I don't know that I have ever seen a better and, at the same time, more reasonable and moderate definition. I am glad you liked Lodge's essays.[2] I had the fourth volume of my book sent you; and have also directed them to send you *my* "Essays" as soon as they come out, which will be shortly.[3] Later, about the 11th of October, I hope to be in New York for a day, and I shall try to see you; but Ninety-third street is dreadfully far up for a man who is on the wing. On Monday would I be apt to be able to get you to lunch down-town, that is, at Delmonico's—Twenty-third Street?

I like your outline of topics in the American literature course very much. I am particularly pleased that you should have put Lincoln in your literature.

In great haste,

Always yours,
Theodore Roosevelt

BMP; 2 pp.; tls.
1. See preceding letter, n. 2.
2. Lodge, *Certain Accepted Heroes and Other Essays in Literature and Politics* (New York: Harper, 1897).
3. *Winning of the West* and *American Ideals,* as mentioned in preceding letter.

To Matthews

NAVY DEPARTMENT
October 26, 1897.

Dear Brander:

I was very glad to get "Outlines in Local Color." I think I have read all the stories, but I shall read them all over again with the keen pleasure I can conscientiously say I always take in your work.

Now, in writing to thank you for your kindness I have got to be a little disagreeable. I don't think I could undertake now to do the work you suggested.[1] I fear it would take a little more time than you believe. Only a few of these old stories are at all well written, and I fear there will have to be a great deal of rewriting done before they will be in passable shape, and I don't dare at present to go into any new work.

The next time I come to New York I have got to, somehow or other, arrange a lunch with you.

Faithfully yours,
Theodore Roosevelt

BMP; 2 pp.; tls.
1. BM apparently tried to recruit TR to do a book of previously published western stories for Longmans, Green, to which BM was advisory editor, for in a letter to George Haven Putnam dated 1 Nov. 1897, TR states that he had rejected book solicitations from that publisher (as well as from Macmillan) in order to complete *Winning of the West* (*LTR,* 1:705).

To Matthews

NAVY DEPARTMENT
November 4, 1897.

Dear Brander:

I was very much pleased with your article, and I was glad of the company I was in.[1] Perhaps the thing that pleased me most was the quotation with which you closed. Of course I know it, but it has been a long time since I had seen it.[2]

Faithfully yours,
Theodore Roosevelt

BMP; 1 p.; tls.

1. BM, "Concerning Certain Contemporary Essayists," *Harper's Weekly* 41 (6 Nov. 1897): 1106. In this review essay, BM maintains that certain American essayists—most notably Lodge and TR—are producing writing worthy of comparison to that of the great English essayists Addison and Steele. BM showers praise on TR, describing him as a "robust writer, not afraid of clear thinking and of plain speaking, and all these essays [in *American Ideals*] are stamped with his vehement sincerity." BM also likens TR's "manly Americanism" to that of Emerson and Lowell.

2. Comparing TR to the English essayist Sir Francis Bacon (1561–1626), BM closes on a martial note with the following quotation from Bacon's "Of the True Greatness of Kingdoms and Estates": "Walled towns, stored arsenals and armories, goodly races of horse, chariots of war, elephants, ordnance, artillery, and the like—all this is but a sheep in lion's skin except the breed and disposition of the people be stout and warlike."

To Matthews

NAVY DEPARTMENT
November 29, 1897.

My dear Brander:

Lodge read me your letter with delight. I shall leave him to make his own apologies. I don't think I can possibly write that piece for the FORUM.[1] You have no conception how busy I am. I wish you were going to be down here in Washington some time.

Faithfully yours,
Theodore Roosevelt

BMP; 1 p.; tls.

1. TR's note to BM of 23 Nov. 1897 (BMP) indicates that BM had solicited an article from him on an unidentified topic.

To Matthews

NAVY DEPARTMENT
December 20, 1897.

Dear Brander:

I am very sorry to hear that you have been laid up with the grippe. My children have been under the weather themselves; I am, as usual, in robust health.

Yes, I read Peck's article, and it struck me as admirable, and I wondered myself if the lunch he alluded to was not that at your house.[1]

The EVENING POST had a characteristically untruthful editorial, with Cabot Lodge as the central figure, last Saturday.[2] What a vindictive sheet it is! I fear that among overeducated[3] people it does a good deal of harm.

Give my warm regards to Mrs. Matthews and Miss Matthews.

Faithfully yours,
Theodore Roosevelt

BMP; 2 pp.; tls.

1. Harry Thurston Peck, "American Newspapers," *Living Age* 215 (11 Dec. 1897): 761–62. To illustrate his thesis that American journalists can be trusted to exercise discretion about what they report, Peck describes a private luncheon he attended at which a political figure revealed confidential information; several journalists were present, but none printed the revelations. This letter suggests that the lunch was at BM's house, and that the free-speaking political figure was perhaps TR.

2. "Literature and Politics," *New York Evening Post*, 18 Dec. 1897, 6. The unsigned editorial argues that political partisanship is incompatible with literary art because politics invariably corrupts character; thus honesty and integrity are rare in writings by professional politicians—including those by Lodge, who is accused of being hypocritical and untruthful in his political dealings.

3. TR, who often expressed contempt for the "overcivilized" or elite class, wrote "uneducated," then scratched out the prefix "un" and replaced it with "over."

To Matthews

NAVY DEPARTMENT
December 27, 1897.

Dear Brander:

There is a certain grim comfort in seeing an intimate friend get a little of the kind of attack I get all the time. That editorial is sufficiently unintelligent to come out of the EVENING POST.[1]

I hope you and yours had a merry Christmas. Mrs. Roosevelt is now all right, and so are all the children.

I shall write to Trent at once.[2]

Faithfully yours,
Theodore Roosevelt

BMP; 1 p.; tls.

1. TR apparently refers to the editorial attacking Lodge mentioned in the preceding letter.
2. TR immediately wrote Trent (27 Dec. 1897, TRP) to congratulate him on the birth of a daughter.

1898–1899

To Matthews

NAVY DEPARTMENT
February 28, 1898.

Dear Brander:

Did I write to tell you how much I like your Lounsbury article?[1]
One of the drawbacks to Washington life is that I don't see you any more.

Give my warm regards to Mrs. Matthews. All this winter Mrs.
Roosevelt and my eldest small boy have been sick.

Faithfully yours,
Theodore Roosevelt

BMP; 1 p.; tls.

1. BM, "An American Scholar: Thomas Raynesford Lounsbury," *Century* 55
   (Feb. 1898): 560–65; a survey of the life and works of Lounsbury, whom BM
   represents as the exemplary scholar.

To Matthews

First Regt. U.S. Volunteer Cavalry,
On Board Transport Miami,
August 14th 1898.

Dear Brander,

I am on my way home and I hope to see you at some not distant
date before we start off on the great Havana campaign.[1] We have had a
great time and this is a regiment of crackerjacks—American from start to
finish, in the best and fullest sense of the term.

I am interested in that McMillan's you sent me.[2] I have forgotten
McMillan's address; would you mind sending the enclosed to them.[3] I
should like to see the original article; it may be that I should like to answer
the gentleman, and therefore I should like to see the May number of the
magazine.

Very sincerely yours,
Theodore Roosevelt

BMP; 1 p.; tls.; pbd. *LTR*, 2:866.

1. TR had accepted appointment as lieutenant colonel and commander of the
   famous Rough Rider volunteer regiment in Apr. 1898, almost immediately

after the U.S. declared war on Spain; the battle of San Juan Hill occurred in July 1898. TR wrote this letter during his return to Montauk, Long Island, apparently not yet aware that the war had ended on Aug. 12. TR's controversial adventures with the Rough Riders are detailed in Morris, *Rise*, 618–61.

2. [David Hannay], "An American Historian of the British Navy," *Macmillan's Magazine* 78 (May 1898): 13–22. Hannay expresses extreme displeasure with the choice of TR to contribute the chapter on the War of 1812 to the British naval history, *The Royal Navy from the Earliest Times to the Present*, ed. William Laird Clowes (Boston: Little, Brown, 1897; London: S. Low, Marston, & Co., 1897). Though he acknowledges that TR's *The Naval War of 1812* was "relatively fair" to the British, Hannay cites numerous examples of what he perceived to be nationalistic bias in TR's account of the naval war.

3. TR enclosed a note dated 14 Aug. 1898 to the editor of *Macmillan's* requesting a copy of the May number, "which I understand contains a review of or attack upon a work of mine" (BMP). After receiving the article (from BM), TR decided that it was not worth answering (TR to BM, 8 Sept. 1898, BMP).

To Matthews

Oyster Bay, L.I.,
Dec. 27, 1898.

Dear Brander;—

I fear I shall not be able to see you until after I get to Albany.¹ Now, can you not pay me a visit at Albany? I should like you to see politics there a little from the inside, and I think it would be useful to you in a way.

Faithfully yours,
Theodore Roosevelt

BMP; 1 p.; tls. (dictated).
1. TR had been elected governor of New York in Nov. 1898; he was sworn into office on 2 Jan. 1899.

To Matthews

EXECUTIVE CHAMBER
May 27th, 1899.

Dear Brander:—

Hearty thanks for yours of the 26th. Now, will you consult Nicholas Murray Butler and find out if he has any plans for me, or if the Committee has?¹ If not I accept with the greatest pleasure.

Always yours,
Theodore Roosevelt

BMP; 1 p.; tls.

1. TR likely refers to his impending visit to Columbia College (7 June 1899), during which he received an honorary LL.D. degree and delivered an address to the alumni eulogizing Hamilton Fish, Jr. (1873?–1898), a Columbia alumnus. Grandson of former Secretary of State Hamilton Fish (1808–93), young Fish had served with TR and the Rough Riders in Cuba, where he was killed in battle.

To Matthews

EXECUTIVE CHAMBER
Aug. 29th, 1899.

Dear Brander:—

Hearty thanks for yours of the 28th. I shall look up that article today. I had seen his former article on North and South and thought it excellent.[1] Our British brother has seen a new light during the past eighteen months, and perhaps we have too, for that matter.

I cannot tell you how I enjoyed the glimpse I got of you last spring, and some how or another I have got to arrange for another this fall.

Always yours,
Theodore Roosevelt

BMP; 1 p.; tls.

1. William Archer, "America To-day: The Republic and the Empire," *Pall Mall Magazine* 19 (Sept. 1899): 95–105; the article that TR had already read was "America To-day: North and South," *Pall Mall Magazine* 18 (Aug. 1899): 462–70. The two pieces are Archer's analysis of Anglo-American relations, based on his observations during a recent visit to the U.S. In the second article ("Republic and Empire"), Archer criticizes his fellow Englishmen for being supercilious and disdainful toward Americans; and he supports his point by quoting a passage from TR's essay "The Monroe Doctrine" (1896; rpt. in *Works*, 13:168–81), in which TR chastises the British for their contempt toward former colonists. "There is," Archer suggests, "no more typical, and probably no more widely respected American at the present moment than Governor Roosevelt, of New York" (105). Archer closes with an appeal for a consolidation, based on mutual respect, of the English-speaking countries of the world.

In a letter to Archer of 31 Aug. 1899, TR expressed great pleasure with the two articles, especially with Archer's emphasis on improved relations between their respective countries (*LTR*, 2:1063–65).

1900–1901

To Matthews

EXECUTIVE CHAMBER

Jany. 25th, 1900.

Dear Brander:—

Many thanks for your note of the 24th. I was much amused at that strawberry. It was delightful to catch even such a brief glimpse of you. But I must make arrangements to see more of you in the future. I have missed you very much.

Hoping that Mrs. Matthews and yourself will have a delightful visit on the other side,[1]

Always yours,
Theodore Roosevelt

BMP; 1 p.; tls.

1. BM took sabbatical leave from Columbia during spring semester 1900; in Feb. he embarked on an extensive tour of Egypt and Europe (*Years*, 422–28). See next letter.

To Roosevelt

GRAND HÔTEL DE RUSSIE
ET DES ILES BRITTANIQUES

Rome, le 15 April 1900

Dear Theodore:[1]

How are you and yours in that far away land where the Eagle is ever twisting the Lion's tail?[2] We are all right—and we have been having a good time in these parts (by which I mean Africa and Asia as well as Europe). All roads lead to Rome; and we came by way of Egypt and Constantinople and Athens. By the way, I discovered two interesting things in Cairo; one is that the fellah still prays to the Sphinx, bowing before him at break of day in earnest supplication; and the other is that the Turk has to have his fez [blocked?] "while he waits."

But I am not writing now to supply you with these interesting items. I found my colleague Munroe Smith[3] here and he lent me *The Political Science Quarterly* for March. In the pressure of your labors you cannot have time to read everything, so I want to call your attention to a paper on "State Administration in New York"—and more especially to the final page or two in which the writer makes two or three suggestions that might or might not approve themselves to your own more intimate knowledge of the case.[4]

I'm sorry for Dewey—and I'm grieved too. In fact, I wish Hazen had not died.[5] As it is, I doubt if the Arch will ever be built—and New York is just pining for that arch.[6] This past week of mine here in Rome has made me feel that I'd like to see a Triumphal Column in New York— to Lincoln, for example, or to Farragut,[7] or even to commemorate the Revolutionary war.

We are going on to Paris by way of Vienna,—and then to London; and I'm hoping to see Sandy Hook toward the end of August.

Here's to you! and to yours!

Brander Matthews

TRP; 4 pp.; als.

1. This is the first extant letter from BM to TR.
2. Symbols of the U.S. and Great Britain, respectively. BM and TR, of course, enjoyed verbally "twisting the tails" of their British counterparts.
3. Edmund Munroe Smith (1854–1926); professor of legal history and later (1922–24) Bryce Professor of European Legal History at Columbia. He contributed articles to the *Political Science Quarterly* and authored many books, including *Bismarck and German Unity* (1898).
4. John A. Fairlie, "State Administration in New York," *Political Science Quarterly* 15 (Mar. 1900): 50–74. In the closing pages, Fairlie (1872–1947), an assistant professor of journalism at the Univ. of Michigan, recommends that the state consolidate, for efficiency, many of its separate bureaus and agencies.
5. After months of hedging, Spanish-American War hero Admiral George Dewey (1837–1917) announced, on 3 Apr. 1900, that he would run for president on the Democratic ticket. His decision dismayed many Republicans, who believed him to be a loyal supporter of President McKinley. TR, who had extolled Dewey in the Oct. 1899 number of *McClure's Magazine* (rpt. in *Works*, 13: 420–29), was infuriated (see, e.g., TR to Lodge, 9 Apr. 1900, *LTR*, 2:1252–53).

   In 1899, Dewey, a widower, had married a wealthy socialite, Mildred Hazen, widow of Gen. William B. Hazen (d. 1887). Many believed that the strong-willed Mildred had pressured her husband into running for president because she desired to be First Lady. Failing to gather much support from Democrats, Dewey soon withdrew from the race, the whole affair being a major embarrassment for him. (See Ronald Spector, *Admiral of the New Empire: The Life and Career of George Dewey* [Columbia: Univ. of South Carolina Press, 1974], 107–16). BM seems to imply that Dewey would have been better off had General Hazen not died, for then Dewey would not have married Mildred and would have escaped the damage done to his reputation as a national hero.

6. In honor of Dewey's victory at the Battle of Manila Bay, the state of New York had erected a wood and plaster arch 70 feet tall, under which Dewey had stood while reviewing his welcome-home parade down Fifth Ave. on 30 Sept. 1899. At the time of this letter, efforts were under way to collect the million dollars needed to construct a permanent arch, modeled on the Arch of Titus in Rome (Spector, *Admiral of the New Empire*, 105–6).

7. Admiral David Glasgow Farragut (1801–70), Union naval hero during the Civil War.

To Matthews

EXECUTIVE CHAMBER
April 30th, 1900.

Dear Brander:—

It was delightful to get your letter. I look forward to hearing about everything when you return. Mrs. Roosevelt, by the way, has just taken a delightful three weeks' trip to Cuba.

Well, I am almost through my thirty day bills, so that the work of my second session is practically closed. For two years now I have worked practically without any let-up and I wish I could get a holiday, but I can't—at least until after January first next, when I fear I shall suffer from exactly the opposite complaint and have too much holiday! I have done good work as Governor. This I think I can conscientiously say, and I think that Nicholas Murray Butler who has been one of my right hand men all through my term will tell you the same.¹ But it is disheartening at times. For example, it is quite on the cards that I shall be beaten for the Governorship this fall, not because of my faults, but largely because of what I have done that is straight.² I have helped the decent element of the democracy time and again, simply because from my standpoint it was impossible to do anything else, and the result has been that I have built up that element, and that the shrewd leaders of the democratic party—men like Hill—seeing this may turn the fact to my own destruction.³ Thus in New York City the best of the City officials was Coler.⁴ Even with Coler it was distinctly a case of the one-eyed being king among the blind; but he did at least have one eye, and so I helped him. The result has been to make him prominent as a candidate for the governorship, and if he is put up, there are very many excellent citizens who in their joy at finding a one-eyed man in Tammany will cheerfully support him against another man with two eyes, on a theory of action that is understandable but in no way defensible. One of the petty, irritating features of the situation is the delight of my own machine men, who of course have always objected strenuously to my helping out the decent democrats and are quite unable to understand that I did it with entire knowledge that the course might turn out to my own personal disadvantage.

I am looking forward to your return. Meanwhile, with best wishes to Mrs. Matthews and yourself, believe me,

Always faithfully yours,
Theodore Roosevelt

BMP; 2 pp.; tls.; pbd. *LTR*, 2:1273.

1. Butler, who like BM had joined the reformers' campaign against the Tammany machine during his undergraduate days at Columbia, was an intimate friend and political advisor of TR throughout his career. See Butler's autobiography, *Across the Busy Years: Recollections and Reflections* (New York: Scribner's, 1939), 1:224–31, 245–46, and *passim*.

2. TR's attempts to increase regulations affecting big business and the state's natural resources, and his refusal to support Republican officials that he considered incompetent, made him a target of powerful business people and politicians, Republicans as well as Democrats. His chief Republican adversary was the powerful boss, Tom Platt. At the Republican National Convention in June 1900, Platt and other Republicans pushed hard for TR's nomination as vice-presidential candidate in order to ensure that he would not run for reelection as governor. The strategy succeeded, and TR—who had insisted that he was not interested in being vice-president—was drafted as McKinley's running mate. See Morris, *Rise*, 711–23.

3. David Bennett Hill (1843–1910). The former New York governor and senator had been TR's political adversary for many years; though he no longer held public office, he remained in control of the state's Democratic machine.

4. Bird Sim Coler (1867–1941), New York City comptroller and a Democrat. TR feared that Coler, who enjoyed the backing of the powerful Hill (see previous note), would be a formidable opponent (see *LTR*, 2:1360, 1384). The Democrats, however, nominated John B. Stanchfield (1855–1921) instead of Coler (who did run for governor in 1902). TR, in any case, dropped out of the race to run for vice-president.

To Roosevelt

681 WEST END AVENUE
Dec 2nd 1900

Dear Theodore:

I see that today is your wedding-day.[1] Let me present my felicitations, as the anti-Dreyfusites would phrase it.[2]

When are you going to be in New York again? I've something to show you when I see you next.

In the mean time I want to know something. My friend, Coquelin, is President of the French Actor's Fund; and the French government has authorized the society to get up a lottery.[3] Of course Coquelin cannot openly offer the tickets of this lottery for sale here. But how far is he doing anything actually illegal in letting his friends pay him for them? To me, the thing seems to be contrary to the letter of the law, to say the least. And yet the authorities wink at raffles etc. And this, being for charity, may stand in some such position. How does it strike you?

Yours Ever
Brander Matthews

TRP; 4 pp.; als.

1. BM of course means that it is TR's wedding anniversary (his 14th).
2. In 1894, Captain Alfred Dreyfus (1859–1935), a French Jew, was unjustly convicted of treason and sentenced to life in prison; anti-Semitism clearly was a factor in the verdict. Many French writers and intellectuals, most notably Zola, rallied to Dreyfus's defense. In 1899 Dreyfus was pardoned and in 1906 retried and found innocent, despite fierce opposition from the anti-Dreyfusites. Both TR and BM deplored the "hideous" wrong done to Dreyfus (*LTR*, 2:1020; *Years*, 194).

   BM's "felicitations" remark is ambiguous; perhaps he is facetiously congratulating TR on his "life sentence" of marriage.
3. Benoit Constant Coquelin (1841–1909), French actor; BM speaks fondly of his long friendship with Coquelin in *Years*, 188–201.

To Matthews

December 4, 1900.

Dear Brander:

I have your letter of the 2nd and thank you heartily.

I hardly know what to say about the lottery business. I think it is undoubtedly illegal, but then I think Church lotteries are also illegal, and yet nobody dreams of interfering with them. Where the line would be drawn it is difficult to say.

I wish I could see you, but when I come to New York I stay at my sister's, No. 422 Madison Avenue,[1] which is a long distance from you. Do you think you could get there next Sunday morning at ten?

TRP; 1 p.; cc.

1. Residence of TR's sister Corinne (Mrs. Douglas Robinson).

To Roosevelt

681 WEST END AVENUE

Dec 27th 1900

Dear Theodore:

Your time will be up soon and your new sentence doesn't begin for two months yet, so I have to catch a glimpse of you during the lucid interval.[1]

I have a letter to show you—a letter of some importance. Are you going to be in town next week?

Yours Ever

Brander Matthews

A Happy New Century to you—and many of them!

TRP; 2 pp.; als.

1. TR's term as governor of New York ended on 31 Dec. 1900, and his "new sentence" as vice-president of the United States began on 4 Mar. 1901.

To Matthews

EXECUTIVE CHAMBER

Dec. 31st, 1900.

Dear Brander:—

I have your note of the 27th inst. As soon as I wind up my last affairs here I am going to spend two months on a lion hunt in Colorado. I shall only be in New York on Friday evening next at the Boone & Crockett dinner. I am afraid you are not sufficiently a devotee of "le sport" to go to it. If you really think I ought to see the letter, it will be the greatest pleasure to catch a glimpse of you at the Metropolitan Club where the dinner takes place, and any time you come there in the evening, before, during or after the dinner, I will at once come out and get you in.

Always yours,

Theodore Roosevelt

BMP; 1 p.; tls.

To Roosevelt

NARRAGANSETT PIER

Sept 22nd 1901

Dear Theodore:

I know that you must be overburdened with correspondence just now,—and yet I do not want any longer to delay assuring you of my sympathy for you in the arduous task, which has been suddenly and most unexpectedly handed over to you.[1]

And I want also to tell you how strong is the confidence of the public in you, in your integrity of purpose, in your firmness of will, and in your ability to do whatsoever may have to be done in the years to come. Not only from the press, but more especially from private talk with all [sorts?] and conditions of men. I am certain that the American people believes that you have proved yourself and that your past makes their future secure.

Do not burden yourself to answer this. But remember that I am
Ever Yours
Brander Matthews

TRP; 3 pp.; als.

1. BM refers to TR's having become president following the death of McKinley on 13 Sept. 1901.

To Matthews

EXECUTIVE MANSION
September 25, 1901.

My dear Brander:
I like your letter so much that I must send you a line to tell you so; when are you coming to Washington?
Faithfully yours,
Theodore Roosevelt

BMP; 1 p.; tls.

To Matthews

October 26, 1901.

My dear Brander:
The essays have come.[1] I am delighted to receive them. Most of them of course I know well.

It was great fun catching a glimpse of you.
Faithfully yours,

TRP; 1 p.; cc.

1. Probably one (or more) of the three collections of essays BM published in 1901: *The Historical Novel and Other Essays*, *Notes on Speech-making*, and *Parts of Speech: Essays on English*.

To Roosevelt

681 WEST END AVENUE
Dec 29th 1901

Dear Theodore:
I've just had a letter from Leigh Hunt, who is laid up in Shanghai—but improving apparently after a hard struggle with death.[1]
Here's the ¶ that may interest you:
"I share with you a perfect confidence in our new President. My only fear is that he will have no thought of self. When you see him, tell him he has a friend, wandering about in the Orient, who prays constantly for his happiness and abundant success."

As you may have heard adverse criticism of your acts, I'll just remark that I have seen no one who does not approve absolutely of your doings in the absurd Schley squabble.[2] I don't happen to know a single Schley partisan—except one, indeed, a peculiar personality who is always on the wrong side.

I wish you a Happy New Year—altho I'm not sure you haven't already had more than your share of fun.

> Yours Ever
> Brander Matthews

TRP; 3 pp.; als.

1. Leigh S. J. Hunt (1855–1933). After going bankrupt in the Panic of 1893, the former owner of the *Seattle Post-Intelligencer* traveled to the Far East, where he earned a fortune developing gold mines in China and Korea and cotton plantations in Egypt and the Sudan; he was captured and nearly killed by bandits in Korea. An expert on Oriental culture, he advised President TR on Far Eastern affairs and later subsidized TR's scientific expeditions.

2. Admiral Winfield Scott Schley (1839–1909); commander of the North Atlantic Squadron during the Spanish-American War. A controversy arose over whether Schley or the chief commander of the naval squadrons blockading Cuba, William T. Sampson (1840–1902), deserved the credit for defeating the Spanish navy at the battle off Santiago on 3 July 1898. (See Margaret Leech, *In the Days of McKinley* [New York: Harper, 1959], 241–59.) The debate was resurrected in June 1901, with the publication of the revised edition of Edgar Stanton Maclay's *History of the United States Navy* (New York: Appleton, 1901), which charged Schley with incompetence and cowardice. Schley requested a review of the charges by the Navy Department, which formed a court of inquiry presided over by Admiral Dewey. After the majority of court officers (with Dewey dissenting) rendered a judgment critical of Schley's conduct during the battle, Schley appealed to President TR, who supported the court's decision (see BM to TR, 26 Feb. 1902). Contrary to BM's remarks, Schley had wide popular support. See next letter.

To Matthews

Personal.
WHITE HOUSE
December 31, 1901.
Dear Brander:

Will you give my warm regards to Hunt? Can't you come on here some day and take dinner or lunch with me? I should so like to go over certain matters with you.

I was really pleased with what you wrote me as to the Miles-Schley business.[1] Taking this whole intricate controversy in a mass, it seems to me that a very large part of our people have turned hysterical, as clearly as the French did in the Boulanger business,[2] and as a large body of the English seem to be doing with Buller.[3] As regards Miles, I feel that any man who fails to back me up is either a fellow wholly incapable of reasoning or else a man who has never taken the trouble to reason, or, finally, a wrong-headed person who deliberately desires the growth of a spirit which would render the army and the navy not merely useless but a menace to the country. The ultra-Schley partisans are simply impervious to reason and indifferent to facts. Many of Schley's opponents have behaved very badly also. Of course the trouble comes, in so far as I am concerned, from the fact that my teeth are being set on edge because other people have eaten sour grapes. Three years ago Miles should have been court-martialed for his insubordinate and improper interview attacking the War Department,[4] and, on the other hand, Eagan should have been dismissed [from] the service with ignominy for his vile outrage against Miles;[5] and at the same time, or before, Schley should have been court-martialed. Sampson committed a capital error in not court-martialing him—and this on the assumption that what Sampson and Sampson's friends now say is true. Instead of this course being followed, the effort was made to make things pleasant for everybody—Alger,[6] Miles, Schley, Sampson, in short, the whole outfit. I understand thoroughly how natural it was to make this effort, and it may well be that under slightly changed circumstances the effort would have succeeded and would have been the wisest thing; but as events have actually turned out nothing but harm has resulted; and the great bulk of our people have become so wedded to their theory in the Schley case that facts make literally no impression upon them whatsoever.

There! I have not written so freely to anyone. Naturally this letter is purely for your private eye. But it was a relief to write it. If you will come on here I will cause you further suffering by telling you about this and all the other incidents of my career as President.

Love to your wife and daughter.

Faithfully yours,
Theodore Roosevelt

BMP; 2 pp.; tls.; pbd. *LTR*, 3:213–14.

1. Gen. Nelson A. Miles (1839–1925); commander-in-chief of the army during the Spanish-American War. Two weeks before this letter, he had publicly expressed his support for Dewey's dissenting opinion in the Schley case, declaring that he had "no sympathy with the efforts which have been made to destroy the honor of an officer under such circumstances" ("Miles Takes Dewey's View," *New-York Daily Tribune*, 17 Dec. 1901, 2). Outraged by Miles's action, TR officially reprimanded him, stirring further controversy ("General Miles Reprimanded," *New-York Daily Tribune*, 22 Dec. 1901, 1).

2. Georges Ernest Boulanger (1837–91); French general whom rebellious factions made their hero during the Third Republic in the late 1880s; but instead of leading a revolt, he accepted the government's sentence of exile and later committed suicide.

3. Sir Redvers Buller (1839–1908) was appointed commander of the British army in South Africa when the Boer War erupted in 1899. Boer victories greatly damaged his reputation as a brilliant general and caused him to lose popular support at home.

4. In 1898, the Dodge Commission was created to investigate charges that the War Department bungled military and supply operations during the war. Testifying before the commission in Dec. 1898, General Miles (a Democrat and opponent of the McKinley administration) accused the Subsistence Department of supplying chemically treated or "embalmed" beef to the troops. The charge shocked the nation and added more fuel to the burning controversy surrounding the War Department's conduct during the war. See Leech, *In the Days of McKinley*, 316–22.

5. Charles Patrick Eagan (1841–1919); commissary general during the war and a direct target of Miles's "embalmed" beef accusations. Eagan denied the charges, contending that he had been "crucified" by Miles. Testifying before the Dodge Commission, Eagan lost control of himself, condemning Miles in such vituperative language that he (Eagan) was court-martialed. Eagan was found guilty and sentenced to dismissal from the service; but McKinley followed the court's recommendation for leniency and reduced the sentence to six years' suspension from duty, the term remaining before Eagan's retirement (Leech, *In the Days of McKinley*, 317–18).

6. Russell Alexander Alger (1836–1907); as secretary of war during the Spanish-American War, he too was implicated in the "beef scandal." Public criticism of Alger's performance as secretary led McKinley to ask for and receive his resignation from that office in 1899.

To Matthews

WHITE HOUSE
February 19, 1902.

Dear Brander:

I have your letter of the 17th instant. I only appoint the sons of army and navy officers as cadets at large to West Point or Annapolis, and so I am afraid I cannot do anything for your friend. I am very sorry.

I thank you most heartily for your kind words about Ted, and am glad to say that he is now all right.[1]

Faithfully yours,
Theodore Roosevelt

BMP; 1 p.; tls.

1. Ted had been seriously ill with pneumonia.

To Roosevelt

681 WEST END AVENUE
Feb 26th 1902

Dear Theodore:

As you are denied the privilege of walking casually down 23rd St you may not have seen the puzzle I enclose. Your daughter may want it for the family archives.

That was a bully note of yours on the Schley question; and I think that you hit the nail on the head so that the ghost can't escape from the coffin again.[1]

It is a gain for the people that you are in the White House—but it is a loss for your friends. Mark Twain and Howells (and enough more to make up the usual octave) are going to lunch here on Friday—and I wish that you were to be 1/8 of the party. But a time will come!

Yours Ever
Brander Matthews

TRP; 4 pp.; als.

1. TR issued his official decision on the Schley case on 18 Feb. 1902; the full text of TR's statement was printed on the front page of the *New York Times* on 20 Feb. 1902, where BM no doubt read it. After explaining in detail his

reasons for endorsing the Court of Inquiry's judgment against Schley, TR closed by saying that "there is no further excuse whatever from either side for any further agitation of this unhappy controversy. To keep it alive would merely do damage to the navy and the country."

To Matthews

February 27, 1902.
Dear Brander:
Thanks for the puzzle, which I think well worth a place in the archives. I do wish I could see you. Can you not make Mark Twain and Howells come down with you and take lunch with me here some day?[1]
Faithfully yours,
Theodore Roosevelt

TRP; 1 p.; ccs.

1. Though they opposed America's war against the Filipino rebels and viewed TR with some ambivalence, Howells and Twain nonetheless supported him at this point; but TR's continuation of the McKinley administration's imperialist foreign policy soon would repel both writers, and they became his outspoken critics. For full discussion of the complex relationship between TR and Howells and Twain, see William M. Gibson, *Theodore Roosevelt Among the Humorists: W. D. Howells, Mark Twain, and Mr. Dooley* (Knoxville: Univ. of Tennessee Press, 1980), 9–42.

To Matthews

June 13, 1902.
Dear Brander:
E. C. Boynton has written a history of West Point,[1] and General Cullum a biographical register of the officers and graduates.[2] I have asked the War Department to send you any offical reports about it.
Faithfully yours,
Theodore Roosevelt

TRP; 1 p.; ccs.

1. Edward Carlisle Boynton, *History of West Point* (New York: D. Van Nostrand, 1863; 2d ed. 1871). BM may have wanted information for the unnamed friend who desired to attend West Point (TR to BM, 19 Feb. 1902).

2. George Washington Cullum, *Biographical Register of the Officers and Graduates of the U.S. Military Academy, at West Point, N.Y., from Its Establishment in 1802, to 1890* (Boston: Houghton, 3d ed. 1891).

TO ROOSEVELT

SAVILE CLUB [London]
July 26th, 1902

Dear Theodore:
Thanks for your promise to send me the Sanger report—if it is accessible.[1] I enclose a copy of verses which may amuse you. The writer is a man named Reeves, who is Agent General for New Zealand.[2] Don't return them—but you might pass them along to Butler, if you happen to be writing to him. The Athenaeum dinner last night & the Orderly Meritorious was interesting.[3] I found Kipling looking at Kitchener eagerly and wanting somebody to introduce him.[4] The best speeches were those of Roberts and Kitchener and Admiral Seymour. I wished you could have been there.
Yours Ever
Brander Matthews

TRP; 3 pp.; als.

1. William Cary Sanger (1853–1921); assistant secretary of war (1901–1903) under TR. The report in question has not been identified.

2. William Pember Reeves (1857–1932) was agent-general for New Zealand (in London) and author of several books, including *New Zealand and Other Poems* (1898). The poem in question is "Coronation Ode," a satirical comment on the impending Coronation of King Edward VII, whose hedonistic lifestyle made him a favorite target for the British press. The Coronation ceremony had been scheduled for June but was postponed until 10 Aug. 1902 because of Edward's bleeding ulcer; thus the ode's opening couplet reads: "Full forty days and four, *plus* three have sped / Since England's heart and Edward's stomach bled." As BM requested, TR sent the poem to Nicholas Murray Butler (Butler to TR, 10 Aug. 1902, TRP).

3. In 1901, BM became the first nonresident American elected into the London Athenaeum, one of England's most exclusive social clubs. (Expatriate Henry James had been admitted earlier.) In celebration of the recent end of the Boer War, the club hosted a dinner on 25 July 1902 honoring the 12 Englishmen awarded the Order of Merit by King Edward. The honorees included the 3 military officers mentioned in this letter: Gen. Horatio Kitchener (1850–1916), Gen. Frederick S. Roberts (1832–1914), and Adm. Edward Seymour (1840–1929), all of whom had served in the Boer War ("The Athenaeum Club and the Order of Merit," London *Times*, 26 July 1902, 12).

4. Describing the Athenaeum dinner in his autobiography, BM remarks that Kipling (also a member of the club) yearned to be introduced to Kitchener. "It seemed to me odd," BM reflects, "that the laureate of the British Empire

should not earlier have met the general who had done so much to make secure the borders of that wide-flung realm" (*Years*, 431–32).

To Roosevelt

HOTEL REGINA

Paris, le 25th Aug 1902

Dear Theodore:

I am dropping you this line merely to enclose a cutting from the *Temps*—which is emphatically the foremost paper of France. I thought that you would be interested to see what a French journalist had been saying about General Wood.[1]

And I am also sending you today the *Revu Bleue* containing the translation into French of your *Century* article.[2]

Don't bother to acknowledge this, as we start for your side of the water in less than three weeks.

Yours Ever

Brander Matthews

TRP; 2 pp.; als.

1. "Lettre des États-Unis," *Le Temps*, 21 Aug. 1902, 1–2. The article (signed "O. G.") is a highly flattering portrait of Gen. Leonard Wood (1860–1927), TR's commander during the Spanish-American War and military governor of Cuba (1899–1902). TR had similarly extolled Wood in an 1899 essay in *Outlook* (rpt. in *Works*, 11:248–58); and Wood later paid tribute to TR in "Roosevelt: Soldier, Statesman, and Friend," which introduces vol. 11 of TR's *Works* (ix–xix).

2. "La Vie Intense," *Revue Bleu* 39 (26 July 1902): 97–102; trans. of "The Strenuous Life," the famous speech TR delivered at the Hamilton Club in Chicago on 10 Apr. 1899 (*Works*, 13:319–31).

To Roosevelt

681 WEST END AVENUE

Feb 4th 1903

Dear Theodore:

Thank you for the invitation to supper which we all three accept with great pleasure.

And thank you also for the prompt reply as to the Whittier correspondence.[1]

I've got lots of things to tell you—if I get a chance!

Yours Ever

Brander Matthews

TRP; 2 pp.; als.

1. Most likely the poet John Greenleaf Whittier (1807–1892); but since BM's letter of inquiry and TR's reply have been lost, one can only speculate.

To Roosevelt

HOTEL GORDON
WASHINGTON, D.C.
Feb 7th 1903

Dear Theodore:

(I begin this way because I am addressing the old friend rather than the President).

We cannot leave Washington without thanking you for the very good time we had on Thursday evening. My wife and my daughter were as pleased as I was that you had us all at your own table and that we had a chance to talk to you again—and better still—to hear you talk. The only trouble was that the time was all too short to chat about half the things we have in mind.

It was a delight also to see Mrs Roosevelt looking so well.

Yours Ever
Brander Matthews

P.S. I've been thinking over that remark of yours that you had done only what any other man could do "if he had a mind"—and it has struck me that this is exactly what Washington himself would have said—and Lincoln too!

BM

TRP; 4 pp.; als.

To Matthews

WHITE HOUSE
March 31, 1903.

Dear Brander:

It was good to hear from you. I regard Burroughs as one of the few bright spots in my trip west.[1]

In July and August I shall not be able to go anywhere. I just can't accept any invitations. I must have a little rest at that time. I am very sorry not to be able to accept.

With warm regards to Mrs. Matthews,

Faithfully yours,
Theodore Roosevelt

BMP; 1 p.; tls.

1. On 1 Apr. 1903, TR launched a hectic two months' tour of the midwestern and western states, during which he had innumerable meetings and gave dozens of speeches. The most pleasant and relaxing part of the trip for TR was the two weeks he camped at Yellowstone National Park with the naturalist John Burroughs (1837–1921), whom he had first met in 1890. During the coming years TR often invited Burroughs to the White House and on camping trips. See *LTR*, 3:447, 463; and Cutright, *Theodore Roosevelt: The Making of a Conservationist*, 242–47.

To Roosevelt

NARRAGANSETT PIER
July 10th 1903

Dear Mr President:

If you haven't seen the current number of the *International Quarterly*, you had better send for a copy on purpose to read Prof. Giddings's striking and suggestive paper on the "American People".[1] It is a paper which the Chief Magistrate of that people will read with deep pleasure.

Leigh Hunt was delighted to have had an evening with you. He said that you riddled him with questions! He is a man of curiously combined strength and gentleness, I think,—a true idealist, who happens also to be a man of affairs.

He gave a dinner to Booker T. a fortnight ago; and I went back to town on the night on purpose to meet the best known citizen of the Southland.[2]

I am glad you met my old pupil, Stewart White; he has eyes to see things and he can see straight.[3] It has pleased me greatly to think that I started him on his present work. I'd like a chance to talk him over with you. But there's the disadvantage of your having the whole country on your hands. Your own friends lose what the other 75000000 gain.

Please recall us all to Mrs Roosevelt. I can't begin to tell you how much we all three enjoyed our evening at the White House.

Yours Ever
Brander Matthews

TRP; 4 pp.; als.

1. Franklin H. Giddings, "The American People," *International Quarterly* 7 (June 1903): 281–99. Professor and chair of the Department of Sociology at Columbia, Giddings (1855–1931) was a firm believer in Anglo-Saxon racial supremacy. In "American People," he assures those who feared (as TR did) that immigrants of non-Anglo stock were polluting the Melting Pot that the United States would remain "essentially English" in its language and ide-

als, and that the country's ability to "convert the most unpromising foreign born citizens" remained as strong as ever. See next letter.

2. Booker T. Washington (1856–1915); the African-American educator, lecturer, and founder of Tuskegee Institute was the undisputed leader of African-Americans who embraced the "accomodationist" approach to racial injustice. Shortly after becoming president in 1901, TR drew a storm of protest from southern racists by inviting Washington to lunch at the White House. In his 1916 essay eulogizing Washington, TR emphasizes Washington's "wise" decision to focus on economic rather than political gains for blacks ("Booker T. Washington," *Works*, 11:273–77). See also Miller, *Theodore Roosevelt*, 361–64, and Oliver, *Brander Matthews*, 39ff.

3. Stewart Edward White (1873–1946), fiction writer and adventurer. The Michigan native and graduate of the Univ. of Michigan (1895) attended Columbia Law School during 1896–97, where BM instructed him in composition. BM encouraged White to submit a short story for publication; its acceptance launched White's prolific career as a writer of adventure novels. His most popular book was *The Blazed Trail* (1902), which TR considered second only to Wister's *The Virginian* among contemporary novels (*LTR*, 3:548). TR met White in Santa Barbara during his trip west, and the two lovers of the "strenuous life" became close friends thereafter. See Judy Alter, *Stewart Edward White* (Boise, Id.: Boise State Univ. Press, 1975), 7–8.

To Matthews

PERSONAL
Oyster Bay, N.Y.,
July 11, 1903.

My dear Brander:

I will send for the INTERNATIONAL QUARTERLY at once.

I was delighted with White. He does you real credit and I both hope and believe that he will go far.

Hunt is a trump. I am very glad you went to his dinner to Booker Washington. There are problems much more intense at the present time than the race problem—the labor problem for instance—but there is none about which I feel so gravely concerned as regards the distant future. I can not be sure what the right solution is, but I am absolutely sure that the wrong solution is inevitable if we fail to treat the individual negro just as we treat the individual white man—that is give him a fair chance; give him a square deal; punish or penalize him as we would a white man if he falls short or goes wrong; and encourage him if he goes right.[1]

With love to Mrs. Matthews,

Faithfully yours,
Theodore Roosevelt

BMP; 1 p.; tls.
1. TR's ambivalent attitudes and actions on the "Negro problem" are examined thoroughly by Dyer, *Theodore Roosevelt and the Idea of Race*, 89–122.

To Roosevelt

NARRAGANSETT PIER
July 25th, 1903

Dear Mr President:
I have just rec'd a telegram from my old friend, H. G. Paine[1] (formerly editor of *Harper's Weekly*) asking me to telegraph you, requesting you to grant an interview to Commander Delano,[2] before acting on the report of the Court Martial on Paymaster Delano.[3] Of course, I have not telegraphed you, for I have complete confidence in your own judgment in such matters,—and I suppose you have a regular order of procedure in such matters.

Leigh Hunt—as you probably found out—is daft about Gen. Gordon[4]; and he has sent us Boulger's biography which I have just read.[5] It has made on me an impression not unlike that I derived from Southey's "Nelson"—an impression of dissatisfaction with the character of the biographer's hero.[6] Gordon seems to me to belong in the class with John Brown[7] and with Torquemada,[8]—men high-minded and unselfish, but arrogant and unscrupulous. He is not the stuff of the true hero,—to my mind, at least. Have you read Boulger's book?—which vindicates Gladstone[9] and scores Wolseley.[10] And what do you think of Gordon? This is the sort of question I hope to have a chance to discuss with you— in six years!

By the way, have you seen a poster of a drink called "Moxie"[11]— with your portrait on it? If you haven't I can send it to you. It seems to me that the Chief Magistrate ought not to be used for advertising—any more than [?].

[Yrs Ever?]
Brander Matthews

P.S.
I hope you liked Giddings's article.[12]

TRP; 4 pp.; als. with postscript in upper-left corner of p. 1.
1. Henry Gallup Paine (1859–1929). The Columbia graduate was managing editor of *Harper's Weekly* from 1893 to 1900, after being associate editor of *Puck* (1887–93).
2. Francis H. Delano (1848–1929); U.S. naval commander, at this time assigned to Court Martial duty.
3. Assistant Paymaster of the Navy P. W. Delano had been court-martialed

because of irregularities in his pay accounts; as TR states in the following letter, he had already decided to accept the Navy Department's recommendation to dismiss Delano from his post ("Dismissed from the Navy," *New-York Daily Tribune,* 28 July 1903, 4).

4. British Gen. Charles George Gordon (1833–85). After serving for many years in China, Gordon was appointed governor-general of the Sudan, where the Mahdi rebels were attempting to drive out the British and establish an independent government. Surrounded at Khartoum, he and his forces were slaughtered in 1885 after a long siege.

5. Demetrius Charles Boulger, *The Life of Gordon,* 2 vols. (London: T. Fisher Unwin, 1896).

6. Robert Southey, *The Life of Nelson* (London: John Murray, 1813); biography of British naval hero Admiral Horatio Nelson (1758–1805). See BM to TR, 16 Jan. 1916, n. 3.

7. John Brown (1800–59); radical Abolitionist who led the failed attack on Harper's Ferry, Va., in 1859. Convicted of and executed for treason, he was considered a martyr by some, a madman by others.

8. Tomás de Torquemada (1420–98); ruthlessly efficient inquisitor general during the Spanish Inquisition.

9. William Gladstone (1809–98); prime minister of England during 1880–85. He was widely criticized for being indecisive during the conflict with the Mahdis in the Sudan (and on foreign policy in general), and many held him directly responsible for Gordon's death. Boulger faults Gladstone for not acting decisively but concludes that "history will . . . acquit Mr. Gladstone and his colleagues of the abandonment of General Gordon personally" (Boulger, *Life of Gordon,* 2:171).

10. Viscount Garnet Joseph Wolseley (1833–1913) commanded the forces sent to rescue the besieged Gordon, who was killed before relief arrived. Wolseley's critics charged that he failed to take the most expeditious route to Khartoum. Boulger contends that Wolseley "was alone responsible" for the failure to reach Khartoum in time to save Gordon (Boulger, *Life of Gordon,* 2:172).

11. American soft drink.

12. See BM to TR, 10 July 1903, n. 1.

To Matthews

Oyster Bay, N.Y.,
July 27, 1903.

Dear Brander:

I had already decided the Delano case.

About Gordon, my judgment exactly agrees with yours. He has never been one of my heroes.

I have seen that Moxie advertisement, and greatly object to it. Nothing can be done in the way of legal steps. It is one of a number of such cases. Sometimes by our protest we succeed in preventing the use of the advertisement, sometimes not. I shall try again in this case.

Faithfully yours,
Theodore Roosevelt

BMP; 1 p.; tls.

To Matthews

PERSONAL
Oyster Bay, N.Y.,
July 30, 1903.

Dear Brander:

I was much interested in your last article.[1] Don't you think that euphony should count for something in the plural of a word like "crisis"? Now, to show that I have profited by the article, I shall ask your advice. At the White House we give in the winter what have been called "musicales." I loathe the word. I should like to call them hereafter "musicals," but I can't find this word in the dictionaries. There is need of the word. I do not wish to use a clumsy paraphrase and invite people to come in the evening and listen to music. I wish to invite them to a "musical." How would you spell it?

Faithfully yours,
Theodore Roosevelt

BMP; 1 p.; tls.

1. BM, "Foreign Words in English Speech," *Harper's Monthly* 107 (Aug. 1903): 476–79. BM's central argument is that foreign words assimilated into the English language should conform to English, not their native language's, rules of grammar. Thus he contends at one point that the plural form of *crisis* should be *crisises,* not *crises* (478).

To Roosevelt

NARRAGANSETT PIER
Aug 3rd 1903

Dear Mr President:

I'm glad you liked that paper in *Harper*. It contained nothing I had not said already in 'Parts of Speech';—but it put some of the old facts in a new way.[1]

I'm inclined to agree with you about *crisis*; and I think I ought to have noted that some foreign plurals, *alumni*, for example, and *phenomena*, are so well established that it is hopeless to try to change them.

Musicale is absurd, of course; the French original is *soirée musicale* or *matinée musicale*,—which are intended to be a little less pretentious than *concert*. So far as I know the French never say *musicale* alone, but only with *soirée* or *matinée*.

I see no reason why you should not call your entertainments *concerts*,—they have State Concerts at Buckingham Palace, you know! Or else *musicals* as you suggest,—on the analogy of church *socials*. It is a common practise of our language to make a noun out of an adjective. I should spell it *musical*. Why not? And if it is the President's English, you may be sure that it will get into the dictionaries promptly.

You will be glad to know that my school book on "American Literature"—the one you so kindly reviewed—continues to sell about 15000 copies a year.[2] It has sold more than 100000 in all.

> Yours Ever
> Brander Matthews

TRP; 4 pp.; als.

1. BM, *Parts of Speech: Essays on English* (New York: Scribner's, 1901); see esp. the chapter titled "The Naturalization of Foreign Words" (165–83).
2. See TR to BM, 6 Dec. 1895, n. 2.

To Matthews

Oyster Bay, N.Y.
September 1, 1903.

Dear Brander:

I have already notified the Moxie people and they have promised to remove the objectionable poster.

I shall be delighted to see Hart's book.[1]

When you get back to New York, if you return this month, could you come out here to lunch?[2] I should so like to see you and talk over some matters.

> Faithfully yours,
> Theodore Roosevelt

BMP; 1 p.; tls.

1. The *LTR* editors identify the book as Albert Bushnell Hart's *Handbook of the History, Diplomacy, and Government of the United States, for Class Use*, which was first published for Harvard Univ. in 1901 (*LTR*, 3:594). However, TR more likely refers to Hart's *Actual Government as Applied under American*

Conditions (New York: Longmans, Green, 1903). In a letter to Hart dated 6 Sept. 1903, TR states that he is reading with "interest and pleasure, your new book" (TRP).

2. BM was vacationing at Narragansett Pier.

To Matthews

October 5, 1903.

My dear Mr. Matthews:

This is to introduce a former member of my regiment, Mr. H. J. Holt.[1] He is a graduate of Harvard and was an admirable man under me. He is a gentleman of the highest character. I take pleasure in giving this note of introduction to you, as he is to live in New York where he is to enter journalism.

Sincerely yours,

TRP; 1 p.; cc.

1. Harrison Jewell Holt (1875–?) served with TR in the Rough Riders and later became a writer. Little else is known about him. A draft of this letter dated 2 Oct. 1903 (TRP) contains the statement that Holt "did first-class work as a correspondent in South Africa." TR cut the remark after Holt informed him that he (Holt) had never served as a correspondent in South Africa, TR apparently having confused him with another Rough Rider (Holt to TR, 3 Oct. 1903, TRP).

To Roosevelt

681 WEST END AVENUE

Oct 7th 1903

Dear Mr President:

It was delightful to have speech with you once more,—and to see that you bear up bravely under the burdens of state. And I was very glad to find Mrs Roosevelt looking so well.

I am writing this chiefly to inclose a paper of Shaler's from the current *International Quarterly*; it seemed to me that there were things in it you would like to see.[1]

And there is an admirable article (in the current *Political Science Quarterly*) on the Coal Strike, which might also interest you and which I shall be glad to send, if you do not happen to have seen it.[2]

Butler has summoned a few of us tomorrow to help solve the problem of a School of Journalism.

Yours Ever

Brander Matthews

TRP; 4 pp.; als.

1. Nathaniel S. Shaler, "The Natural History of War," *International Quarterly* 8 (Sept. 1903): 17–30. Professor of geology at Harvard, Shaler (1841–1906) had been one of TR's instructors there during his undergraduate days; Shaler's theories of social evolution and Anglo-Saxon racial superiority had exerted a strong influence on young TR's thinking (Dyer, *Theodore Roosevelt and the Idea of Race*, 6–7). Shaler's central argument in "The Natural History of War" is that war is a "shameful relic of savagery" and "thwarts the highest purpose of the commonwealth which is to insure life and happiness to its citizens" (30). He decries the "folly" of the recent Spanish-American War and deplores literature that promotes the warrior ideal. Obviously, TR, who believed that battle developed the "manly" virtues and toughened the national as well as individual character, would have found much to quarrel with in the article.

2. E. Dana Durand, "The Anthracite Coal Strike and Its Settlement," *Political Science Quarterly* 18 (Sept. 1903): 385–414. In 1902, a strike by the United Mine Workers crippled the anthracite coal industry. Though he had no legal authority to intervene, TR succeeded in convincing the union and coal operators to allow a special commission appointed by him to investigate the dispute and make recommendations; the miners returned to work, and the commission's final report to TR in 1903 granted many, but not all, of their demands. The settlement of the strike was a great political triumph for TR. Analyzing the complex strike and settlement in depth, Durand lauds TR and suggests that the commission established important precedents for binding arbitration between coal unions and operators in the future. See Gould, *The Presidency of Theodore Roosevelt*, 66–71.

To Matthews

WHITE HOUSE
October 8, 1903.

Dear Brander:

I was much interested in the article you enclosed. I shall get a copy of the Political Science Quarterly at once.

I thoroughly enjoyed catching a glimpse of you.

Faithfully yours,
Theodore Roosevelt

BMP; 1 p.; tls.

1904

To Roosevelt

681 WEST END AVENUE
Jan 25th 1904

Dear Mr President:

It is very good of you and Mrs. Roosevelt to ask us to the White House again; and we enjoyed our supper so much last year that we should be delighted if we could accept. But this black border tells you why we are not good company just now. My mother was carried off by a swift and sudden attack of pneumonia; and we buried her the day after Christmas.[1] That is a bereavement that came to you years ago; and you know yourself how irreparable the loss is. Fortunately it was the painless death she would have chosen, without warning and without struggle.

Have you seen the French translation of your "New York"?[2] It seems to me pretty well done. And Jules Lemaitre has chosen your "Vie Intense" to praise[3]—so that he had dispraise the President of his own republic.[4]

Please remember us all to Mrs Roosevelt.

Yours Ever
Brander Matthews

TRP; 4 pp.; als.

1. BM's mother, Virginia Brander Matthews, died on 22 Dec. 1903. TR had lost his mother in 1884.

2. TR, *New-York,* trans. Albert Savine (Paris: F. Juven, 1903).

3. French critic Jules Lemaître (1853–1914), whose literary criticism BM greatly admired (see, e.g., BM's essay on Lemaître in *Books and Play-Books,* 117–37). Lemaître praises TR and *The Strenuous Life* ("Tous les Français cultivés devraient lire la *Vie intense*") in "Un Président de République," *Théories et Impressions,* by Lemaître (Paris: Société Française d'Imprimerie et de Librairie, 1903), 56–59. See BM to TR, 29 Jan. 1904.

4. Émile Loubet (1838–1929), president of France from 1899 to 1906. BM's sentence is ungrammatical; he may have meant to write "had to dispraise."

To Matthews

WHITE HOUSE
January 27, 1904.

Dear Brander:

I am very very sorry to hear of your mother's death. There is nothing one can say, even to one's close friends, under such circumstances that will in any way comfort them. It was very good of you under such conditions to remember about the French translation of my books. No, I have not seen the translation of the New York and I cannot imagine what interest it could have for French people; nor have I seen the article by Jules Lemaitre. Do you happen to have it handy?

With warm regards to Mrs. Matthews, believe me,

Sincerely yours,
Theodore Roosevelt

BMP; 1 p.; tls.

To Roosevelt

681 WEST END AVENUE
Jan 29th 1904

Dear Mr President:

I have succeeded in getting a copy of your "New York" in French; and I have written your name in it. The note on p. 284 suggests that there is no French equivalent for the Golden Rule.[1]

I am sending you also my copy of Lemaitre's book.[2] Keep this also, as I can get another copy. As I wrote you, his article on you is a covert attack on his own President. He is a violent anti-Dreyfussard, as you could guess by the essay on the Jews—as clever as it is unfair.[3]

Yours Ever
Brander Matthews

TRP; 3 pp.; als.

1. In chapter 14 of New York, TR quotes a cynical politician's assertion that the Golden Rule has no place in a political campaign (*Works*, 10:533). Savine translates "Golden Rule" as "les Vers dorés," or golden verse, and in a footnote refers the reader to the moral precepts of Pythagoras: "Recueil versifié des precepts moraux de Pythagore" (*New-York*, 284n.).

2. See TR to BM, 25 Jan. 1904, n. 3.

3. A royalist and anti-Semite, Lemaître was a bitter enemy of Dreyfus and of the moderate President Loubet, under whose administration Dreyfus was

eventually vindicated. The essay on the Jews to which BM refers is "L'Esprit Juif," *Théories et Impressions*, 133–39. Modern readers may not find the piece very clever, but they certainly will find it unfair, for it is blatantly anti-Semitic. Lemaître strikes a pose of objectivity at the beginning of the essay; but he then proceeds to accuse the Jews of being the enemies of Christianity and of French nationalism, and he makes them a scapegoat for France's political and social problems. Though TR and BM deplored such vicious prejudice, they were not entirely free of anti-Semitic feelings (see Oliver, *Brander Matthews*, 176, and Dyer, *Theodore Roosevelt and the Idea of Race*, 124–25).

To Matthews

WHITE HOUSE
February 1, 1904.

Dear Brander:

Thank you so much for the two volumes. You are awfully good to have taken such trouble. I am interested and curious in reference to the translation of "New York," and the LeMaitre I shall read with real pleasure. I am rather amused that I, who have always championed Dreyfus, or to speak more correctly, reprobated the attack on him, should be selected as a club by an anti-Dreyfus man.[1]

Always yours,
Theodore Roosevelt

BMP; 1 p.; tls.; pbd. *LTR*, 4:714.

1. See, for example, TR's letter (10 June 1899) to several American supporters of Dreyfus, lauding them for attempting to redress the "hideous wrong" done to the French Jew (*LTR*, 2:1020).

To Roosevelt

681 WEST END AVENUE
Feb 5th 1904

Dear Mr President:

I have taken the liberty of giving a letter of introduction to M. Louis Aubert,—a young Frenchman who holds a travelling fellowship from the University of Paris and who has chosen as the theme of his report "the spirit of expansion in America."[1]

I understand of course how busy you are; and I shall not be surprised—nor will M. Aubert—if you are unable to give him any of your time.

But in addition to my desire to have an intelligent Frenchman see for himself what manner of man we have in the White House, I have thought also that it might interest you to hear M. Aubert's impressions—which seem to me unusually acute. He has sized up the Bostonians with obvious shrewdness.

Yours Ever
Brander Matthews

TRP; 4 pp.; als.

1. Louis Aubert (1876–?); the French author and historian would later publish *Paix Japonaise* (1906), *Américains et Japonais* (1908), and other works on political history of interest to TR. See BM to TR, 16 May 1906.

To Matthews

WHITE HOUSE
February 8, 1904.

Dear Brander:

Of course I shall be delighted to see your young French friend whenever he comes on with a letter from you.

I have been greatly interested in LeMaitre's criticisms. Later, if you can get on to Washington, I want you to come to lunch and I shall discuss some of them with you.

Always yours,
Theodore Roosevelt

BMP; 1 p.; tls.

To Roosevelt

681 WEST END AVENUE
Feb 22nd 1904

Dear Mr President:

It seems that a namesake of mine in London has a keen eye to the main [chance?] and a shrewd insight into our weaknesses on this side of the water. I enclose the specimen page in which he deals with you—getting his dates wrong, owing to a British misunderstanding of the interval between election and entry into office.[1]

I hope you saw the open letter in which Butler held the *Evening Post* up to scorn. It was a job that it was well to have done;—and he did it to perfection.[2]

I hope that my French friend was able to get speech with you, for I thought you would be interested in seeing how acutely he had sized us up. How did he strike you? I thought him to have the intelligence of his race, with more openmindedness than is common to the Gaul.

Yours Ever
Brander Matthews

TRP; 4 pp.; als.

1. BM enclosed pages from *Matthews' American Armoury and Blue Book* (London: J. Matthews, 1903), by John Matthews, a London genealogist. The book, advertised as a register and authentic record of "American Families bearing Arms, with information as to lineage," appealed to the American "weakness" of desiring to be related to Old World aristocracy, to be a "blue blood." The specimen page contains the entry for TR; it confuses the years in which TR was elected to office (as mayor, governor, and vice president) with those in which he began to serve his elected terms.

2. On 3 Feb. 1904, the *New York Evening Post* reported that Edward MacDowell (1861–1908), Columbia's first professor of music, was resigning from the faculty as a result of a dispute with President Butler regarding MacDowell's proposal to restructure the Department of Music ("MacDowell to Resign," *Evening Post*, 3 Feb. 1904, 1). In a letter to Butler dated 4 Feb. 1904, MacDowell denied making statements attributed to him in the *Evening Post* article. Butler then wrote a long, angry letter to the *New York Times* accusing the *Evening Post* of making a "wholly false and unjustifiable attack upon Columbia University, its influence, and its teaching staff" ("Denial from President Butler," *New York Times*, 8 Feb. 1904, 8). The controversy continued for weeks and was covered by newspapers around the country, causing much embarrassment to Columbia. MacDowell resigned, and in 1905 suffered a mental collapse. See Douglas Moore, "The Department of Music," in *A History of the Faculty of Philosophy, Columbia University,* ed. Jacques Barzun (New York: Columbia Univ. Press, 1957), 271–74.

To Matthews

WHITE HOUSE
February 23, 1904.

Dear Brander:

I am much obliged to you; and am amused at your British namesake having included me in his armoury.

Did not Butler do up the Evening Post in fine shape? I liked your French friend very much, and I wish my work had given me a chance to see a little of him.

Faithfully yours,
Theodore Roosevelt

BMP; 1 p.; tls.

To Roosevelt

681 WEST END AVENUE
April 10th 1904

Dear Mr President:

It is an honor to know you and it was a joy to have a chat with you at Oyster Bay six months ago; but all honorable joys have to be paid for. The receipt of letters like the enclosed is a part of the price I pay for the joyous honor. I send this letter because I believe that Woodward would make a very good Secretary, indeed.[1] I heard in Paris in 1900 high praise for his energy and efficiency.

Did you see Prof. Burgess's article in the latest *Political Science Quarterly* on the ethnic and ethical solidarity of the U.S.—Great Britain and Germany?[2] As it expressed forcibly things I had vaguely felt, I naturally thought it interesting; and I think it would interest you. Can I send it to you?

I am glad to see that there begins to be a chance for a worthy candidate to run against you.[3] That will raise the plane of the campaign; and it will strengthen the opposition—the power of which is as necessary to the proper working as the greater power of the Administration.

Yours Ever
Brander Matthews

TRP; 4 pp.; als.

1. Benjamin D. Woodward (1868–1948), professor of French at Columbia (where he had received his Ph.D. in 1891). Woodward, who had been executive assistant commissioner general for the U.S. Commission to the Paris Exposition of 1900, wrote BM on 8 Apr. 1904 (TRP), asking him to urge TR to appoint him secretary of the Panama Canal Commission. The appointment was not made, however (see next letter).

2. John W. Burgess, "Germany, Great Britain, and the United States," *Political Science Quarterly* 19 (1904): 1–19. Professor and dean of political science and international law at Columbia, Burgess (1844–1931) was a pioneer in his field and the founder of the *Political Science Quarterly*. His belief that the Teutonic race had a special genius for political organization left a lasting imprint on TR, who studied under Burgess during his year at Columbia (see Dyer, *Theodore Roosevelt and the Idea of Race*, 7–8). "Germany, Great Britain, and the United States" is fervently Teutonic and imperialistic, Burgess arguing that the three great heirs to the "Teutonic genius and Teutonic conscience" should unite in their efforts to extend their superior civilization into the "dark places of the earth for the enlightenment and advancement of the inhabitants of these dark places."

3. TR's Democratic opponent in the 1904 presidential election was Judge Alton
   B. Parker (1852–1926) of New York. The Democrats considered him a strong
   contender, but in Nov. TR won by a landslide (336 electoral votes to 140).

To Matthews

WHITE HOUSE
April 11, 1904.

Dear Brander:

I have your letter of the 10th. I should like much to see Burgess's
article.

I receive many letters for Woodward. There are, however, one or
two points against him which I shall tell you when we meet.

With warm regards to Mrs. Matthews,

> Faithfully yours,
> Theodore Roosevelt

BMP; 1 p.; tls.

To Roosevelt

681 WEST END AVENUE
April 12th 1904

Dear Mr President:

I am sending you today the *Political Science Quarterly* with Burgess's
article.

And I enclose (for your own amusement) a correspondence which
appeared in the *Evening Post* a few days ago.[1]

I hope you did not suppose that I was urging Woodward's appointment. He asked me to write to you; and I did. But I want you always
to count me among the small group of your old friends who never ask
anything from the President.

> Yours Ever
> Brander Matthews

TRP; 3 pp.; als.

1. Editorials and letters to the editor focusing on TR appeared almost daily in
   the *New York Evening Post,* so certain identification is impossible. BM may
   have sent TR a sharp-edged *Evening Post* editorial dated 8 Apr. 1904 concerning TR's speech the night before at a banquet of the Periodical Publishers Association, in Washington, D.C. The anonymous author noted that
   many of TR's complaints about inflammatory rhetoric applied to his own

writings and speeches. The editorial begins: "Mr. Roosevelt, the well-known author, openly censured in his speech . . . some of the tendencies of Mr. Roosevelt the President." A cutting of the editorial is in the TRP (reel 473, vol. 12, p. 72).

To Matthews

WHITE HOUSE
April 13, 1904.

Dear Brander:

Indeed, I understood about Woodward absolutely. Cannot you get on here some time? I should so like to talk over various matters with you.

I was much amused with the printed correspondence.

Faithfully yours,
Theodore Roosevelt

TRP; 1 p.; tls.

To Roosevelt

681 WEST END AVENUE
May 20th 1904

Dear Mr President:

Since Bunner died, it has not been necessary to read *Puck*; but I acquired the habit a quarter of a century ago.[1] And I was rewarded yesterday by the enclosed skits on the estimable Mabie and the inestimable Hearst.[2] I showed them to Butler; and he suggested that they might amuse you.

And I seize the occasion to thank you for your kindness in granting an interview to Sir James Reckitt.[3]

Don't bother to acknowledge this. We are off to the other side early in June—but I shall return in good time to register!

Yours Ever
Brander Matthews

TRP; 3 pp.; als.

1. Bunner died in 1896.
2. Hamilton W. Mabie (1845–1916); influential literary critic and personal friend of BM. The wealthy newspaperman William Randolph Hearst (1863–1951), the king of "yellow journalism" of his era, had a political as well as a journalistic career; at this time he was a New York congressman, with aspirations of being the Democratic nominee for president.

The (anonymous) "skits" in question appeared in *Puck* 55 (18 May 1904), n.p. The Mabie piece is a two-stanza humorous poem responding to a *Ladies' Home Journal* announcement that Mabie was preparing to recommend books for summer reading ("Mute inquiry is in men's looks; / Everybody is holding his breath— / *Mabie is reading the Summer books*"). Titled "The Idol of the Proletariat," the short satire of Hearst, supposedly an extract from an admiring biography, portrays him as a simple working man, who rises late to breakfast on squab chicken, then goes off to his "daily toil in a simple Tuxedo, and carrying a modest dinner pail of champagne."

3. Sir James Reckitt (1833–1924), English businessman, philanthropist, and art collector.

To Matthews

WHITE HOUSE
May 21, 1904.

Dear Brander:

I was immensely amused at both skits. Of course, professionally, the Hearst business appealed to me even more than the other! That particular bit of trifling bites, because it has got solid truth behind it.

A pleasant voyage to you.

Always yours,
Theodore Roosevelt

BMP; 1 p.; tls.

To Matthews

WHITE HOUSE
June 7, 1904.
Personal.

Dear Brander:

I simply must send you this choice bit of wisdom from a British brother. It comes in a letter of Mrs. Edith Wharton's[1] to young Lodge:[2]

"I sat last night next to a Mr. Fildes, Lord Saye and Sele's son who had been all over the South African War and was very keen about military matters.[3] We talked about Conan Doyle's book,[4] and then I asked him if he had ever read Sir George Trevelyan's history of the *American Revolution*.[5] No, he hadn't, but would make a note of it. Capital book, eh! I said the descriptions of the fights were wonderful; that I had told Sir G. T. that I thought his *battle* of *Bunker Hill* was the best battle picture I knew and he had answered that Lord Wolseley had told him the same thing.

"Mr. Fildes (keenly interested) 'Oh, really? I must read that. Trevelyan's an army man himself, I suppose?'

"Me. 'No, I think not. You know he was—'

"Mr. Fildes. 'Oh, of course. Out there as a correspondent, I suppose.'"!!!

Is not this really too good to be true?

Sincerely yours,

Theodore Roosevelt

BMP; 2 pp.; tls.; pbd. *LTR*, 4:823.

1. American novelist Edith Wharton (1862–1937); she had known TR since her youth and was a second cousin of Edith Roosevelt. Wharton discusses her friendship with TR, and the dinner party mentioned in this letter, in her autobiography *A Backward Glance* (New York: Scribner's, 1933; reprint ed. 1964), 311–17, 217–18.

2. George ("Bay") Cabot Lodge (1873–1909), eldest son of Henry Cabot Lodge, chose poetry over politics as a career. TR was very fond of Bay and encouraged his literary pursuits (see John W. Crowley, "'Dear Bay': Theodore Roosevelt's Letters to George Cabot Lodge," *New York History* 53 [1972]: 177–94). Wharton shared TR's fondness for Bay, who was among her inner circle of friends in Washington, D.C. (Wharton, *Backward Glance,* 149–51).

3. The page from Wharton's letter that Bay Lodge sent to TR (George Lodge to TR, 6 June 1904, TRP) is accurately transcribed by TR, but the reference to Fildes as the son of Lord Saye and Sele (1830–1907) is confusing. Wharton may have sat next to the English painter and illustrator Sir Luke Fildes (1844–1927), but he was the son of James Fildes. Wharton may have confused his lineage with that of Sir Eustace Fiennes (1864–1943), who was Lord Saye and Sele's second son and who did serve in South Africa during the Boer War.

4. The famous British mystery writer Sir Arthur Conan Doyle (1859–1930) served as a physician in South Africa during the Boer War. Wharton probably discussed over dinner his *The War in South Africa* (Leipzig: Brenard Tauchnitz, 1902), or perhaps his earlier book, *The Great Boer War* (New York: T. Nelson, 1900; rev. ed. 1903).

5. English historian George Trevelyan (1838–1928), author of *The American Revolution* (New York: Longmans, Green, pt. 1, 1899; pt. 2 [2 vols.], 1903–5).

To Roosevelt

681 WEST END AVENUE

June 8th, 1904

Dear Mr President:

I hasten to thank you for the quotation; and I shall show it to Butler with whom I dine tonight.[1]

McKim and Root got degrees at our Commencement this morning,—and you would have been mighty pleased to hear the fit words with which Burgess presented Root,—to the real satisfaction of the audience![2] We sail on the *Celtic* on Friday; and we leave behind our best wishes for your summer!

Yours Ever

Brander Matthews

P.S. By way of a swap for your quotation, I send you Oliver Herford's latest limerick:—

> There was a young man of St. Paul,
> Who went to a *British* masked ball;
>   Their mirth to provoke,
>   He went as a joke,—
> And nobody saw him at all!

N.B. Herford is an Englishman by birth.[3]

TRP; 4 pp.; als.

1. See preceding letter.
2. New York architect Charles Follen McKim (1847–1909), whose many famous designs include those of the original campus of Columbia College at Morningside Heights, and Elihu Root (1845–1937), former secretary of war, were awarded honorary doctoral degrees at Columbia commencement ceremonies on 8 June 1904. Presenting the degree to Root, Dean John Burgess stated:

   > As a man and a citizen he is, like the knight of old, without fear and without reproach; as a lawyer and a jurist he stands in the very forefront of the American bar; as an orator he has no superior, and as a statesman and an administrator he has taught two great lessons . . . one that an American civilian can organize the armed forces of his nation more perfectly and more effectively than any purely military man the nation has ever produced, and the other that a free republic can discharge imperial duties successfully and honorably, without sacrificing or impairing or imperiling its own historic liberties. (Quoted in "Nearly 1,000 Degrees Conferred by Columbia," *New York Times*, 9 June 1904, 5)

3. Oliver Brooke Herford (1863–1935). Born in Sheffield, England, Herford at this time was a prominent New York author, illustrator, and wit; he was on the staff of *Life* and *Harper's Weekly*, and was a member of the Players.

To Roosevelt

681 WEST END AVENUE
Nov 27th 1904

Dear Mr President:

I've come late to avoid the rush. I've waited till the White House staff has run a snow-plow through the avalanche of congratulations.[1] And now that you may have got the sidewalks cleared, I want to offer my congratulations—not merely on your election, for that seemed to me inevitable. No,—rather because you are the chief of a people that knows a good man when they see him,—a people compounded now (as ever) from all the other peoples of the world—and yet remaining (or acquiring) the old Anglo-Saxon respect for character and courage and straightforwardness. And I don't want that foreign mission, either!

I enclose a postal card I picked up in Paris three months ago,—and also a caricature of McCutcheon's that you may not have seen.[2] And have you seen—Oh, have you seen?—the poem on the alleged pair of leather-breeches that once belonged to you?[3] If you haven't, I'll send it to you, as I cut it from the St. Louis paper when we were there.

I hear the news from Butler, whose affection for you is stronger than ever. But there will be compensations when you live in a house, whatever its color, not so far off.

Yours Ever
Brander Matthews

TRP; 4 pp.; als.

1. A reference to TR's landslide victory in the 1904 election.
2. John Tinney McCutcheon (1870–1949), political cartoonist for the *Chicago Tribune*. Since he drew many cartoons of TR, it is impossible to identify which one BM sent; it might have been a cartoon of TR arriving at the Louisiana Purchase Exposition in St. Louis, which had appeared on the front page of the *Tribune* the day before BM wrote this letter ("De-light-ed," *Chicago Tribune*, 26 Nov. 1904, 1). McCutcheon later collected his drawings of TR into a volume, *T. R. in Cartoons* (Chicago: McClurg, 1910). The postal card is unidentified.
3. During TR's visit to the St. Louis Exposition on 26 Nov., he was delighted to find an old pair of his riding breeches on display, their pockets stuffed with visiting cards (see "In a Twinkling of an Eye," *Chicago Tribune*, 27 Nov. 1904, 2). BM's letter below of 1 Dec. seems to suggest that he somehow got hold of the breeches (or a different pair?) and sent them to TR.

To Matthews

WHITE HOUSE
November 29, 1904.

Dear Brander:
I loved the cartoon and the postal card. I have not seen the poem on the leather breeches, and should like to.
Now can't you and Mrs. Matthews get on here for dinner on the night of December 8th? We are to have a little musical afterwards, and it would be such a pleasure if we could see you both at dinner.
Faithfully yours,
Theodore Roosevelt

BMP; 1 p.; tls.

To Roosevelt

681 WEST END AVENUE
Dec 1st 1904

Dear Mr President:
Of course, we shall be delighted to dine with you on the 8th. We are far too loyal to dispute an invitation from the Chef d'Etat—even if it [is] not a command. Mrs Matthews and I will register at the new Willard State on Wednesday, probably. It was very good of you to ask and we shall be glad indeed to have a glimpse of you and of the Lady of the White House.
In the mean while I send you herewith the leather breeches—with a poem not by the Secretary of State.[1] I invite your careful attention to the various inscriptions contributed by your admiring fellow citizens.
Yours Ever
Brander Matthews

TRP; 4 pp.; als.

1. John Hay (1838–1905) was secretary of state from 1898 to 1905, dying in office. A man of letters as well as a diplomat and statesman, Hay published many poems, including, in 1902, a sonnet to TR (*The Complete Poetical Works of John Hay* [Boston: Houghton Mifflin, 1917], 232). BM's puzzling use of the phrase "not by" may imply that the poem on TR's breeches was published anonymously, as Hay's controversial novel *The Bread-winners* (1884) had been.

To Matthews

WHITE HOUSE
December 2, 1904.

Dear Brander:

That poem is really funny, and I enjoyed it. I am so glad Mrs. Matthews and you can come on to dinner on the 8th.

Faithfully yours,
Theodore Roosevelt

BMP; 1 p.; tls.

To Roosevelt

681 WEST END AVENUE
Dec 10th 1904

Dear Mr President:

We greatly enjoyed our dinner at the White House; and we have recorded it on the tablets of memory as a Historic Occasion—for us. And we were both delighted to find you and Mrs Roosevelt looking so well—and so happy.

I enclose the little drawing of Oliver Herford's that I spoke about. I don't know why it seems to me so funny; but it does.

That Lucerne "Peace & War Museum" (of which I gave you the catalog) is visited by thousands every summer; and I was sorry to see that we had nothing there to show.[1] I don't know what we could show; but it seemed to me a little forlorn that we should be represented solely by the portrait of Andrew Carnegie!—even if he is—what William Black once called him—"The star-spangled Scotchman."[2]

Have you seen my little book of curiosities of literature?—the 'Recreations of an Anthologist'? If you haven't, I'd like to send it to you, for there is an article collecting American epigrams that might interest you.[3]

Yours Ever
Brander Matthews

TRP; 4 pp.; als.

1. The Museum of War and Peace in Lucerne, Switzerland, which opened in 1902, was the creation of the Polish banker, author, and antiwar activist Ivan Bloch (1836–1902). The exhibits included a large collection of ancient and modern weapons, bullet-riddled skulls, pieces of fortifications, battle plans, and other material objects related to war.

2. Andrew Carnegie (1835–1919), the Scotch-American immigrant who became a self-made millionaire and the foremost spokesperson for the "Gospel of Wealth" during the Gilded Age, returned to Great Britain for a widely publicized tour in 1884, during which he often extolled the virtues of American democracy and capitalism. His fellow travellers included the Scottish novelist William Black (1841–1898), who wrote an account of the trip ("A Few Days' Driving," *Harper's Monthly* 70 [Dec. 1884], 21–36) in which he refers to Carnegie as the "Star-spangled American." Both TR and BM were personal friends of Carnegie, who financially supported the Simplified Spelling Board (see BM to TR, 16 May 1906, n. 1) and other projects in which the two men were directly involved.

3. BM, *Recreations of an Anthologist* (New York: Dodd, 1904). The essay "American Epigrams" (103–29) argues that the "plain people" invent and sustain linguistic meaning, despite the attempts by "precisians" to control the language.

To Matthews

WHITE HOUSE
December 12, 1904.

Dear Brander:

I was amused with the picture, and if you will send me that book I shall be very much obliged. It was delightful having you both here. In great haste

Faithfully yours,
Theodore Roosevelt

BMP; 1 p.; tls.

1905

To Roosevelt

681 WEST END AVENUE
Jan 1st 1905

Dear Mr President:

A Happy New Year to you and yours!—and four happy years for the nation.

In the mean while I want to know if you have seen the December *Political Science Quarterly*? There are two articles that would interest you,—one a striking review of Steffens's book,[1] and the other the address on the "Problems of Constitutional Law" that Burgess delivered at St. Louis.[2] If you like, I'll send you the number.

It may possibly be of value to know that a Frenchman here expressed to me his sincere hope that Mr Meyer would not take Gen. Porter's place,—for the sole reason that the German *name* would produce a bad effect on the French.[3] And they are rather touchy at times,—and rather inclined to misunderstand. Did you see Brunetiere's wrongheaded paper on "L'Ame Americaine"?[4]

Yours Ever

Brander Matthews

TRP; 4 pp.; als.

1. Henry Jones Ford, "Municipal Corruption," *Political Science Quarterly* 19 (Dec. 1904): 673–86, a review of Lincoln Steffens's *The Shame of the Cities* (1904); Ford is highly critical of Steffens's muckraking journalism, arguing that "national hypochondria is a worse evil than national corruption."

2. John W. Burgess, "Present Problems of Constitutional Law," *Political Science Quarterly* 19 (Dec. 1904): 545–78. Burgess's analysis of several issues in Constitutional law concludes with a ringing endorsement of American territorial expansion and a recommendation that the Constitution be amended to "meet the exigencies of a colonial or imperial policy" (574).

3. Boston banker George von Lengerke Meyer (1858–1918), a personal friend and political ally of Lodge, was at this point the American ambassador to Italy (1900–1905); Gen. Horace Porter (1837–1921), ambassador to France since 1897, was stepping down from that post. TR considered appointing Meyer as Porter's replacement, but decided instead to make him his emissary to St. Petersburg (see *LTR*, 4:890). In that capacity, Meyer helped ne-

gotiate TR's proposals for ending the Russo-Japanese war; the successful results of those proposals earned TR the Nobel Peace Prize in 1906.
4. Ferdinand Brunetière (1849–1906), French literary critic and editor-in-chief
of *Revue des Deux Mondes*. His "L'Ame Américaine"—a review essay on
M. Edmond de Nevers's *L'Âme Américaine* (Paris: Jouve & Boyer, 1900)—
was originally published in 1901 and was reprinted in his *Variétés Littéraires*
(Paris: Calmann-Levy, 1904), 97–163, BM's source. (An English translation of Brunetière's essay ["The American Spirit"] may be found in *The
Living Age* 230 [3–10 Aug. 1901]: 265–75, 374–86.) Brunetière contends that
there is no distinctively American race, language, literature, or even history;
i.e., the U.S. is merely an offshoot of Anglo-European history and culture.
His ideas would certainly have seemed "wrongheaded" to the author of "True
Americanism" and "American Ideals." During the next several years, BM
published a series of essays ("American Character," "American Manners,"
"American Humor") that implicitly rebut Brunetière's essay; they are collected in *The American of the Future and Other Essays* (New York: Scribner's,
1909). See BM to TR, 1 Feb. 1905.

To Matthews

WHITE HOUSE
January 3, 1905.

Dear Brander:
   No, I have not seen the December Political Science Quarterly. If
you happen to have it please send it to me. Nor have I seen Brunetière's
piece. I do not think Meyer will go to Paris.
   Happy New Year to you and yours!
                     Faithfully yours,
                     Theodore Roosevelt

BMP; 1 p.; tls.

To Roosevelt

681 WEST END AVENUE
Jan 4th 1905

Dear Mr President:
   I am posting to you (with this) the December *Political Science Quar-
terly*—in which I have marked the two articles.
   The Brunetiere book is lent now; but you shall have it when I can
lay hands on a copy.
   Did you ever receive my little 'Recreations of an Anthologist'?

I thought that the paper on American epigrams might amuse you—
and also the collection of Bunner's verses.[1]

Yours Ever
Brander Matthews

TRP; 3 pp.; als.

1. See BM to TR, 10 Dec. 1904. *Recreations* includes "The Uncollected Poems of
H. C. Bunner" (186–208)—a sampling, with commentary, of poems not included in BM's edition of *The Poems of H. C. Bunner* (New York: Scribner's,
1899).

To Matthews

January 7, 1905.

Dear Brander:

I thank you for the Quarterly. I enjoyed "Recreations" greatly; not
merely the essay on American epigrams; and of all the other articles I
am tempted to say I liked best the one on Bunner.

Always yours,
Theodore Roosevelt

TRP; 1 p.; ccs.

To Roosevelt

681 WEST END AVENUE
Feb 1st 1905

Dear Mr President:

I am sending you today a copy of Brunetière's book—the first I have
been able to lay hands on. The article on "L'Ame Américaine" is the
one I drew your attention to. It is shrewd and able,—and yet curiously
wrong. Distance in space is as misleading often as remoteness in time;
and Brunetière is very likely no more astray than we are when we seek
to reconstruct Elizabethan England or Horatian Rome, from facts which
are never final or complete.

And I enclose a cutting from *Puck*—having fun with the *Post.*[1]

Yours Ever
Brander Matthews

TRP; 4 pp.; als.

1. "As It Was in the Beginning," *Puck* 57 (1 Feb. 1905), n.p. (author not specified).
This biting satire of the *New York Evening Post* is presented as an extract from

the "Eden Evening Post" complaining about God's handling of the Creation. The piece reads in part: "It is regrettable that the *Evening Post* was not created first; its advice and criticism would have prevented the mistakes that one now sees. . . . Primarily we should have protested against crowding the work of Creation into six days, and should have advised at least a fortnight. The ill effects of haste are everywhere so apparent that the future is full of gloom, and the *Evening Post* is committed to an eternity of criticism and fault-finding."

To Matthews

WHITE HOUSE
Personal
February 3, 1905.

Dear Brander:
  That is an amusing clipping; and I shall read Brunetière's book with real pleasure. I have time for but a line, as there are any number of things pressing upon my attention at present—most of them disagreeably so.
    Always yours,
    Theodore Roosevelt

  BMP; 1 p.; tls.

To Roosevelt

681 WEST END AVENUE
March 16th 1905

Dear Mr President:
  I suppose that no mere elected chief magistrate has any magic in his touch—whether for the King's Evil or the King's English;—but it is a fact that the kindly welcome Miss Butler received from you and from Mrs Roosevelt has done her a lot of good, and sent her home refreshed and renewed. Butler himself has slipped his collar and is cavorting through space, way off on the occidental horizon.[1]
  I want to congratulate you—not, of course, on your inauguration as President, for that is something that the rest of us have a right to be congratulated on,—but on your election as one of the first 15 of the National Academy of Arts & Letters.[2] No other President could possibly have been considered as eligible—except perhaps Jefferson (Thomas). And that reminds me, that when you 15 choose the next 5, and when the 20 pick out 10 more, I hope you will not overlook Jefferson (Joseph).[3] His book and his pictures may not entitle him to election; but his histrionic record and his most impressive personality seem to me to justify

it. The choice of Lounsbury as one of your colleagues somewhat allevi-
ates my disgust at the selection also of that literary parasite, Norton.[4]

As you liked my 'Recreations of an Anthologist,' I've asked Mills to
send you my "American Familiar Verse"—from Franklin to Bunner.[5]
There's an introduction of mine that you needn't read.

Our triplicate remembrances to the Lady of the White House—
Yours Ever
Brander Matthews

TRP; 4 pp.; als.

1. Since Nicholas Murray Butler's only daughter, Sarah Schuyler Butler (b.
   1893), was a mere child, the Miss Butler who visited TR was most likely
   Nicholas's spinster aunt, Rosa Butler (d. 1913), of whom he speaks affection-
   ately in his autobiography (Butler, *Across the Busy Years*, 44–45). Butler's
   "occidental horizon" was the American West—he was on a three-week trip
   to Arizona and California (Butler to TR, 30 Mar. 1905, TRP).

2. Founded in 1904, the National Academy of Arts and Letters was the upper
   chamber of the National Institute of Arts and Letters, which BM helped
   organize in 1898. The academy's 7 original members (who included Howells,
   Twain, and John Hay) were empowered to elect 8 more; TR was among the
   8 chosen. Election to the academy was, of course, a matter of great prestige
   and honor. See *Years*, 447–50.

3. Joseph Jefferson (1829–1905) was one of the most popular American stage
   actors of the late nineteenth century, his most famous role being that of Rip
   Van Winkle. He was, along with BM, one of the founding members of the
   Players, and was elected its president after the death of Edwin Booth. BM
   portrays him as a genial and modest man in *Years* (370–73). Jefferson died
   several weeks after this letter was written, on 23 Apr.

4. Charles Eliot Norton (1827–1908); professor of English at Harvard (1873–
   97), literary critic, and one of the founders of the *Nation*. Norton was an
   outspoken opponent of the Spanish-American War, American imperialism,
   and President TR; as a literary critic, he was Anglophilic, ignoring or depre-
   ciating many American writers whom BM and TR admired. BM detested
   Norton. See Oliver, *Brander Matthews*, 68–69.

5. *American Familiar Verse*, ed. BM (New York: Longmans, Green, 1904); an
   anthology of playful poems by several dozen American writers, including
   many of BM's contemporaries. In his introduction (1–37), BM defines and
   traces the evolution of this literary form, contending that the American "species" differs in essential ways from its Anglo-European counterparts.

To Matthews

WHITE HOUSE
March 18, 1905.

Dear Brander:

I look forward to the book on "American Familiar Verse," and shall keep in mind what you say about Jefferson. It was such a pleasure to see Miss Butler.

In great haste,

faithfully yours,
Theodore Roosevelt

BMP; 1 p.; tls.

To Matthews

Personal
March 20, 1905.

Dear Brander:

I greatly like the book of American verse, including both your introduction and the choice of poems. What a loss Bunner was! It is a real misfortune that he did not live.

Always yours,

TRP; 1 p.; cc.

To Roosevelt

681 West End Avenue
N.Y.
June 11th 1905

Dear Mr President:

Here is an article of mine, which you might care to glance at. And here also is a little pamphlet for your personal collection.[1]

Blessed are the peacemakers! For a man with a big stick, you seem to be fairly successful at least in persuading others to give over fighting.[2]

Butler made a very good speech at the banquet to Choate the night before last.[3] He is steadily deepening the impression he has made on the community.

He dined here a month ago to meet the Leigh Hunts. And Hunt's latest effort to colonize coons in Khartoum has a certain resemblance to carrying coals to Newcastle.[4] But he is as enthusiastic as ever about it.

I hope that you are going to get a little real rest at Oyster Bay, for these are strenuous days in which we are living; and it is well to store up reserves of strength for the hour of struggle.

Yours Ever

Brander Matthews

TRP; 4 pp.; als.

1. BM probably enclosed his recently published article "Apology for Technic," *North American Review* 180 (June 1905): 869–79. Anticipating the New Criticism of mid-century, BM advises critics to devote more attention to analyzing the technical merits, rather than the themes and moral value, of art works. The pamphlet cannot be identified.

2. TR's efforts to end the Russo-Japanese War, which had begun in Feb. 1904, reaped results in early June, with the two adversaries agreeing to enter direct negotiations. But three more months of skillful mediation and diplomacy by TR were required to secure the peace treaty, signed on 2 Sept. 1905. TR, of course, coined the aphorism, "Speak softly and carry a big stick," and the image became inextricably connected to his foreign policy. See Gould, *Presidency of Theodore Roosevelt*, 180–87.

3. Joseph Hodges Choate (1832–1917) had recently returned to the U.S. after six years' service as ambassador to Great Britain. Butler was one of the speakers at a banquet, held at the Waldorf-Astoria on 9 June, welcoming Choate home; the affair attracted about 350 friends and supporters of Choate, including many prominent political figures ("Pilgrims Bid Mr. Choate Warm Welcome Home," *New York Times*, 10 June 1905, 9).

4. In 1902, after his adventure developing gold mines in Korea, Leigh S. J. Hunt traveled to Sudan to begin building his dream of establishing cotton plantations along the Nile. A major part of his grand scheme was to hire African Americans—whom BM refers to here as "coons"—to work the plantations, giving them economic opportunity and him skilled labor. This idea was enthusiastically supported by Booker T. Washington and TR. Several Tuskegee graduates did, in fact, join the plantations at Zeidab and Khartoum in 1905; despite setbacks caused by malaria and destructive insects, the plantations eventually succeeded. The mass migration of American blacks that Hunt envisioned never took place, however, and Booker T. was severely criticized by some of his peers for endorsing such "deportation" of African Americans. Disputes with other investors led Hunt to resign his post as director of the Sudan Plantations Syndicate Board in 1909. See Laurance B. Rand, *High Stakes: The Life and Times of Leigh S. J. Hunt* (New York: Peter Lang, 1989), 179–252.

To Matthews

WHITE HOUSE
June 12, 1905.

Dear Brander:

I enjoyed your letter, and I shall enjoy the article and the pamphlet, too.

I wish I could have gotten the Leigh Hunts on here to spend a night. Things have moved so fast the past few days that I have had no other time when I could have them visit the White House, except just to come for lunch or dinner, if they were in Washington. Hunt has not been able to get hold of Mrs. Hunt, and I am only afraid that now it will be too late for us to get them down here if they are able to come.

With love to Mrs. Brander.

Theodore Roosevelt

BMP; 1 p.; tls.

To Roosevelt

Narragansett Pier, R.I.
August 31st 1905

Dear Mr President:

I think it must tickle your sense of humor, that it is the Man with the Big Stick at whose word a great war has ceased.[1] After all, Sam Patch was right when he said that "Some things can be done as well as others."[2]

The one dark spot in the outlook is that there is nothing now left for you to do. You had made war; you have made peace; and I needn't say anything about the hearts of your countrymen. Things have been coming your way so abundantly and so frequently of late, that I don't see how you can better the record in the future.

In the ample leisure of the summer I've been reading Jusserand's admirable history of English literature,—clear and sane like all French criticism.[3] And in one of the notes I found that Bacon suggested the Hague Court of Arbitration. At least, he wrote to the King in 1617 expressing the pious hope that "There will be erected a tribunal, or praetorian power, to decide controversies which may arise amongst the princes and estates of christendom without effusion of christian blood."[4]

The Leigh Hunts came down here to see us last week. He then expressed his certain conviction that your conference would result in peace.

I suppose you have seen Howells's tribute to Hay in the *North*

American Review.[5] I'm going to send you my ϑBX address at Columbia on "American Character."[6]

In the mean while, my wife and daughter "desire their compliments"—as our Southern grandmothers used to say—to you and to Mrs Roosevelt.

Ever Yours

Brander Matthews

TRP; 4 pp.; als.

1. On 29 Aug. 1905, at the Portsmouth Conference, Russia and Japan agreed on the terms of the treaty signed four days later.

2. Sam Patch (1807–1829) was a daredevil, famous for diving off high places and for the apothegm BM quotes here. Some things, however, could not be done: Patch was killed after plunging from the brink of Genesee Falls on 13 Nov. 1829.

3. Jean Jules Jusserand, *A Literary History of the English People,* 3 vols. (1895; reprint ed. New York: Benjamin Blom, 1968). In addition to being a literary historian, Jusserand (1855–1932) was a diplomat; he had been the French ambassador to the U.S. since 1902. He and TR greatly respected and admired one another.

4. The Hague Tribunal, a court for settling international disputes peaceably, was established in 1899; Sir Francis Bacon's remark anticipating such a world court of arbitration is quoted in Jusserand's *Literary History,* 3:530n.

5. Howells, "John Hay in Literature," *North American Review* 181 (Sept. 1905): 343–51. Howells suggests that the recently deceased Hay (1 July 1905) could have been as great an author as he was a statesman had he chosen the literary instead of the public-service path in life.

6. Titled "American Character," the address was later included in BM's *The American of the Future,* 25–56. Seeking to rebut claims that Americans are materialistic, acquisitive, and warlike, BM contends that Americans are ethical, idealistic, peace-loving (but willing to fight for right), generous, and so on. The patriotic speech glosses over or ignores the darker side of the "American character." See BM to TR, 6 Mar. 1906.

To Matthews

Oyster Bay, N.Y.,

September 2, 1905.

Dear Brander:

It was good to receive your note. You know Jusserand personally, do you not? He is a splendid fellow, and even more interesting when he talks than when he writes.

I am going to read Howell's article on Hay, and will read your address with pleasure.

With love to your wife and daughter, believe me,
      Faithfully yours,
      Theodore Roosevelt

P.S.
I picked up "Democracy" the other day.[1] What a mean and foolish novel it is, and how events have given it the lie!

    BMP; 1 p.; tls. with handwritten postscript.

    1. Published anonymously in 1880, *Democracy: An American Novel* was the first of two novels by Henry Adams. The book is a scathing indictment of Washington politics and of the corrupting influence of power. Writing Lodge on 2 Sept. 1905, TR describes *Democracy*—which he believed had been written by Godkin with assistance from Mrs. Henry Adams—as having a "superficial rotten cleverness" and being "essentially false" (*LTR,* 5:10).

To Roosevelt

    681 West End Avenue
    N.Y.
    Nov 20th 1905

Dear Mr President:

Let me express the hope that the advertisement I enclose was not authorized by you.[1] You may be the American Xenophon—altho the Rough Riders were not Ten Thousand and did not retreat;[2] and you may be the American Herodotus[3] or even the American Thucydides.[4] But the American Homer! Really the sycophancy of some toadies is appalling. As I like always to think well of my friends—especially when they are practical politicians—I shall try to believe that this advertisement is wholly unauthorized. Indeed, I shall expect you to disavow it promptly. And I can only hope that the Evening *Post* will fail to see it.

All the same I am,
      Ever Yours
      Brander Matthews

    Scribner Papers, Princeton Univ. Libraries (Author Files I, Box 124, Folder 3); 4 pp.; als.

    1. BM enclosed a Scribner's advertisement for TR's *Outdoor Pastimes of an American Hunter* (1905) mistitled as *Outdoor Pastimes of an American Homer.* BM is of course being facetious in this letter, as is TR in his response to it.

    2. Xenophon (434?–355? B.C.), Greek soldier and historian; when a force

of 10,000 Greek soldiers was stranded in Persia, he led them on a 1,500-mile retreat.

3. Herodotus (484?–425? B.C.), Greek historian, often referred to as the "Father of History."

4. Thucydides (460?–400? B.C.), Greek historian.

To Matthews

WHITE HOUSE
Personal
November 21, 1905.

Dear Brander:

I am hurt and grieved at your evident jealousy of my poetic reputation. Evidently you have not read my notable review of the epic poems of Mr. Robinson,[1] or you would appreciate that, even though I have not written poetry myself, I have yet shown such keen appreciation of the poetry of other great poets that I felt justified in securing the insertion of that advertisement.

If you saw my review of Mr. Robinson's poems you may have noticed that I refrained from calling him "our American Homer". This was simply due to the fact that I hoped some discerning friend would see where the epithet ought to go; less perhaps as an acknowledgment of what I have actually done, than as an inspiration and prophecy concerning the future.

Regretfully and reproachfully yours,
T.R.

When are you coming on here?

BMP; 1 p.; tls. with handwritten postscript; pbd. *LTR,* 5:86.

1. American poet Edwin Arlington Robinson (1869–1935) was virtually unknown when TR reviewed *Children of the Night* (1897), Robinson's second book of poetry, in the *Outlook* 80 (12 Aug. 1905): 913–14 (rpt. in *Works,* 12:296–99). Though TR generally did not appreciate the kind of somber poetry found in Robinson's volume, the poems struck a chord; they displayed, TR declared, an "undoubted touch of genius." In addition to writing the review, which helped get Robinson's poetry the attention it deserved, TR secured Robinson (who had been working as a timekeeper on a New York City construction project) a federal job so that he could devote the necessary time to his poetry.

To Roosevelt

681 West End Avenue
N.Y.
Nov. 26th 1905

Dear Mr President:
    Really, that press-agent of yours ought to lose his job. Just look at this from *McClure's*! First, he mixes you up with Homer; and now you appear with Woodberry![1] I think this is going too far. What have you ever done to deserve a place on the same page as Woodberry? It is true that you are said to be "athletic but not an athlete," and he is an esthete but not esthetic. All the same, you are not in his class,—and he knows it, even if you fail to see it. To put you with Lafarge might be justified, I suppose, but with Woodberry![2]
    It's good of you to ask when I can be in Washington; and I wish I knew. I may be able to run down about New Years; but I doubt if we can break away from the meshes of New York until the midyear examinations, which fill the final week of January.
    Why don't you come on for the Century Twelfth Night?
                                            Yours Ever
                                            Brander Matthews

    TRP; 4 pp; als.
    1. BM enclosed an advertisement page for *McClure's Magazine*'s offerings for 1906 (TRP). The ad includes an announcement of a series of literary articles by George Woodberry. Poet and critic, Woodberry (1855–1930) had been a professor of comparative literature at Columbia from 1891 to 1904; his decision to retire early from the faculty in 1904 was largely due to a long and bitter feud between him and his archenemy, BM. Details of their nasty conflict are presented in Oscar James Campbell, "The Department of English and Comparative Literature," in *A History of the Faculty of Philosophy, Columbia University*, ed. Jacques Barzun (New York: Columbia Univ. Press, 1957), 71–79.
        The ad also announces a forthcoming article by sports writer Henry Beach Needham titled "Theodore Roosevelt—An Outdoor Man," quoting the comment that TR was "athletic but not an athlete." The article would appear in *McClure's* 26 (Jan. 1906): 230–52, the phrase quoted above occurring on 252.
    2. The *McClure's* ad for Woodberry's series of articles states that John LaFarge "is doing for the masters of painting what Professor Woodberry does for the masters of writing."

1906

To Roosevelt

681 West End Avenue
New York
Jan 1st 1906

Dear Mr President:

This is just to convey our triplicate greetings and good-wishes to you and to Mrs Roosevelt!

But I seize the occasion to enclose the advertisement of a French book, which I haven't yet seen. The translation of your big stick saying does not seem to me felicitous. *Gentiment* is not quite what you meant.[1]

By the way, if you happen to see the January *Munsey* you will find a paper of mine on "The Supreme Leaders"—in all departments of human endeavor.[2] Butler and LaFarge and Mahan all helped me to make the selection. I wonder how it will strike you.

You are the busiest man in the world, and therefore you must have time for your friends. That's why I venture to butt in, now and again, with these needless epistles.

Yours Ever
Brander Matthews

TRP; 3 pp.; als.

1. The advertisement, from an undated issue of *De La Librairie Plon,* was for *De Monroe à Roosevelt, 1823–1905* (1905) by Horace Dominique de Barral de Montferrat. The abstract suggests that the book portrays TR as personifying the American spirit of imperialism—an American Caesar. TR's "speak softly" phrase is translated as "On peut parler gentiment" (i.e., "speak gracefully").

2. BM, "The Supreme Leaders," *Munsey's Magazine* 34 (Jan. 1906): 460–65. BM offers his list of (Western) civilization's greatest writers, artists, composers, orators, military leaders, and scientists. (Neither TR nor any other contemporary of BM is mentioned.)

To Matthews

WHITE HOUSE

January 2, 1906.

Dear Brander:

Somebody sent me that book.[1] I found difficulty in recognizing my-self as this particular other man saw me.

I shall look up Munsey's at once. I am sure I shall like your article. Wishing many happy new years to you and yours, believe me,

Your friend,

Theodore Roosevelt

BMP; 1 p.; tls.

1. See preceding letter, n. 1.

To Roosevelt

681 West End Avenue

N.Y.

Feb 1st 1906

Dear Mr President:

Of late I've seen a good deal of Frank Sprague the electrical inventor.[1] As you know, he is an Annapolis man;—and he is also a good citi-zen, with a fine public spirit.

He feels very strongly about Niagara and about the need for im-mediate action to save it. Of course it ought to be saved;—and if not saved, it ought to be *sold*. There is no possible advantage in *giving* it away.

As the result of my last talk with Sprague, he has sent me the en-closed letter, which I take the liberty of sending to you.[2] (Don't return it.)

Last week's *Outlook*—the February Magazine number—contained a careful statement of the present situation at Niagara, so far as the grants already made are concerned.[3]

Yours Ever

Brander Matthews

PS. At the risk of seeming to butt in, I'd like to suggest that Sprague would make a useful member of the Board of Visitors to the Naval Academy.[4]

BM

TRP; 4 pp.; als.

1. Frank J. Sprague (1857–1934), electrical engineer and pioneer in development of electric trains and elevators. After graduating from Annapolis (1878) and

serving in the navy (until 1883), he worked for a year in Thomas Edison's laboratories, then formed his own company. He resided in New York City, where his public service included membership on the Commission for Electrification of Grand Central Terminal (1903–8).

2. Like many other Americans (and Canadians), Sprague was concerned that increasing diversion of water from the Niagara River for power and manufacturing plants would eventually have a devastating effect on Niagara Falls, one of the world's great natural treasures. In his letter to BM of 31 Jan. 1906 (TRP), which BM enclosed with this letter, Sprague, reacting to news that the New York state legislature was considering a bill to create a commission for preserving the Falls, stated that he wanted to write TR to express his support for the commission and to suggest that an electrical or hydraulic engineer be appointed to it. Noting that the President receives thousands of such unsolicited letters, Sprague asked BM to be his mediator if BM thought his ideas had merit.

3. Charles M. Dow, "How to Protect Niagara," *Outlook* 82 (27 Jan. 1906): 179–89. (This is clearly the article to which BM refers, though it appeared in the Jan., not Feb., number.) Dow's detailed analysis of the deteriorating condition of the falls, due to commercial development, contains much hard scientific data; he notes, for example, that existing permits allowed power and manufacturing companies to divert 60,000 cubic feet of water per second from the American side of the river alone. The granting of additional permits, he argues, would soon bring the falls to the point of extinction.

4. See postscript to next letter.

To Matthews

February 2, 1906.

Dear Brander:

The Naval Academy visitors are already chosen.

I shall do all I can and am doing all I can about Niagara, but what I shall be able to accomplish I do not know. I can not pass laws. Congress must do that, and there must be a big popular feeling to urge them to do it. As you know, I recommended action about Niagara in my message.[1] Does Sprague mean that I should appoint such a commission, to serve without pay? I would gladly do it, but I hesitate to ask men to incur the expense and travel. You see, unless Congress acts I could pay nobody anything.

Ever yours,
Theodore Roosevelt

P.S.

Good luck! One visitor gave out, & I have put on Sprague.

TRP; 1 p.; ccs. with handwritten postscript.

1. In his State of the Union Message to Congress on 4 Dec. 1905, TR declared that Niagara Falls must be preserved, and he suggested that if the state of New York could not protect the falls, then the federal government should assume the responsibility.

To Roosevelt

681 West End Avenue
N.Y.
March 6th 1906

Dear Mr President:

I'm sending you today the *Columbia University Quarterly*, with a ΦBX address of mine on "American Character."[1] Butler liked it; and there are some things in it that might interest you.

You had my heartful sympathy a little while ago when you were looking forward to the wedding,—for I am undergoing the same experience. My daughter is to be married the last of next month,—and she is my only child.

She is to be the wife of Nelson Macy[2] who served under Cowles[3] on the *Topeka*,—a manly fellow whom we have long known.

There are lots of interesting things I'd like to talk over with you. But you are a long way off!

Yours Ever
Brander Matthews

Brownell has written a fine article on Cooper for the April *Scribner*.[4]

TRP; 4 pp.; als.

1. See BM to TR, 31 Aug. 1905, n. 6.

2. Edith Brander Matthews wed Nelson Macy (1869–1957) on 30 Apr. 1906. Scion of a prominent New York family, Macy was president of the paper firm Corlies Macy & Co., and was a decorated naval veteran of the Spanish-American War, during which he served on the cruiser *Topeka* off Cuba.

3. William Sheffield Cowles (1846–1923), career naval officer and husband of TR's sister Anna (Bamie). TR had been instrumental in securing Cowles his position as captain of the *Topeka* in 1898 (*LTR*, 2:821).

4. William Crary Brownell (1851–1928); literary critic, and editor and literary advisor to Charles Scribner's Sons from 1888 until his death. His "Cooper" appeared in *Scribner's Monthly* 39 (Apr. 1906): 455–68.

To Matthews

March 7, 1906.

Dear Brander:

I am very much pleased. Give my warm regards to your daughter. I am glad she is to be connected with the Navy, and it is an eminently fitting connection for you, for no better American walks this country.

Can't you, as soon as possible after the wedding, get on here and let me talk over all kinds of things with you!

Faithfully yours,
Theodore Roosevelt

TRP; 1 p.; ccs.

To Matthews

March 20, 1906.

Dear Brander:

I shall read that article by Giddings with great interest.[1] I am afraid Stickney cannot tell me much about railroad rates.[2]

Did I not write you how much I liked your article on American character?[3] I certainly intended to do so, for it delighted me.

I shall surely read the article on Cooper in April Scribner's.

Ever yours,
Theodore Roosevelt

TRP; 1 p.; ccs.

1. Franklin H. Giddings, "Sovereignty and Government," *Political Science Quarterly* 21 (Mar. 1906): 1–27. After analyzing various conceptions of sovereignty, Giddings warns against the trend toward absolute submission to authority, and concludes that if the "ultimate democracy [in the United States] is to be liberal, cherishing true freedom and perfecting individual life, there must be a great broadening of economic opportunity,—through public ownership, or otherwise—a wholesale destruction of state-controlled privilege, a wider distribution of power, and a leveling up of educational attainment" (27).

2. Most likely Albert Stickney (1839–1908); New York attorney and author of *State Control of Trade and Commerce by National or State Authority* (1897). TR knew and corresponded with him (see TR to Stickney, 3 Apr. 1907, TRP, and *LTR*, 6:1421).

To Roosevelt

681 WEST END AVENUE
April 22nd 1906

Dear Mr President:
That was a good piece you spoke about the Man with the Muck-Rake.[1] And you spoke it at the right moment, so that the name will stick. It is not a bad thing for a country to have a President who knows how to read and write.

But I'm writing this for the sake of an anecdote bearing on your suggestion that we must hobble the [mare?] that makes the money go.[2] A friend of mine in London told me that when Vernon Harcourt was forcing the death-duties thru Parliament, a wealthy aristocrat protested that this was putting too heavy a burden on the landed proprietor.[3] Harcourt faced him with this: "That's just what I intend. I *mean* to bring your order down! And these death duties will do it!"

Yours Ever
Brander Matthews

TRP; 4 pp.; als.

1. "The Man with the Muck-Rake," address at the laying of the cornerstone of the office building of the House of Representatives on 14 Apr. 1906 (pbd. *Works*, 16:415–24). Taking aim at David Graham Phillips (1867–1911) and other journalists preoccupied with exposing political corruption, TR reached for an image out of John Bunyan's *Pilgrim's Progress*: the Man with the Muck-rake, who typifies the man "who in this life consistently refuses to see aught that is lofty, and fixes his eyes with solemn intentness only on that which is vile and debasing" (*Works*, 16:416). Such reformers, in TR's view, do more harm that good in the battle against corruption because they breed public cynicism; TR emphasizes that he is not denouncing truthful investigative reporting, only reckless "mud-slinging." BM's prediction that the name would stick proved correct.

2. The metaphor of a hobbled mare does not occur in "The Man with the Muck-Rake," but BM apparently refers to TR's call in that speech for a progressive income tax and an inheritance tax—notions considered radical at the time. As a front-page article ("Roosevelt for Tax on Wealth") in the *New York Times*, 15 Apr. 1906, observed, the tax proposals created a storm of controversy and overshadowed the attack on the muckrakers.

3. Sir William Vernon Harcourt (1827–1904), English radical Whig; as chancellor of the exchequer, he succeeded in imposing (via the Finance Act of 1894) heavy "death duties," or inheritance taxes, on the wealthy, as TR in his "Muck-Rake" address suggested the U.S. should do.

To Matthews

WHITE HOUSE
April 23, 1906.

Dear Brander:

I have your note of the 22d and am glad you liked that speech. It represented several very sincere convictions of mine.

That is an excellent anecdote of Vernon Harcourt and it just exactly expresses my attitude. I do not like the yellow rich!

Always yours,
Theodore Roosevelt

BMP; 1 p.; tls.

To Roosevelt

681 WEST END AVENUE
May 16th 1906

Dear Mr President:

I enclose a little thing of mine,—altho' I hope you do not need to be converted to the good cause.[1]

And I've recently rec'd a book on Japan and on the situation in the Orient by a very clever and clearheaded Frenchman, Aubert, who has held a traveling scholarship and who writes without bias.[2] I think it would interest you. Shall I send it to you?

This is a lonely household, now that the only child has been amputated by matrimony.

It was very good of you and Mrs Roosevelt to send her those flowers from the White House conservatories.

Yours Ever
Brander Matthews

TRP; 4 pp.; als.

1. As TR's reply letter indicates, the "good cause" was simplified spelling; the unidentified article BM enclosed, therefore, was most likely his recently published essay on the topic, "The Spelling of Yesterday and To-morrow," *Outlook* 82 (14 Apr. 1906): 848–53. After repeating arguments from earlier essays advocating simplified spelling, BM announces the creation and explains the objectives of the Simplified Spelling Board, which BM helped form (in 1906) and which he initially chaired; the board was funded for three years by BM's friend and admirer, Andrew Carnegie. TR not only joined the organization, but in Aug. 1906 issued orders for the Public Printer to adopt the board's 300 simplified spellings—an act which ignited a firestorm of protest. See

Years, 441–47; Oliver, *Brander Matthews,* 125–27; and TR to BM, 22 Aug. 1906.

2. See BM to TR, 5 Feb. 1904. Aubert had just published *Paix Japonaise* (Paris: Colin, 1906).

To Matthews

WHITE HOUSE
May 17, 1906.

Dear Brander:

Can't you come to Washington some time when we can have an evening together and talk over everything from spelling to the Japanese? Of course I am with you on the spelling, and I would like very much to see that Frenchman's article on the Japanese.

Always yours,
Theodore Roosevelt

BMP; 1 p.; tls.

To Matthews

Oyster Bay, N.Y.,
August 22, 1906.

Dear Brander:

It may interest you to know that the Public Printer has been instructed to follow the rules of your new Spelling Reform Association,[1] and that Mr. Loeb, himself an advanced spelling reformer, will hereafter see that the President in his correspondence spells the way you say he ought to![2]

With love to Mrs. Matthews, believe me,

Always yours,
Theodore Roosevelt

BMP; 1 p.; tls.

1. In a letter dated 20 Aug. 1906, TR instructed the government printer, Charles Arthur Stillings, to write BM for a copy of the Simplified Spelling Board's pamphlet listing the 300 recommended simplified spellings, and to then ensure that "all Government publications, including the President's messages, are spelt in accordance" with the recommendations (*LTR,* 5:378). TR issued an official order on the matter to Stillings on 27 Aug. 1906 (*LTR,* 5:389–90). TR's effort failed, however, as the Supreme Court ignored his recommendations, and the House of Representatives eventually passed a law forbid-

ding departures from standard spellings in government publications; many of TR's opponents in Congress and in newspaper rooms, moreover, took great pleasure in satirizing his scheme. TR thus was forced to accept defeat. See TR to BM, 16 Dec. 1906.

2. William Loeb (1866–1937), TR's personal secretary. As instructed by TR, Loeb sent several letters to BM requesting information and advice on spelling reform (21 and 24 Aug. 1906, BMP); in a letter to BM dated 27 Aug. 1906 (BMP), Loeb enclosed a draft of TR's official order to Stillings, for BM's "comment, amplification, elision, and return."

To Roosevelt

681 WEST END AVENUE
Sept 22nd 1906

Dear Mr President:

As you are a very busy man, of course, you have lots of spare time. That's one reason why I hope you will read a paper of mine on 'Reform & Reformers' in today's *North American Review*.[1] I wrote it with the memory of many things you have said. And I had the *Evening Post* crowd in plain view!

I don't know whether you will have occasion again to say anything about simplified spelling. But I've just heard a new argument, which would have great [weight?] coming from you:—So long as the foreign voter can't read, he is the prey of the henchman and the hecler. But anything which makes it easier for him to read, helps just so much toward his thinking for himself, free from the semi-hypnotic appeal of the oral argument.

I'm glad that Kwig[2]—if I may so spell it, with your permission—, is down and out.

Yours Ever
Brander Matthews

TRP; 4 pp.; als.

1. BM, "Reform and Reformers," *North American Review* 183 (21 Sept. 1906): 461–73; rpt. in *The American of the Future*, 283–305. BM commends public-spirited citizens and the "better class of politicians" who are intent on fighting corruption and serving the public good; but, echoing TR's condemnation of the "muckrakers" (one of whose major outlets was the *New York Evening Post*) BM attacks radical reformers—"the faddists, the freaks, the cranks, who take up with every passing whim of the moment and who tag themselves to the tail of every cause, whether it is wise or otherwise" (*American of the Future*, 297).

2. BM's simplified spelling of "Quigg," Lemuel Ely Quigg (1863–1919), prominent New York lawyer and former Republican congressman. In 1906 Quigg, supported by the Republican machine, reentered the political arena in an attempt to unseat fellow Republican Congressman Herbert Parsons (1869–1925), the reform candidate. TR publicly endorsed Parsons, who beat Quigg soundly in the primary election, ending his political career.

To Matthews

Oyster Bay, N.Y.,
September 24, 1906.

Dear Brander:
I will look up that article in the North American Review at once. As for the simplified spelling business, at present I see no need for my saying anything more. We are all right, surely.
Sincerely yours,
Theodore Roosevelt

BMP; 1 p.; tls.

To Matthews

Oyster Bay, N.Y.,
September 27, 1906.

My dear Brander:
That article of yours on reform and reformers is the very best thing of the kind I have ever yet seen done.[1] It is complete in every way. I only wish it could be sufficiently widely read.
Faithfully yours,
Theodore Roosevelt

TRP; 1 p.; ccs.
1. See BM to TR, 22 Sept. 1906.

To Matthews

WHITE HOUSE
December 16, 1906.

Dear Brander:
I could not by fighting have kept the new spelling in, and it was evidently worse than useless to go into an undignified contest when I was beaten.[1] Do you know I think that the one word as to which I

thought the new spelling was wrong—thru—was more responsible than anything else for our discomfiture? But I am mighty glad I did the thing anyhow. In my own correspondence I shall continue using the new spelling.

Faithfully yours,
Theodore Roosevelt

BMP; 1 p.; tls.; pbd. *LTR*, 5:527.

1. After heated debate, the House of Representatives on 12 Dec. 1906 passed a bill against, as the *New York Times* put it, the "Brander Matthewized printing office," prohibiting the Public Printer from implementing TR's executive order ("House Bans Spelling in President's Style," *New York Times*, 13 Dec. 1906, 3).

1907

To Matthews

January 8, 1907.

Dear Brander:

The enclosed letter explains itself.[1] Pray accept my heartiest congratulations.

Ever yours,
Theodore Roosevelt

TRP; 1 p.; ccs.
1. A letter from French Ambassador Jusserand stating that BM had been awarded the French Legion of Honor.

To Roosevelt

681 WEST END AVENUE
Jan 9th 1907

Dear Mr President:

It was very good of you to send me Jusserand's letter at once; and I have taken a double pleasure in the honor because you were the transmitter of the glad tidings.

I saw a New Year's card the other day with your portrait on it, and Rockefeller's[1] and Jim Jeffries'![2] And the legend wished the recipient to have your luck, John D's money and Jim's health. I don't think you need envy Jim his health or John his money![3]

Our best New Year's wishes to you and to the Lady of the White House!

Yours Ever
Brander Matthews

TRP; 3 pp.; als.
1. John D. Rockefeller (1839–1937), industrialist and philanthropist, was one of the nation's wealthiest persons.
2. James J. Jeffries (1875–1953), heavyweight boxing champion from 1899 to 1905; his name was synonymous with health and physical strength.
3. TR was affluent, if not a millionaire, and he was a virtual fanatic about physical fitness.

To Matthews

WHITE HOUSE

April 1, 1907.

Dear Brander:

It is horrid to have to refuse the request for even a "pair of old pants," but I do not think it best that just at present I should say anything more about the simplified spelling.[1] I am using it myself. I used it for the Nation until Congress stopt it. Then I accepted an election on the Simplified Spelling Board. Now I do not think it wise for me to talk about it any more.

Always yours,

Theodore Roosevelt

BMP; 1 p.; tls.

1. BM, in a letter that has been lost, apparently asked TR to speak (or perhaps provide a written statement) on spelling reform at the meeting of the Simplified Spelling Board mentioned in the next letter. TR's refusal is understandable, in light of the storm of criticism and ridicule that greeted his executive order to the Public Printer.

To Roosevelt

681 WEST END AVENUE

April 2nd 1907

Dear Mr President:

Behind your unwillingess to give me even a "pair of old pants", I seem to detect a suspicion that I was using them as a cover to "pull your leg."

But I'm going to heap coals of fire on your head by sending you the enclosed,—our special souvenir for tomorrow's banquet.[1] Perhaps some of the verses will take your mind off the cares of state.

I'll see that you have a copy of the most interesting report I am to make tomorrow as the first Chairman of the Board. We expect to elect Lounsbury to the Chairmanship for next year.[2]

Yours Ever

Brander Matthews

TRP; 3 pp.; als.

1. The Simplified Spelling Board held a banquet at the Waldorf-Astoria on 3 Apr. 1906, with Andrew Carnegie as toastmaster. The souvenir which BM enclosed was a miniature reproduction of the *New-England Primer*, with many of its verses replaced with poems written especially for the occasion,

and with all spellings brought into conformity with the recommendations of the Board. The first verse (for the letter A), for example, was:

> Since Andrew [Carnegie] fell
> Beneath the spell
> Reform's lookt well.

("New Spellers Meet," *New York Times*, 4 Apr. 1907, 5.)
2. BM's banquet speech on the history and accomplishments of the Simplified Spelling Board paid special tribute to TR, who had recently been elected to the Board. TR's public support of simplified spelling, BM noted, had "arrested the attention of the civilized world." Despite the setback caused by Congress, BM and his fellow Board members believed, incorrectly as it turned out, that their cause would eventually prevail. Deciding that it needed a president rather than a chairman, the Board elected Thomas Lounsbury to that position ("New Spellers Meet").

To Roosevelt

681 WEST END AVENUE
May 6th 1907

Dear Mr President:

Cooperstown is to celebrate the centenary of its incorporation in August; and I have been asked to deliver the oration on Cooper.[1]

Have you any thing to add to what Riis has reported as to your admiration for our first novelist?[2] If there are any aspects of the man you think I ought to emphasize I'd be delighted to profit by your hints.

I remember that you told me that you thought his Indians accurate except that he did not bring out their callous cruelty & their other weak points.[3]

Read Lounsbury on Spelling in the May *Atlantic*. It is delightful,— and it gives you the credit you deserve.[4]

Yours Ever
Brander Matthews

TRP; 3 pp.; als.
1. See TR to BM, 2 Sept. 1907.
2. Jacob A. Riis (1849–1914); Danish-American journalist and social reformer. In his biography of TR, Riis, who greatly admired James Fenimore Cooper's fiction, reports that TR once told him that Cooper's novels were superb— "nothing like them"—and that the creator of Leatherstocking deserved a higher standing in American literature than he then held (Riis, *Theodore Roosevelt, the Citizen* [New York: Outlook, 1904], 19–20).

3. TR discusses and provides examples of the Indians' alleged "love of cruelty for cruelty's sake" in vol. 1, *Winning of the West* (*Works*, 8:68–69, 75–76).

4. Lounsbury, "Confessions of a Spelling Reformer," *Atlantic Monthly* 99 (May 1907): 614–31. Looking back on the controversy stemming from TR's attempt to have all government publications conform to the recommendations of the Simplified Spelling Board, Lounsbury commends the president and chastises those who opposed and ridiculed his efforts.

To Matthews

WHITE HOUSE
May 7, 1907.

Dear Brander:

Lounsbury's article did me good.

No, I have nothing to add about Cooper. If you happen to have my "Winning of the West," I speak there of some of his extraordinarily lifelike backwoodsmen.[1] I am very glad you are to speak about him. With warm regards to Mrs. Brander, believe me,

Faithfully yours,
Theodore Roosevelt

BMP; 1 p.; tls.
1. See next letter.

To Matthews

WHITE HOUSE
May 12, 1907.

Dear Brander:

In "Wilderness Hunter" page 455, and the first volume of "Winning of the West" page 127, you will find allusions to Cooper's frontiersmen.[1] I feel sure I have somewhere made an allusion to his Indians, but for the life of me I can not remember where.

Ever yours,
Theodore Roosevelt

BMP; 1 p.; tls.
1. Speaking in *The Wilderness Hunter* of American writers' fictional portraits of the frontier, TR singles out Cooper for preserving "for always the likenesses of these stark pioneer settlers and backwoods hunters. . . . As for Leatherstocking, he is one of the undying men of story; grand, simple, kindly, pure-minded, stanchly loyal, the type of the steel-thewed and iron-willed hunter-warrior" (*Works*, 1:358). In the first volume of *Winning of the West*, he

remarks that Cooper's "pictures of white frontiersmen are generally true to life; in his noted Indian characters he is much less fortunate" (*Works,* 8:380–81n.) The influence of Cooper's frontier novels on TR's "myth-ideological system" is examined in Richard Slotkin, "Nostalgia and Progress: Theodore Roosevelt's Myth of the Frontier," *American Quarterly* 33 (1981): 608–37. TR's overall attitude and actions toward Native Americans are discussed in detail in Dyer, *Theodore Roosevelt and the Idea of Race,* 69–88.

To Matthews

Oyster Bay, N.Y.,
July 20, 1907.

Dear Brander:

What delightful reading Lang always is! Your letter, with his essay on the American President of the future, was sandwiched in this morning between internal politics and our relations with Japan; and I appreciated the diversion.[1] Who but Lang could write with such genuine humor, and be so amusing, and yet leave no sting behind?

Faithfully yours,
Theodore Roosevelt

By the way, I wish Lang could tell me if there really *is* an "Aryan" race; Aryan speech, yes; Aryan race—well, I am *very* doubtful.

TRP; 1 p.; ccs. with handwritten postscript; pbd. *LTR,* 5:723.

1. BM's letter is not in the TRP, and the Lang article remains unidentified.

To Matthews

Oyster Bay, N.Y.,
September 2, 1907.

Dear Brander:

I had already read that article in the Atlantic Monthly, and of course liked it immensely.[1] You know how absolutely I agree with you on Cooper. You brought out point after point that I did not know.

I am amused at what you say about your trouble in the fight to drive out the gamblers and the argument advanced for them that gambling helps prosperity.[2] Heney is attacked in California because it is said that honesty hurts business in a city;[3] and Wall Street takes precisely the same view about my enforcing the law against the rich malefactors.

Ever yours,

TRP; 1 p.; cc.

1. BM, "Fenimore Cooper," *Atlantic Monthly* 100 (Sept. 1907): 329–41; rpt. in

BM, *Gateways to Literature,* 243–76. This is the published version of the address that BM delivered at the centenary of the incorporation of Cooperstown on 8 Aug. 1907. In this often insightful analysis of Cooper's life and works, BM extols Cooper's powers as a storyteller and mythmaker, while acknowledging his faults as an artist. Discussing Cooper's portraits of Indians, BM echoes TR's judgment that the novelist glossed over the "Indian's ferocity and his cruelty" (270); see BM to TR, 6 May 1907.

2. At this time, New York District Attorney William Travers Jerome (1859–1934) was leading an antigambling crusade that was opposed not only by the powerful gambling interests but also by corrupt city officials and police.

3. Francis Joseph Heney (1859–1937). In 1906, after gaining national notoriety for prosecuting land-fraud cases in Oregon, Heney was appointed deputy district attorney of San Francisco. His vigorous investigations of municipal corruption won him the admiration of TR and other Progressives. In 1908, he was nearly killed by an assassin's bullet. See TR to Heney, 11 Dec. 1908 (*LTR,* 6:1419–20).

To Roosevelt

681 WEST END AVENUE
Sept 26th 1907

Dear Mr President:

Could Mrs Matthews and I dine at the White House on Thursday, Dec 5th and spend the night? We could; and we shall be delighted to accept.[1]

I don't know whether you see the *Independent* or not. But on the chance that you didn't, I enclose a cutting from the issue of Aug 29th. It is an editorial; but I happen to know that it was written by an infrequent contributor, my colleague, Professor Giddings, the sociologist.[2]

He is a Cape Codder by descent—as I am; and he stood only a few yards from you at Provincetown. I think that you may like to see what a man of his training—and of his stock—thinks of you. And perhaps Mrs Roosevelt might be pleased with it!

Mrs Matthews joins me in desiring to be remembered to her.

Yours Ever
Brander Matthews

TRP; 4 pp.; als.

1. BM is responding to TR's invitation of 23 Sept. 1907 (TRP) inviting him and Mrs. Matthews to dine at the White House with Lodge, Lounsbury, and the Jusserands.

2. On 20 Aug. 1907, TR laid the cornerstone of the Cape Cod Pilgrims Memorial Monument at Provincetown, Mass., and delivered a speech entitled "The Puritan Spirit and the Regulation of Corporations" (*Works*, 16:76–85), in which he vowed to continue his fight against the "rich malefactors" whose unfair business practices were destabilizing the stock market and threatening the American economy.

The *Independent* of 29 Aug. 1907 printed two anonymous editorials praising TR's speech; the style and content of the second editorial, titled "The Roosevelt Personality" (518–20), suggest that it was by Giddings. Declaring the speech "history-making," the editorial expresses strong support for TR's stance against the plutocrats, and portrays him as a courageous and sincere ally of the American people in their conflict with the "predatory rich."

To Matthews

September 27, 1907.

Dear Brander:

I have your letter of the 26th instant. I am greatly interested in the editorial, and especially in learning that it is from Giddings. Coming from him it gratified me peculiarly, and I am sure it will Mrs. Roosevelt.

With warm regards,

Faithfully yours,
Theodore Roosevelt

TRP; 1 p.; ccs.

To Roosevelt

681 WEST END AVENUE
Nov 25th 1907

Dear Mr President:

Does our friend, Lummis, the poet-lariat of Los Angeles, send you his monthly *Out West*?[1] If he doesn't, I'd like to inflict on you a recent number, in which I've spankt him for his casual remarks about the simple-minded spellers and in which he tries to wriggle from under the chastisement.[2]

You will be glad to know that Lounsbury seems to be better of late. He has been coming to the meetings of the Simplified Spelling Board.

On the other hand, Butler is beginning to look a little tired. He is so full of energy that he is tempted to burn the candle at both ends—

·and *le jeu vie haut pas la chandelle*[3] (as we members of the Légion d' Honneur say).

I hope you are not worrying over the financial situation. From all I hear, there has been a return of cheerfulness during the past week.[4]

Yours very truly
Brander Matthews

TRP; 4 pp.; als.

1. Charles Fletcher Lummis (1859–1928), poet, journalist, and explorer of the American Southwest; a native of Mass., he moved to Calif. in 1885, and in 1894 founded *Out West* (titled *Land of Sunshine* until 1902), the leading monthly magazine of the Los Angeles area. He had been a friend and correspondent of TR and BM for many years.

2. Lummis was an opponent of what he sarcastically termed the "Deformed Spelling" movement. The Oct. 1907 number of *Out West* contains a letter by BM defending spelling reform and lightly chastising Lummis for ridiculing the movement; BM notes that the Simplified Spelling Board members included many eminent scholars and President TR. BM's letter is followed by Lummis's lengthy rebuttal, in which he good humoredly accuses BM (why not "Brandr Mathuz"? he asks) and his fellow spelling reformers for promoting linguistic anarchy ("In the Lion's Den," *Out West* 27 [Oct. 1907]: 365–78).

3. Loosely translated: "It's not worth it."

4. In Mar. 1907, stock prices plunged, and the stock exchanges remained chaotic during the months that followed; a banking panic in New York City sent stock prices diving again in Oct. The country seemed to be sliding into a depression similar to the Panic of 1893, and many blamed TR for the financial problems (see Gould, *Presidency of Theodore Roosevelt*, 246–50). The crisis had largely abated by late Nov., however, and two days after BM wrote this letter, a *New York Times* article confirmed his observation that investors were cautious but "cheerful" overall ("Improvement in Sentiment," *New York Times*, 27 Nov. 1907, 11).

To Roosevelt

681 WEST END AVENUE
Dec 10th 1907

Dear Mr President:

Mrs Matthews has already written to Mrs Roosevelt to express the pleasure we had last week in visiting the White House and in having the privilege of seeing you, seated at the center of things.

Mrs Matthews wants me now to transmit her thanks for the return of the little fan she carelessly left behind her.

I have askt my French bookseller to see[1] you Boissier's 'Conspiracy of Catiline'.[2] But I think that Boissier's volume on 'Cicero and his Friends' is quite as interesting. In fact, all Boissier's books reveal an intimate knowledge of Roman life and of Latin modes of thought; and I think you will soon send for the rest of them.

    With renewed thanks I am

Ever Yours
Brander Matthews

TRP; 4 pp.; als.

1. TR obviously meant to write "send."
2. Gaston Boissier (1823–1908), eminent French scholar of Latin antiquity. His many books, several of which were translated into English, include *Cicéron et Ses Amis* (Paris: Hachette, 1865; trans. *Cicero and His Friends* [2d ed., New York: Putnam's, 1903]), and *La Conjuration de Catilina* (2d ed., Paris: Hachette, 1908). See BM to TR, 23 Mar. 1915.

To Roosevelt

681 WEST END AVENUE
Dec 15th 1907

Dear Mr President:

    There isn't a copy of Boissier's 'Catiline' to be had in [town?], so Christern[1] reports to me; and I've had to send you instead his 'Cicero'.

    And I'm going to send you also the new *Political Science Quarterly* with a paper on "Railroad Valuation" which dispassionately discusses the question with a conclusion in favor of your proposals.[2]

Yours Ever
Brander Matthews

TRP; 3 pp.; als.

1. The New York bookstore F. W. Christern was very popular among book collectors, esp. those interested in foreign books; its founder, Frederick W. Christern, died in 1891, but the business continued after his death.
2. William Z. Ripley, "Railroad Valuation," *Political Science Quarterly* 22 (Dec. 1907): 577–610. Ripley contends that the Hepburn Act of 1906, which gave the government the power to regulate railroad rates, should be broadened to include regulation of railroad property and stocks. TR had pushed hard for regulation of the railroads (see Gould, *Presidency of Theodore Roosevelt*, 149–64).

To Matthews

WHITE HOUSE
December 18, 1907.

Dear Brander:

The Cicero has just been received, and I shall order the Catiline myself. Jusserand says that both books are simply thrilling and as amusing as possible. I will glance at (altho I can not say that I will read) the article in the Political Science Quarterly. What spare time I devote to reading is apt to be devoted to *lighter* reading than railroad literature, with which I have to deal officially!

Ever yours,
Theodore Roosevelt

BMP; 1 p.; tls.

1908–1910

To Matthews

Oyster Bay, N.Y.,
Private.
September 1, 1908.

Dear Brander:
I think that silhouette warrants all you say in your letter.[1]
I am doing all I can to get the leaders to nominate Hughes.[2] I think
I shall succeed, but I can not be sure, for Hughes has some real and grave
elements of weakness, and he has acted with worse than folly in insult-
ing thoroly reputable men interested in politics and making them feel
it incompatible with their self-respect further to support him.
Give my warm regards to Mrs. Matthews.
Faithfully yours,
Theodore Roosevelt

BMP; 1 p.; tls.
1. The letter has not been located and is probably not extant.
2. Charles Evans Hughes (1862–1948), who had defeated William Randolph
   Hearst in 1906 in the New York gubernatorial election, was among several
   contenders for the Republican party's presidential nomination in 1908; Hughes
   enjoyed the support of many progressive-minded Republicans, but not of
   TR, who considered him "an objectionable type of public man" and an arrogant "mugwump" (*LTR*, 6:1160–61). TR backed the more conservative William Howard Taft (1857–1930). After Hughes had lost the nomination battle
   to Taft at the Republican National Convention (in June 1908), TR reluc-
   tantly endorsed his renomination as New York governor. Both Taft and
   Hughes were victorious in the Nov. elections. See *LTR*, 6:1207–8, and Gould,
   Presidency of Theodore Roosevelt, 271–88.

To Matthews

WHITE HOUSE
November 2, 1908.

Dear Brander:
I was glad to receive your letter.[1] Indeed nobody has had a better
time—I am tempted to say that nobody has had as good a time as I

have had in the last fifty years, and what is more, I am looking forward to a very good time in the future.

By the way, John L. Sullivan also remembered my birthday and sent me a rabbit's foot which I am to take with me to Africa![2]

Of course I know Lavengro, but I either have never seen or have forgotten that Rough-Rider quotation.[3] It is interesting.

With love to Mrs. Matthews,
Ever yours,
Theodore Roosevelt

BMP; 1 p.; tls.

1. BM apparently sent TR a letter, now lost, congratulating him on his 50th birthday (27 Oct. 1908).

2. John L. Sullivan (1858–1918), former world heavyweight boxing champion (1882–92). On 23 Mar. 1909, shortly after leaving office, TR embarked on an extended tour of Africa and Europe, returning to Oyster Bay on 18 June 1910.

3. Lavengro was the pseudonym of the eccentric English writer George Henry Borrow (1803–81). His autobiographical narrative *Lavengro, The Scholar—The Gypsy—The Priest* (first published in 1851 and reprinted many times) recounts his experiences during a walking tour of the British Isles in 1825, during which he was nearly poisoned to death, engaged in a fistfight, and spent time among the Gypsies and other members of the British lower classes. The Rough Rider quotation is unidentified.

To MATTHEWS

WHITE HOUSE
December 15, 1908.

Dear Brander:

In an address I am to make on Saint Gaudens this evening, I shall use an idea of your own about New York City, so I hope you will look at what I say.[1]

Ever yours,
T. R.

BMP; 1 p.; tls.

1. TR delivered a speech honoring the American sculptor Augustus Saint-Gaudens (1848–1907) at the Saint-Gaudens Exhibition, Corcoran Art Gallery, Washington, D.C., on 15 Dec. 1908 ("Augustus Saint Gaudens," *Works*, 11:282–87). Contending that America's industrial development has created scenes worthy of artistic representation, TR echoes BM's cel-

ebration of the New York City skyline in his preface to *Vignettes of Manhattan* (see TR to BM, 13 Oct. 1894, n. 1). "A great artist," TR suggested in his speech, "will yet arise to bring before our eyes the powerful irregular sky-line of the great city at sunset, or in the noonday brightness, and, above all, at night" (*Works*, 11:283).

To Roosevelt

681 WEST END AVENUE

Dec 16th 1908

Dear Mr President:

I have received a communication on White House paper signed "T. R." In Great Britain I have seen communications from the Chief of State signed "V. R." and "E. R." I confess that my democratic Soul is shockt to find you putting on these imperialistic airs!

But that's a mighty good speech of yours about Saint Gaudens,— and I was delighted that you found a suggestion of mine worth using.

Your mention of Louis XIV reminds me that in a history of Versailles I read about a queer thing, very characteristic of those times.[1] Bernini,—at least, I think it was Bernini—made an equestrian statue of the monarch in Roman togs as usual.[2] The King was supposed to be "climbing the mount of Fame". But he didn't like the statue, yet he had to keep it. So the sculptor carved a few flames amid the rocks, and the statue immediately became "Curtius approaching the fiery gulf."

Yours Ever

Brander Matthews

TRP; 4 pp.; als.

1. In his Saint-Gaudens speech, TR cites sculptures of George Washington in a toga and "Louis XIV, with his peruke, in a Roman corselet" as examples of the foolish attempt to represent modern subjects in the classical style (*Works*, 11:286).

2. Giovanni Lorenzo Bernini (1598–1680), Italian sculptor and painter. BM's anecdote is slightly inaccurate. Bernini did sculpt a marble equestrian statue of Louis XIV in Roman garb (ca. 1673), and the King did not like it. But it was the French sculptor François Girardon (1628–1715) who in 1688 (after Bernini's death) transformed the figure from the Sun King into Marcus Curtius on the verge of the fiery abyss. A detailed account of the curious event may be found in Cecil Gould, *Bernini in France* (Princeton, N.J.: Princeton Univ. Press, 1982), 122–31.

To Matthews

WHITE HOUSE
January 4, 1909.
Dear Brander:
I thank you for the letter from Johnson.[1] I shall take up his case at once and see if it is possible to do something for him.
Ever yours,
Theodore Roosevelt

BMP; 1 p.; tls.

1. BM's letter to TR of 3 Jan. 1913 indicates that the reference is to the African-American writer, songwriter, and diplomat James Weldon Johnson (1871–1938), to whom BM was a friend and mentor (see Oliver, *Brander Matthews,* 47–62). TR had appointed Johnson, a Republican who had worked for TR's election in the 1904 campaign, as U.S. consul to Puerto Cabello, Venezuela, in 1906. In June 1908, Johnson was promoted to a better position as consul to Corinto, Nicaragua, but six months later he was still in Venezuela awaiting his replacement. Late in 1908, Johnson wrote BM a letter in which he stated that if he were not soon transferred he would resign from the diplomatic service and return to New York (Johnson to BM, [Nov.? 1908], James Weldon Johnson Papers, Beineke Library, Yale Univ.). BM apparently sent the letter to TR, who was in the final weeks of his presidency, asking him to intercede. Johnson finally left Venezuela for Nicaragua in Apr. 1909. See also BM to TR, 2 Dec. 1912, and 12 Apr. 1918.

To Matthews

The Outlook[1]
March 15th 1909.
Dear Brander:
My today's mail contained another copy of the editorial from the London "Times", together with yours.[2] It is a very pleasant editorial.
I am sorry to hear you have been suffering from the grip; but for Heaven's sake don't ask me to write "a few lines" for *any* occasion! You have no conception of the hundreds of such requests I have received.
Sincerely yours,
Theodore Roosevelt

BMP; 1 p.; tls.

1. After his term as president had expired, TR accepted a position as contributing editor to the *Outlook,* a weekly magazine published in New York City and edited by Lyman Abbot (1835–1922).

2. The *London Times* printed an editorial titled "Mr. Roosevelt as a Journalist" on 5 Mar. 1909, 10, announcing that TR would begin writing for the *Outlook* and providing a summary of his first contribution, "Why I Believe in the Kind of American Journalism for which the *Outlook* Stands," which appeared in the *Outlook* on 6 Mar. 1909, 510–11. The editorial also praised TR for being open with the press during his presidency.

To Roosevelt

681 WEST END AVENUE
June 21st 1910

Dear Theodore:

I've just had a card from Rudyard Kipling,—and the half about you I copy on the back of this, thinking you might like to see it.

That was a mighty pretty wedding yesterday.[1]

Yours Ever
Brander Matthews

[On back of page:]
R.K. to B.M.: June, 1910

"Roosevelt has come & gone & done our state great service.[2] Here you have one simple, single-minded person, saying today quite casually, things which ought to set the world flaming. Instead of which the world says:—'Thank you! Please do it again!'

His Egyptian speech was, from certain points of view, the biggest thing he has ever done.[3] I saw him for a hectic half-hour in London, & a little at Oxford. Take care of him. He's scarce & valuable."

TRP; 2 pp.; als.

1. Theodore Roosevelt III (1887–1944), married Eleanor Alexander on 20 June 1910 in New York City.
2. TR concluded his long tour of Africa and Europe with a three-weeks' visit to London (16 May to 8 June 1910), during which he met with numerous British notables, received honorary degrees from Cambridge and Oxford universities, delivered lectures, and was much in the news (see Miller, *Theodore Roosevelt*, 508–11).
3. On 31 May 1910, TR, after being presented with the Honorary Freedom of the City of London, spoke on British colonialism, particularly as regarded Egypt, which was then experiencing a surge of nationalism. In developing his central thesis that "the civilized nations who are conquering for civilization savage lands should work together in a spirit of hearty mutual good will," TR condemned the Egyptian Nationalist Movement as a threat to world civilization, and urged the English to maintain firm control of the country; he also warned that "weakness, timidity, and sentimentality" would

only cause more harm and injustice. The *London Times*, which printed the full text of the speech, reports that TR was interrupted several times by cheers ("Mr. Roosevelt in the City," *London Times,* 1 June 1910, 9).

To Matthews

The Outlook
October 6th 1910.

Dear Brander:

I am really obliged to you for sending me The Times' review, and appreciate it.[1] As soon as election is over, I hope to see you.[2]

In great haste,

Faithfully yours,

T. R.

BMP; 1 p.; tls.

1. Perhaps a review of John Callan O'Laughlin's *From the Jungle Through Europe with Roosevelt* (Boston: Cahpple, 1910) that appeared in the *New York Times,* 17 Sept. 1910, 502. O'Laughlin (1873–1949), TR's secretary during his travels in Africa and Europe, lavishes praise upon the former president.
2. TR had recently been elected temporary chairman of the New York State Republican Committee. Despite his strenuous campaigning, however, the Republicans lost badly in the Nov. gubernatorial and congressional elections throughout the country.

1911–1912

To Roosevelt

681 WEST END AVENUE
May 26th 1911

Dear Theodore:
  Mrs Matthews and I both regret extremely that we cannot lunch with you and Mrs Roosevelt on June 1st. Unfortunately I am making graduation addresses at two She-schools on that day—one in the outskirts of New York and the other in the outskirts of Philadelphia.[1]
  Have you read Faguet's "Les Préjugés Nécessaires"?[2] There are incidental remarks on the historic influence of war, which would interest you, I think.
                    Yours Ever
                    Brander Matthews

  TRP; 3 pp.; als.
  1. Unidentified.
  2. Émile Faguet, *Les Préjuges Nécessaires* (Paris: Société Française d'Limprimerie et de Librairie, 1911). Faguet (1847–1916) was a French literary historian and critic.

To Roosevelt

681 WEST END AVENUE
June 18th 1911

Dear Theodore:
  That U. of Calif. address was worthy of the Greek theater wherein it was delivered.[1] Can I say more?
  Could I say less?—seeing that you gave me the pamphlet. The least I can do [is] to return two pamphlets for one. I enclose them—and I'll send the 'Notes on Speech-Making' as soon as I can get it.[2] In fact, I'll give you good measure,—I'll send you also my new 'Study of Versification', a guide-book for [spring?] poets.[3]
  It was bully to see you and Mrs Roosevelt looking so peart (if that's the way it's spelt.) My wife and I agreed that you two had changed mighty little in twenty years.

Have you seen the article on *War* in the new Britannica? It is by Henderson (biographer of Stonewall Jackson); and I think it echoes things you have said.[4]

Yours Ever

Brander Matthews

TRP; 4 pp.; als.

1. During 24–28 Mar. 1911, TR was Earl Lecturer at the Univ. of California at Berkeley, delivering a speech each day in the Greek Theater there to an audience of thousands. The five lectures—"Realizable Ideals," "The Home and the Child," "The Bible and the Life of the People," "The Public Servant and the Eighth Commandment," and "The Shaping of Public Opinion and the Ninth Commandment"—were collectively published under the title *Realizable Ideals* (San Francisco: Whitaker, 1911; rpt. in *Works,* 13:615–74).

2. BM, *Notes on Speech-making;* orig. published in 1901 (New York: Longmans, Green), BM's collection of essays on making speeches was reprinted in 1910. The two pamphlets mentioned are unidentified.

3. *A Study of Versification* (Boston: Houghton Mifflin, 1911); a collection of BM's critical essays on the craft of poetry.

4. George F. R. Henderson, "War," *Encyclopaedia Britannica,* 11th ed. (1910–11), 28:305–11. Henderson (1854–1903), author of *Stonewall Jackson and the American Civil War* (New York: Longmans, Green, 1900), argues that military organization has evolved into a science, and that officers must therefore be trained as rigorously as lawyers and doctors; he further maintains that intelligence and education are more important than courage and experience in modern warfare.

To Matthews

The Outlook

June 21st, 1911.

Dear Brander:

I must get that article on "War" in the Brittanica. I shall read both the pamphlets with the utmost interest; & the little book.

It was fine having you and dear Mrs. Matthews out the other day.

Ever yours,

T. R.

BMP; 1 p.; tls.

To Matthews

The Outlook
June 30th, 1911.

Dear Brander:
I thank you for sending me those two documents. I never heard of the book, nor of the author, and on the two documents there is no statement as to where to address the author. I have written saying that it is an impudent forgery;[1] so you won't have to send the documents to the Evening Post!

Since I last wrote you, the volume on versification came, and I am really delighted with it. I have been reading it with the utmost interest. Let me say again what a pleasure it was to see you both the other day.

Faithfully yours,
Theodore Roosevelt

BMP; 1 p.; tls.
1. The documents, author, and alleged forgery are unidentified.

To Roosevelt

681 WEST END AVENUE
Oct 19th 1911

Dear Theodore:
We have both been greatly grieved by Mrs Roosevelt's accident, and we are very glad to know that she is now out of pain and on the road to recovery.[1]

Have you seen a volume just publisht by my colleag W. W. Lawrence on "Medieval Story"?[2] I can send it to you, if you like. I think it is a book you would like to read—& perhaps to write about, for it deals with the medieval ideals which helpt to make us so called AngloSaxons what we are. The "melting pot" of our race was put on the fire centuries ago.

Lawrence dedicated the book to me—but that is not the only reason I like it. And I feel sure that it will interest you.

Yours Ever
Brander Matthews

TRP; 4 pp.; als.
1. Edith Roosevelt suffered a serious head injury after being thrown from her horse on 30 Sept.; her recovery took weeks, and she completely lost her sense of smell.
2. William W. Lawrence, *Medieval Story and the Beginnings of the Social Ideals of English-Speaking People* (New York: Columbia Univ. Press, 1911); the book

is dedicated to "Brander Matthews, interpreter of the literature and life of modern times." Lawrence (1876–1958), professor of English at Columbia from 1910 to 1936, contends that the "foundations of our [melting-pot] republic rest on the sterling virtues of English character," which was itself a fusion of the Germanic, Scandinavian, French, and Celtic races that occurred in the British Isles (11).

To Matthews

October 20th, 1911.
Dear Brander:
    Mrs Roosevelt is really better. I should particularly like to see Lawrence's volume. Now do not send it to me unless it is convenient for I can get a copy myself.
    Give my love to Mrs Matthews.
    In great haste,
                    Sincerely yours,

    TRP; 1 p.; cc.

To Roosevelt

681 WEST END AVENUE
Jan 4th 1912
Dear Theodore:
    The enclosed is from yesterday's *Puck*. It seems to me that you have made a pretty good Score!¹
    A Happy New Year to you both from us both.
                    Yours Ever
                    Brander Matthews

    TRP; 2 pp.; ans.
    1. The 3 Jan. 1912 number of *Puck* contains a cartoon, titled "The Twenty Greatest Men in the World's History," composed of twenty caricatures of TR in different outfits suggesting his numerous roles (soldier, woodsman, gentleman, cowboy, etc.).

To Matthews

The Outlook
January 5th 1912.
Dear Brander:
    I was immensely amused over that picture from Puck, but Heav-

ens and Earth! what a frightful mouth I must have!¹ Thanks to the comic papers, I *am* given the gift to see myself as others see me.
Many happy New Years to you and Mrs Matthews, the daughter and the son-in-law, and the family unto the third and fourth generation.
Ever yours,
T. R.

BMP; 1 p.; tls.
1. The *Puck* cartoon images of TR accentuate his moustache and jowls, giving him a walrus-like appearance.

To Roosevelt

681 WEST END AVENUE
Dec 2nd 1912
Dear Theodore:
Now [that] this cruel war is over I am sending you (for your archives) the oriflamme my wife has flaunted all thru the campaign.¹ And I put with it my privately printed verses so that you can discover that your sister is not the only host of the muses on Manhattan Island.²
I'm delighted that you are going to write your autobiography.³ As Longfellow once said, "Autobiography is what biography ought to be."⁴ And I've thought of writing mine, sooner or later.⁵ What are you going to call yours? "From Cowboy to Cop,"—this would be striking, at any rate.
Did you ever read the "Autobiography of an Ex-Colored Man" that I sent you six months ago?⁶ If you did, I'd like to know your opinion of it.
Yours Ever
Brander Matthews

TRP; 4 pp.; als.
1. TR reentered national politics in 1912 as the Progressive party's presidential candidate, and the "war" was indeed "cruel" for him: not only was the campaign nasty, but on 14 Oct. he was shot in an attempted assassination outside the Hotel Gilpatrick in Milwaukee. He swiftly recovered from his wound, but was soundly defeated by the Democratic candidate, Woodrow Wilson, in the Nov. election. Apparently, Mrs. Matthews showed her support for TR during the campaign by wearing an oriflamme, the red banner of Saint Denis (near Paris), which was carried before early French kings as a military ensign.
2. BM's collection of poems, *Fugitives from Justice*, was privately printed (99 copies) in 1912 by his son-in-law's firm, Corlies, Macy & Co. (New York). TR's sister Corinne, a poet since her adolescent years and a lifelong resident

of New York City, had recently published her first book of poetry, *The Call of Brotherhood* (New York: Scribner's, 1912).

3. TR's autobiography was published a year later, blandly titled *Theodore Roosevelt: An Autobiography* (1913; rpt. in *Works*, vol. 22).

4. In his journal entry of 21 Feb. 1848, Henry Wadsworth Longfellow wrote: "What is *Autobio*graphy? What biography *ought to be*" (*Life of Henry Wadsworth Longfellow with Extracts from His Journals and Correspondence*, ed. Samuel Longfellow, 3 vols. [Boston: Houghton Mifflin, 1891], 2:114).

5. BM's autobiography *These Many Years* appeared five years later, in 1917.

6. James Weldon Johnson, *The Autobiography of an Ex-Colored Man* (1912). Though now considered a classic of African-American literature, Johnson's novel, published anonymously in 1912, was virtually ignored until the Harlem Renaissance of the 1920s. BM, however, favorably reviewed the book in the Aug. 1913 number of *Munsey's Magazine* and recommended it to several friends in addition to TR (see Oliver, *Brander Matthews*, 54–56).

To Matthews

December 6th, 1912.

Dear Brander:

I was delighted with the letter, the book and the flag—perhaps especially with the book!

At present I seem to be more busy than ever. In a little while I shall hope to see you and talk over many of those things.

Sincerely yours,

Theodore Roosevelt

TRP; 1 p.; ccs.

To Roosevelt

681 West End Ave N.Y.
(where I expect to be this afternoon)[1]
Jan 3rd 1913

Dear Theodore:

Happy New Year!

You have been President of the U.S.—& also of the Am. Hist. Ass.[2] I have been President of the Modern Language Ass. and I am President of the National Institute of Arts & Letters.[3] Thus do we slowly broaden down from President to President!

I don't know whether you noted the enclosed stanzas in the *N.Y. Times* of Jan 1st.[4] If you didn't, you will be glad to see them. The writer is that colored man of letters for whom I said a good word to you five or six years ago.[5] And he is also the author of that anonymous "Auto-biography of an Ex-Colored Man" that I sent you last year when you were in the throes of Progressing. If you haven't read it, look it up, for it will interest you. It is not exactly fact—but it is the truth.[6] And it lets the light into some dark and curious places.

Yours Ever
Brander Matthews

TRP; 4 pp.; als.

1. This letter is written on letterhead stationery from the Hotel Brighton, At-lantic City; BM crossed out the printed return address, and inserted his home address and the parenthetical note.

2. TR was elected president of the American Historical Association in 1912, after having served a year as its vice-president.

3. BM served as president of the Modern Language Association from 1910 to 1911 and of the National Institute of Arts and Letters from 1912 to 1914.

4. James Weldon Johnson, "Fifty Years," *New York Times*, 1 Jan. 1913; rpt. in Johnson's *Fifty Years & Other Poems*, with an introduction by BM (Boston: Cornhill, 1917), 1–5. The patriotic poem commemorates the 50th anniversary of the signing of the Emancipation Proclamation. In a letter to Johnson of 2 Jan. 1913, BM states that he will send the poem to TR and also to Rudyard Kipling (James Weldon Johnson Collection).

5. See TR to BM, 4 Jan. 1909.

6. Unlike many readers of the anonymously published *Autobiography*, BM knew that the work was a novel, not an autobiography.

To Matthews

The Outlook
January 7th, 1913.

Dear Brander:

I am very glad you sent me that poem. It is a striking thing. I read the autobiography that you sent me, and was much impressed by it.[1] Ugh! There is not any more puzzling problem in this country than the problem of color. It is not as urgent, or as menacing, as other problems, but it seems more utterly insoluble. The trouble is that the conflict in many of its phases is not between right and wrong, but between two rights.

A little later, Brander, I wish to have the chance to see you. There is so much I want to talk over with you.

With love to Mrs Matthews, and wishing you many happy New Years, I am

> Faithfully yours,
> Theodore Roosevelt

BMP; 1 p.; tls.

1. Writing to Johnson on 8 Jan. 1913 (James Weldon Johnson Collection), BM quoted the opening three sentences of this letter by TR but withheld TR's subsequent comments about the "problem of color."

To Roosevelt

681 WEST END AVENUE
Feb 16th 1913

Dear Theodore:

My wife and I don't know whether to congratulate you and Mrs Roosevelt on the engagement of your daughter—or to commiserate you.[1] This amputation of our offspring by matrimony is a pleasant pain and a painful pleasure. But *we* had only our ewe-lamb; and *your* sheepfold will not be empty.[2] And then there is always the delightful prospect of grandchildren—the coupons on the bonds of matrimony.

The American Academy of Arts & Letters holds its joint meeting with the National Institute of Arts & Letters (of which I am President this year) at Chicago Nov 13th & 14th! Hamlin Garland has probably askt you to speak a piece on "The West in Literature"—or any other non-inflammable theme.³ And I sincerely hope that you will accede to this request. Your presence in your loyal city of Chicago would place the cap of glory on my administration.

Yours Ever
Brander Matthews

TRP; 4 pp.; als.

1. TR's daughter Ethel (1891–1977) became engaged to Dr. Richard Derby (1881–1963), a Manhattan surgeon; the two were married on 4 Apr. 1913 at Oyster Bay.
2. BM and his wife had only one child; TR and Edith had five children (and TR had another child, Alice Lee, by his first wife).
3. Garland, who was determined to develop the literary culture of Chicago and the Midwest region, was a member of the institute and chaired the joint meeting's program committee. A central topic of discussion at the convention was the growing influence of the West in American literature and art. Though it drew national attention, the meeting did not, in Garland's eyes, significantly change the intellectual life of Chicago. See his *Companions on the Trail: A Literary Chronicle* (New York: Macmillan, 1931), 511–24.

To Matthews

The Outlook
February 18th, 1913.

Dear Brander:

It is very good to hear from you. Having, as you say, a sheepfold full, my happiness is really unalloyed. Young Dick Derby is the very finest young fellow I know, without any exception, and I am always overjoyed if any boy or girl of mine makes a good marriage; for I do not regard life as a success for either a single man or a single woman!

I guess I will have to come out to that meeting in November. I was weakening at Hamlin Garland's request, and now that you make the request, I suppose I will simply *have* to throw up my hands. But do'n't ask me to make a definite promise yet.¹

Sincerely yours,
Theodore Roosevelt

BMP; 1 p.; tls.

1. TR did not attend the Nov. meeting in Chicago; in Oct. he embarked on extensive travels through South America.

To Roosevelt

681 WEST END AVENUE
Feb 19th 1913

Dear Theodore:
You can sit on the fence—only on condition that you finally fall off on our side! You must have lots of things to say about the "West in Literature"—things that need to be said and that nobody but you can say as they ought to be said.
Besides, we mean to build our program up to you and around you! So there—
I knew "Dick Derby's" father[1]—and he was a fine fellow too!
Yours Ever
Brander Matthews

TRP; 2 pp.; als.
1. Richard Henry Derby, New York physician.

To Matthews

The Outlook
February 26th 1913.

Dear Brander:
I have received a letter from Mr. R. U. Johnson about the meeting next November.[1] He asks me to speak for twenty minutes apparently in the course of a series of addresses by a number of others. I am no use in speaking in a symposium, so to speak, and I don't like to speak unless, as our Methodist brethren say, "it is borne in on me", and then it is out of the question to limit myself to any time, either to make it as short or as long as is artificially required. It does not seem to me that it would be wise for me to try to make a speech under these conditions.
Always yours,
Theodore Roosevelt

BMP; 1 p.; tls.
1. Robert Underwood Johnson (1853–1937); respected editor of the *Century* magazine and secretary of the American Academy of Arts and Letters (which he helped found).

To Roosevelt

681 WEST END AVENUE
Sept 27th 1913

Dear Theodore:
Once upon a time a cub-reporter of the *Herald* was sent to interview Ex-President Hayes[1]; and after the end of the talk the innocent cub askt,—"By the way, Mr Hayes, what was it you were president of?"

Now, you *were* President of the U.S. but I *am* President of the National Institute which holds a joint meeting with the Academy of Arts & Letters in Chicago in November. You avoided the speech you promised by sneaking away to South America where extradition is unfashionable. Your topic was the "West in Literature". Now, won't you write us a letter on that theme—to be read at the meeting and to be printed in the Proceedings. Or if not on that theme, then on any other. Please![2]

Lodge's 'Early Memories' are delightful—and I hope he will prepare 'Later Memories'.[3] I'm going to review his book and Dewey's and yours in *Munsey*.[4] By the by, you got Dewey appointed to the Asiatic Squadron. Did Lodge have anything to do with your appointment to the Navy Department?[5]

I shall also say something about your volume of essays—but if you don't write the letter I'm asking for, my opinion of you may be lowered. And I shall have to express my opinion in the article.
Yours Ever
Brander Matthews

TRP; 4 pp.; als.
1. Rutherford B. Hayes (1822–93), 19th president of the United States.
2. TR apparently did not write the letter, for none is listed in *Proceedings of the American Academy of Arts and Letters and of the National Institute of Arts and Letters*, No. 7: *1914* (New York: American Academy of Arts and Letters, 1914). President Wilson, however, did send a letter expressing his support for the organizations (6).
3. Henry Cabot Lodge, *Early Memories* (New York: Scribner's, 1913). Lodge's memoirs begin with his childhood and end with his entry into political life (ca. 1880); in the book's closing sentence he remarks that he might continue his memoirs "if time and strength permit" (351), but he never did.
4. George Dewey, *The Autobiography of George Dewey, Admiral of the Navy* (New York: Scribner's, 1913). BM reviewed *Theodore Roosevelt: An Autobiography* (1913) and TR's *History as Literature and Other Essays* (1913) not in *Munsey's* but in the *Bookman* 38 (Dec. 1913): 418–22. The opening section of the review mentions Lodge's *Early Memories* (which BM had reviewed in the *Bookman* the month before [38: 288–90]) and Dewey's autobiography,

but the rest of the essay focuses on the two TR books, upon which BM, not unexpectedly, heaps praise. See TR to BM, 25 May 1914.

5. Lodge was among several of TR's friends who lobbied hard for his appointment, in 1897, as assistant secretary of the navy (see Miller, *Theodore Roosevelt*, 246–48).

To Matthews

ON BOARD THE "VANDYCK",[1]
October 15th 1913.

Dear Brander:

I have enjoyed "Shakespeare as a Playwright" so much that I must write to tell you so.[2] I had not anticipated caring much for it because I am anything but a good Shakespearian, Macbeth being about the only play that I habitually re-read in its entirety. But your book strikes me as one of the best things you have done—and when I say that I mean to speak in very high praise.

Give my love to Mrs Matthews, and tell her that when I come back I want to discuss with her and you the irrelevant sentence in your volume in which you exalt the prodigal son at the expense of the one who stayed at home.[3] My dear Brander, I know there are exceptions, and I know that some frightful prigs and sneaks and cold-blooded dogs stay at home and look virtuous and respectable, and that some of the so-called prodigal sons are merely wild adventurous young fellows of the best type; but I have too often seen the prodigal son at close quarters, when he was the son of a kinsman or friend, not to have a very pronounced dislike of the genus as an entity.

Always yours,
Theodore Roosevelt

BMP; 1 p.; tls.

1. TR was en route on the *S. S. Vandyck* to Brazil.

2. *Shakspere as a Playwright* (New York: Scribner's, 1913); BM brought his immense knowledge of the drama to this study of Shakespeare's dramaturgy.

3. Noting the popularity of Shakespeare's Prince Hal with the English people, BM asserts that "the sure instinct of mankind has always recognized the larger possibilities of good in the Prodigal Son, preferring him to this staid and sober elder brother, to whom there seems to cling a taint of the Pharisee" (*Shakspere as a Playwright*, 118).

To Matthews

The Outlook
May 25th 1914.

Dear Brander:

I have just seen your review of my book. I like it so much that I must tell you so. By the way, I entirely agree with you in your view of the mechanical part of the book.¹ I was very much disappointed in it. It should have been done as Scribners did with the "Life Histories" and put into two volumes on good paper and with the pictures in decent shape.²

Give my love to Mrs Matthews. Sometime soon I am going to get you to bring her and Professor Trent out to lunch at Oyster Bay.

Faithfully yours,
T. Roosevelt

BMP; 1 p.; tls.

1. See TR to BM, 27 Sept. 1913. In his review of TR's *Autobiography*, BM waxes enthusiastic about TR the man and the writer; but he lambasts the publisher (Macmillan) for the book's "mechanical setting," complaining that the volume is "undeniably ugly" and likening it to "an ill-made subscription book cluttered with haphazard process-cuts" (*Bookman* 38 [Dec. 1913]: 421).

2. Charles Scribner's Sons, which had established a reputation for producing handsome, high-quality volumes, and which would later publish the National Edition of TR's *Works*, had recently published TR's two-volume *Life-Histories of African Game Animals* (1914; rpt. in *Works*, vol. 4).

To Roosevelt

337 WEST 87TH STREET¹
Nov 24th 1914

Dear Theodore:

Your note about Brieux did not get to me till a week ago today; & I could not speak to him till Thursday night.²

When I askt if he would like to meet you, his face lighted up; and he said you were the one man in America he did want to meet!

I saw him again yesterday. He has your invitation and he goes to you on Sunday. I wish I could go with him, but we are on duty, taking charge of our only grandchild. You have several grandchildren, but ours is Unique!—in the exact sense of that much abused word.

You will like Brieux. He is our sort. I've found him simple, direct, wholly unaffected—a very fine type of his race, and more Norman than Celtic.

I'm glad that Mrs Roosevelt continues to find nourishment in my 'Shakspere'. Of course, this is only a recognition of the obvious fact that I wrote it specially for her! My wife joins me in best wishes to you both.
Yours Ever
Brander Matthews

TRP; 4 pp.; als.
1. BM's new residence.
2. Eugène Brieux (1858–1932), popular French playwright. Brieux was visiting New York City as a special delegate of the French Academy to the 6th annual joint meeting of the National Institute of Arts and Letters and the American Academy of Arts and Letters, held during 19 and 20 Nov. 1914 (see *Years*, 449). In his note to BM of 14 Nov. 1914 (BMP), TR suggested that BM bring Brieux to lunch at Sagamore Hill, and BM agreed to do so (BM to TR, 18 Nov. 1914, TRP). TR then sent a personal invitation to Brieux (20 Nov. 1914, TRP), but it is not known whether the Frenchman actually made the trip to Long Island.

TO ROOSEVELT

337 WEST 87TH STREET
Dec 8th 1914

Dear Theodore:
I'm going to give your Brazilian book to two (2) boys this Xmas;[1] and I wonder if you would be so obliging as to scribble a few words in your fine Italian hand, duly authenticated by your copper plate signature, for me to set in the forefront of those two (2) books for those two (2) books.[2] They will read that far, any how!
I haven't seen Brieux since he made a date with you;—and I hope he was able to keep it and to have a powwow with you.
Our duplicate best wishes to Mrs Roosevelt!
And I am, of course,
Yours Ever
Brander Matthews

TRP; 4 pp.; als.
1. *Through the Brazilian Wilderness* (1914; rpt. in *Works*, vol. 5); TR's account (which had been serialized in *Scribner's* in Apr.–Nov. 1914) of his exploratory expedition through the Brazilian jungles and down the River of Doubt (Mato Grosso) early in 1914. During the adventure, TR badly injured his leg, contracted dysentery and malaria, and lost 57 pounds; the ordeal did lasting damage to his health. See Miller, *Theodore Roosevelt*, 535–38.
2. BM appears to have made a slip of the pen, ending the sentence with "books" instead of "boys."

1915–1916

To Matthews

THEODORE ROOSEVELT
THIRTY EAST FORTY SECOND STREET[1]
New York City
February 3rd, 1915.

Dear Brander:

I will read that book of Boas with the greatest pleasure.[2] What is he—a German or a Jew or what? I am familiar with his name; but with very little else. Love to the Lady!

Faithfully yours,

T. R.

BMP; 1 p.; tls.

1. Headquarters of the Progressive party.

2. Franz Boas (1858–1942); internationally renowned ethnologist, sometimes referred to as the "father of modern anthropology." Born in Westphalia of Jewish parents and educated in German universities, Boas took up permanent residency in the U.S. in 1886. In 1896 he became a lecturer, and in 1899 a professor, at Columbia University, where he remained for the rest of his career, ceaselessly challenging the theory of Anglo-Saxon racial superiority embraced by TR and BM (and most of the rest of the Western world). Though TR in this letter states that he will read Boas's "book," BM's next letter (see below) indicates that the publication was actually a pamphlet. Dyer suggests that TR was unacquainted with Boas's work (*Theodore Roosevelt and the Idea of Race,* 17–18); but, assuming that TR did read the pamphlet that BM sent, then he was familiar with at least one of Boas's works.

To Roosevelt

337 WEST 87TH STREET
Feb 7th 1915

Dear Theodore:

Boas *was* a German; but he *is* an American. He's our Columbia professor of anthropology—and he has made his subject really popular with undergraduates.

The reading of the pamphlet I sent you will give you no clue to his sympathies in the present war.[1]

The Lady returns your love with interest. And she joins me in
sending ours to your Lady.
Yours Ever
Brander Matthews

TRP; 2 pp.; als.

1. The pamphlet was likely Boas's *Race and Nationality* (New York: Assoc. for
International Conciliation, Jan. 1915), one of a series of pamphlets and bulle-
tins published by the Assocation for International Conciliation, an organization whose purpose was to promote international understanding and good
will. BM sat on the association's Council of Direction, and in 1916 contributed a pamphlet of his own to the series: *Do We Want Half the Hemisphere?*
(no. 107, Oct. 1916).

Boas's pamphlet contains more than a clue to his sympathies toward
Germany and Austria, though his main purpose is to condemn war in general
(see Marshall Hyatt, *Franz Boas: Social Activist* [Westport, Conn.: Green-
wood, 1990], 123–38). He argues that the war raging in Europe was not, as
was often suggested, the result of hostility between the Anglo-Saxon, Teutonic, Slavic, and Latin races (no such pure racial types exist, he observes);
rather, the conflict stemmed from an aggressive, unreasoning nationalism—
which was as evident in the U.S. as in Europe. To avoid future wars, Boas
concludes, a "federation of nations" must develop. TR, of course, held quite
different views on the war and on racial types.

To Roosevelt

337 WEST 87TH STREET
March 23rd 1915

Dear Theodore:

That's mighty interesting reading—that paper of yours in the
Homely Ladies Journal.[1] And I was delighted to see you swat Carlyle,
whom I detest uncritically & who anticipated all the recent German
apologists.[2]

Sloane[3] told me once that Taine[4] held Macaulay[5] to be one of the
half-dozen great historians of the world,—ranking among moderns
with Voltaire[6] and Gibbon.[7]

But I wondered a little that you failed to mention Gaston Boissier.[8]
To me he is the master interpreter of Roman life.

My wife "desires her compliments" to your wife.
Yours Ever
Brander Matthews

TRP; 3 pp.; als.

1. "Books That I Read, and When and How I Do My Reading," *Ladies' Home Journal* 32 (Apr. 1915): 7, 72. TR comments on dozens of his most and least favorite writers, explaining that since personal tastes vary, there can never be a list of the world's best books; he also argues that the reading of "vicious" books should be eliminated. BM's substitution of *"Homely Ladies"* for *"Ladies' Home" Journal* betrays his antipathy for the women's movement (see Oliver, *Brander Matthews*, 77–81).

2. Thomas Carlyle (1795–1881); Scottish historian, biographer, and social critic. Carlyle was steeped in and wrote major books on German literature and history, including the 6-volume *History of Frederick II of Prussia, Called Frederick the Great* (1858–65), which epitomizes the hero-worship that Carlyle trumpeted. His social and political beliefs were indisputably conservative, at times totalitarian, thus making him attractive to those in sympathy with Germany during World War I, the historical context for this letter and TR's "Books That I Read."

   In "Books That I Read," TR praises Carlyle's *Frederick the Great* for its "splendid descriptions of the battles" and for its portrait of the "iron-tempered king"; but he objects to Carlyle's "screaming deification of able brutality in the name of morality" and his "suppression and falsification of the truth under the pretense of preaching veracity" (7).

3. William Milligan Sloane (1850–1928); BM's colleague at Columbia, where he held the Seth Low Professorship in History (1896–1916). A former president of the American Historical Association (1911), he at this time was chancellor of the American Academy of Arts and Letters.

4. Hippolyte Taine (1828–93); French literary historian and critic. Taine's theory of "race, moment, and milieu," which he developed in *History of English Literature* (1864), profoundly influenced the literary criticism of BM and many other American critics (see Oliver, *Brander Matthews*, 9–12).

5. Thomas Babington Macaulay (1800–59); English historian and statesman. TR commends Macaulay's *Frederic the Great* (1878) in "Books That I Read," counterpointing Macaulay's highly critical portrait of the Prussian king to Carlyle's idolizing one (7). See BM to TR, 16 Jan. 1916.

6. Voltaire; pen name of François Marie Arouet (1694–1778), French historian, philosopher, and satirist.

7. Edward Gibbon (1737–1794); English historian, best known for his 6-volume work, *The History of the Decline and Fall of the Roman Empire* (1776–88).

8. See BM to TR, 10 Dec. 1907.

To Matthews

SAGAMORE HILL.
Oct 4th 1915

Dear Brander,
Can you give me the name of the editor of Harper's Monthly who passes on contributions?[1] I have written an article on "Prehistoric Man; and the Horse, the Lion and the Elephant" (yes, it *does* remind one of the "Parrot who talked in his sleep"). It is too long—16,000 words— and I can't compress it, and am doubtful about dividing it; Fair Osborn[2] is the only human being to whom it might appeal, and to him only that he might pull it in pieces; even the long suffering Scribners does'n't want it. But it is possible the Harper's editor may not be quite sober, or something, and may take it; and as I am not conscientious I wish to give him the chance.[3]
Love to Mrs. Brander and all the descendants. I must see you soon.
Ever yours
Theodore Roosevelt

BMP; 2 pp.; als.; pbd. *LTR*, 8:973.

1. As BM states in the next letter, Henry M. Alden (1836–1919) was the editor of *Harper's Monthly*, from 1869 until his death.

2. Henry Fairfield Osborn (1857–1935); professor of paleontology at Princeton (1881–91) and then at Columbia (1891–1907), where he organized the biology department and also the American Museum of Natural History. TR had sent a draft of an essay on Prehistoric Man—which seems to have been intended as a chapter in a planned book on the subject—to Osborn for his remarks. Osborn responded that the handwritten draft was too difficult to read to allow him to judge the contents, though he found what he could decipher to be interesting. He suggested that TR indicate to prospective publishers that the book was only in the "suggestive stage." In closing, Osborn stated that he would send a copy of his forthcoming book, *Men of the Old Stone Age* (New York: Scribner's, 1916); he did so several weeks later (Osborn to TR, 4 Oct. and 15 Nov. 1915, TRP). See next note.

3. Alden apparently rejected the essay, if TR did submit it (there is no record in the TRP); but TR later published an article, "How Old Is Man?," in *National Geographic Magazine* 29 (Feb. 1916): 111–27, which may have incorporated material from "Prehistoric Man." The published essay devotes much attention to Osborn's *Men of the Old Stone Age*, TR praising it as the "most important book on the evolution of our species . . . since Darwin's 'Descent of Man'" (114).

To Roosevelt

337 WEST 87TH STREET
Oct 6th 1915
Dear Theodore:
His name is Henry M. Alden—and he has held the job down for forty years or more. And altho he would rejoice to have your name on his list of contributors, I fear he would shrink from 16000 words, even when these discuss a topic of "contemporaneous human interest" (to borrow a phrase from the late Augustin Daly).[1]
If you could suggest that your paper might be printed in two instalments and if it will illustrate, I think you would improve your chances at *Harpers*.
And there is always the *Yale Review* to fall back on, one of the best and most interesting of our reviews,—perhaps the best. (I myself have a most readable paper in the October number![2])
Mrs Matthews and I "desire our compliments" (as our respective Southern grandmothers would have phrased it) to Mrs Roosevelt.
Yours Ever
Brander Matthews

TRP; 4 pp.; als.
1. Augustin Daly (1838–99); playwright, producer, and theater-owner. BM credits him with helping to develop American drama during the late 19th century (*Years*, 141–43).
2. BM, "'Hamlet' with Hamlet Left out," *Yale Review* 5 (Oct. 1915): 117–26. BM discusses several plays in which the main character is not bodily present on stage. The *Yale Review* had been founded in 1892 as a journal of history and politics, but broadened its scope to include literary essays such as this one.

To Matthews

SAGAMORE HILL.
Jan 10th 1916
Dear Brander,
Just a line to tell you how much Mrs. Roosevelt and I have enjoyed the delightful little Mrs. Siddons volume.[1] It is charming.
When spring comes I shall again try to get Mrs. Matthews and you out here; and we'll hold a [commiseration?] service over the Germans and Wilson.[2]
Always yours
Theodore Roosevelt

BMP; 1 p.; als.

1. Between 1914 and 1926, the Brander Matthews Dramatic Museum at Columbia, under the general direction of BM, published a series of 21 small volumes on the theater, including a reprinted edition of Fleeming Jenkin's essays on the great English actress Mrs. Sarah Kemble Siddons (1775–1831): *Mrs. Siddons as Lady Macbeth and as Queen Katharine* (New York: Dramatic Museum of Columbia Univ., 1915), with an introduction by BM.

2. TR and BM were severely critical of President Wilson's policy of neutrality toward the warring European countries, esp. toward Germany after one of her submarines sank the *Lusitania* (in May 1915), killing 128 Americans.

To Roosevelt

337 WEST 87TH STREET

Jan 16th 1916

Dear Theodore:

It's a long time since I've had a letter from you writ by your own right hand; and I'm glad that you and Mrs Roosevelt liked the Lady Macbeth booklet. (I liked it myself).

Of course, we shall be delighted, my wife & I, to run out to you and Kuss the Kaiser in Koncert.[1]

And that leads me to inclose a little unsigned essaylet of mine in the February *Scribner's*, which was suggested by a casual remark of yours on the Macaulay & Carlyle treatment of Frederick the Great,—a genius but no gentleman.[2] I only wonder whether you will accept my opinion of Nelson.[3]

Yours Ever

Brander Matthews

TRP; 3 pp.; als.

1. Kaiser Friedrich Wilhelm Victor Albert (1859–1941), emperor of Germany from 1888 to 1918; his militaristic actions were largely responsible for the outbreak of World War I.

2. BM's unsigned article, a brief comparative analysis of national heroes, appears in the "Point of View" section of *Scribner's* 59 (Feb. 1916): 254–56. While acknowledging that Frederick the Great was one of the world's greatest soldiers, BM concurs with, and quotes at length, Macaulay's damning assessment (in his *Frederic the Great*) of the Prussian king. Americans, BM suggests, can take much more pride in George Washington and Abraham Lincoln than the Germans can in Frederick (and in Bismarck), whose evil ambitions resulted in bloody war and immense suffering. See BM to TR, 23 Mar. 1915, n. 2.

3. In the *Scribner's* piece, BM lauds Nelson's seafighting abilities, but finds him as a man to be a "pitiful creature, vain, egotistic, selfish, avid of glory, insubordinate, intolerant of control, and regardless of the elementary dictates of domestic morality" (255). See BM to TR, 25 July 1903.

To Matthews

SAGAMORE HILL.
Jan 18th16

Dear Brander,

That is excellent; except that you should credit Nelson (in utter contradistinction to Wellington[1]) with his wonderful care of and affection for his subordinates. He called his captains "a band of brothers." Morally he was not much better than Henry IV; he was much more of the French class than the English type.[2]

Ever yours
T. R.

BMP; 1 p.; als.

1. Arthur Wellesley, 1st Duke of Wellington (1769–1852); British general who defeated Napoleon at Waterloo in 1815. His reputation for being a stern disciplinarian earned him the nickname "the Iron Duke."

2. Nelson's notorious affair with Lady Emma Hamilton broke up his marriage and sullied his professional reputation. Nelson's great affection toward those who served under him is emphasized in Southey's *Life of Nelson* (1813; reprint ed. London: Dent, 1951), in which is quoted Nelson's "band of brothers" remark (233).

1917–1918

To Roosevelt

337 WEST 87TH STREET
Jan 8th 1917

Dear Theodore:

You may not approve of all the opinions in this little article of mine—but I think that you will not dislike the point of view.[1]

I'm just finishing your "obituary" for the new Edition of Warner's 'Library of the World's Worst Literature'; & I've said that your 'Winning of the West' is obviously a continuation of Parkman's histories.[2] Isn't this the fact?

By the way, you write better now than you did when you wrote vol i of the 'W. of the West.' Your vocabulary is complex and your choice of words more certain. This I discovered by scientific analysis.

Yours Ever (as usual)

Brander Matthews

TRP; 2 pp.; als.

1. BM's most recent short article was "Irish Plays and Irish Playwrights," *Scribner's* 61 (Jan. 1917): 85–90, in which he argues that the burgeoning of Irish and of Irish-American drama is evidence that an ethnic or dialect literature can enrich a national literature without leading toward cultural separatism.

2. In 1896, Charles Dudley Warner (1829–1900) and his brother George (1833–1919) published the 30-volume *Library of the World's Best Literature*, commonly referred to as the Warner Library. As BM indicates in this letter, the *Library* was revised in 1917 (New York: Knickerbocker Press for the Warner Library Co.). Excerpts from TR's *Winning of the West* were included in vol. 20 of the new edition (pp.12385d–96r), with an introduction by BM (pp. 12384–85d), who was a member of the *Library*'s Advisory Council. In his essay, which emphasizes TR's general achievements as a man of letters, BM describes TR as "the loyal follower" of Francis Parkman, adding that TR's praise of Parkman's books equally applies to his own histories, esp. *Winning of the West*. After TR's death, BM revised and expanded this essay into "Theodore Roosevelt as a Man of Letters," which, as the introduction to

vol. 12 (*Literary Essays*) of the National Edition of TR's *Works, is* a sort of literary "obituary." See BM to TR, 31 Aug. 1917.

To Roosevelt

337 WEST 87TH STREET

March 11th 1917

Dear Theodore:

Lanson told me yesterday that in the latest number of the *Revue des Deux Mondes* (just rec'd over here) he has something on your address before the Academy last November.[1] As yet I haven't seen it. But it ought to be interesting.

Yrs Ever (as usual)

Brander Matthews

TRP; 2 pp.; ans.

1. Gustave Lanson (1857–1934), French literary historian and professor at the Univ. of Paris. He had delivered a paper at the 1916 joint meeting of the American Academy of Arts and Letters and the National Institute of Arts and Letters in New York at which TR read his address on "Nationalism in Literature and Art" (*Works*, 12:325–36). Lanson summarizes and quotes from his and TR's addresses in his article "Deux 'Lectures' Académiques à New-York," *Revue des Deux Mondes* 37 (Feb. 1917): 800–812; he expresses great admiration for the content and delivery of TR's speech.

To Matthews

METROPOLITAN[1]

432 FOURTH AVENUE NEW YORK

March 15, 1917.

Dear Brander:

With your note came the Revue, and I am really pleased with the article. It is pleasant to hear from you. Love to dear Mrs. Matthews.

Faithfully yours,

T. R.

BMP; 1 p.; als.

1. TR had resigned from his position with the *Outlook* in 1914, and had then signed a three-year contract to write exclusively for *Metropolitan Magazine*, beginning in 1915 (see *LTR*, 7:768–69).

To Roosevelt

337 WEST 87TH STREET

Aug 31st 1917

Dear Theodore:

I think I told you that I was charged with the pleasant duty of outlining your achievements as a man of letters for the revised edition of Warner's "Library of the World's Best Literature." And I've done it as best I could. And here it is.[1] Don't bother to return it, as it is already in type. Ours to yours—

Yours Ever

Brander Matthews

TRP; 2 pp.; als.

1. BM enclosed the typed draft, with handwritten corrections, of "Theodore Roosevelt" (TRP), the essay mentioned in BM to TR, 8 Jan. 1917.

To Matthews

OYSTER BAY

LONG ISLAND, N.Y.

September 4, 1917.

Dear Brander:

I am very much obliged to you, my dear fellow, for that article. I am very proud that you felt you could write it. Naturally, I am pleased that you laid as much stress as you did upon the "Winning of the West". How could I help being pleased? This is praise from Sir Hubert![1] Are you and Mrs. Matthews able sometime to come to lunch in New York, or at Sagamore Hill? There are as usual very many things I would like to talk over with you.

Always yours,

Theodore Roosevelt

BMP; 1 p.; tls.

1. TR probably refers to Sir Walter Hubert (d. 1205), who was the archbishop of Canterbury, papal legate, justiciar of King Richard I, and chancellor of King John. After Hubert's death, King John is reported to have exclaimed: "Now for the first time am I truly king of England" (quoted in Kate Norgate, *England Under the Angevin Kings* [1887; reprint ed. New York: Haskell House, 1969], 2:428–29).

To Roosevelt

337 WEST 87TH STREET
Sept 19th 1917

Dear Theodore:
 If you read the circular, you will see that the sailors rest-house is to be establisht in our old home,—681 West End Avenue, where you have dropt in to lunch on not a few joyous occasions. Perhaps, if you happen to be in town on October 1st, you will drop in again. You needn't speak a piece but you can extend the glad hand.
 I've lots of things that I want to talk over with you; and after Columbia opens we shall hold you to that welcome invitation to luncheon.[1]
 In the mean time I prostrate myself at the feet of Mrs Roosevelt.
                Yours Ever
                Brander Matthews

TRP; 3 pp.; als.
1. TR was unable to accept, due to other commitments (TR to BM, 20 Sept. 1917, TRP).

To Roosevelt

337 WEST 87TH STREET
April 2nd 1918

Dear Theodore:
 I'm just out of St Luke's Hospital, where I underwent a slight operation at the skilful hands of Dr Downes,—who had a hand also in carving you.[1]
 He has been proposed for the Century,—& I wish you would drop a note to the Committee on Admissions, vouching for his desirability.[2]
 I hope that you are taking care of yourself. You are a national asset;—and you must regard yourself as a thrift stamp (raised to the nth).[3]
 Have you heard of the proposed regiment of Kilties, to be recruited only from the Jews? It is to be called the Jordan Highlanders,—and its motto is to be "No advance without security." Every rifle is to fire [three?] balls; and the privates will receive the regular pay, while the officers will also get their commissions.[4]
 My wife joins me in desiring to be remembered most cordially to Mrs Roosevelt.
                Yours Ever
                Brander Matthews

TRP; 4 pp.; als.
1. Dr. William Augustus Downes (1872–1948); attending surgeon at St. Luke's

Hospital, New York City, from 1915 to 1927. Downes had received his M.D. degree from Columbia Univ. in 1895, and had been professor of clinical surgery there since 1913. His specialty was hernia operations.

2. TR wrote the letter of recommendation, noting that Downes was a personal friend and had "attended me professionally" (TR to Century Admissions Committee, 4 Apr. 1918, TRP). Downes was admitted to the Century Club in 1919.

3. After the U.S. entered World War I, the Wilson administration sought to raise revenues and encourage savings by issuing thrift cards and stamps, which earned interest at four percent annum compounded.

4. The Kilties were the Scottish Highlanders regiment of the British army, so nicknamed because they wore their native kilts into battle. BM's little "joke" reflects his anti-Semitic prejudices.

To Matthews

April 4, 1918.

Dear Brander:

I am concerned to learn that you have been in the hospital but very glad to learn that you are out of it. I will write at once for Dr. Downes as you request. I loved your page about the Jordan Highlanders. Give my love to your dear wife.

Faithfully yours,

TRP; 1 p.; cc.

To Roosevelt

337 WEST 87TH STREET

April 12th 1918

Dear Theodore:

J W Johnson, author of "Fifty Years" writes me that you told him that if I'd write to you & request it, you would express in writing your high opinion of his poems. So I hereby formally present this request.[1]

I said what I thought about the high merit of 'Fifty Years' in my brief introduction.[2]

I suppose we have no right to expect better weather from this administration!

Yours Ever

Brander Matthews

TRP; 2 pp.; als.

1. James Weldon Johnson and TR exchanged several letters during 1917–18, and Johnson sent TR an autographed copy of his *Fifty Years & Other Poems* in

Jan. 1918 (Johnson to TR, 17 Jan. 1918, TRP). In early April, Johnson requested a personal meeting with TR in New York City, where Johnson was
field secretary for the NAACP, and TR accepted (Johnson to TR, 5 Apr.
1918, TR's secretary to Johnson, 6 Apr. 1918, TRP). When they met, TR
apparently suggested that Johnson write to BM to request TR's written
opinion of *Fifty Years*; why TR did not simply write the letter directly to
Johnson is a mystery. In any case, TR honored BM's request, and BM for-
warded TR's letter to Johnson (TR to BM, 17 Apr. 1918, below; BM to
Johnson, 21 Apr. 1918, James Weldon Johnson Collection).

2. In his introduction to *Fifty Years*, BM lavishes praise on "Fifty Years"
and on a group of other poems in which Johnson "has been nobly suc-
cessful in expressing the higher aspiration of his own people" (xi–xiv).
Some of BM's well-intentioned remarks about Johnson and African-
American art and literature in general, however, are patronizing (see Oliver,
Brander Matthews, 59–61).

To Matthews

THE KANSAS CITY STAR[1]
April 17, 1918.

My dear Brander:
    I have received the poems of Mr. Johnson with your foreword. I
wish to say how very much pleased I have been with them. They more
than warrant your high opinion of them. I am exceedingly glad that you
have written the introduction for them, and I hope they will be widely
circulated.
                    Faithfully yours,
                    Theodore Roosevelt

James Weldon Johnson Collection; 1 p.; tls.
    1. TR wrote a weekly syndicated column for the *Star*, from the paper's New
York City Office.

To Roosevelt

KENT HOUSE
GREENWICH CONNECTICUT
July 20th 1918

Dear Theodore:
    I postponed writing to you, with the hope that the dread news might
be contradicted.[1] But now I can delay no longer.
    My wife and I want to assure you and Mrs Roosevelt of our deep-
est sympathy and at the same time to send you our congratulations on

the costliness of the sacrifice you have laid on the altar of patriotism.[2] Words cannot assuage your grief; but pride may help you better to bear it,—and to that stern pride no one has a better right than you.

We recall yours as an unusually happy family. Knit by loftiness of purpose as well as by an abundance of love; and we have had the thought of you in our hearts constantly these last few days.

> Yours (now more than ever)
> Brander Matthews

TRP; 2 pp.; als.

1. All four of TR's sons served in World War I. On 17 July 1918, unofficial news dispatches reported that Quentin Roosevelt (1897–1918), a combat pilot, had been shot down behind German lines; his death was confirmed on 20 July. TR would later state that it was "dreadful that [Quentin] should have been killed; it would have been worse if he had not gone" (*LTR*, 8:1368).

2. BM echoes Abraham Lincoln's famous letter of sympathy to Lydia Parker Bixby, who was reported to have lost all five of her sons in battle during the Civil War (only two, as it turned out, had been killed). Lincoln wrote that the bereaved mother's grief would one day be assuaged, leaving only the "solemn pride that must be yours to have laid so costly a sacrifice upon the altar of freedom" (see Carl Sandburg, *Abraham Lincoln: The War Years* [New York: Harcourt, Brace, 1939], 3:666–68). BM printed a facsimile of the letter in his chapter on Lincoln in the 1918 edition of *An Introduction to the Study of American Literature* (see BM to TR, 20 Sept. 1918).

To Matthews

THE KANSAS CITY STAR
July 24th, 1918.

Dear Brander:

I thank you and Mrs. Matthews with all my heart. There isn't any more for me to say.

> Always yours,
> Theodore Roosevelt

BMP; 1 p.; tls.

To Roosevelt

337 WEST 87TH STREET

Sept 6th 1918

Dear Theodore:

It was good to get a glimpse of you, however fleeting.[1] And it will be better to have speech with you. But—if you hold to the opinions I know as I hold to the opinions you know—our [uncensored?] conversation would corruscate with the fireworks of invective. It is a comfort, however, to remember that the mills of God grind slowly—but they grind exceeding fine—sooner or later.[2]

Our loves to Mrs Roosevelt.

Yrs Ever

Brander Matthews

TRP; 2 pp.; als.

1. BM probably caught a glimpse of TR at New York City Hall on 6 Sept. 1918, for TR was the principal speaker that day during celebrations of Lafayette Day and the anniversary of the first Battle of the Marne. TR used the occasion to blast President Wilson's peace plan and to express his opposition to the League of Nations ("Spirit of Victory Marks Marne Day," *New York Times*, 7 Sept. 1918, 3).

2. As the next letter indicates, the invective would have been directed at President Wilson, whom BM despised as much as did TR. The mills did gradually grind Wilson down: on 25 Sept. 1919, he suffered a severe stroke; on 19 Mar. 1920, the Senate handed Wilson a stinging defeat when it rejected the Treaty of Versailles and U.S. membership in the League of Nations.

To Matthews

THE KANSAS CITY STAR

September 13, 1918.

Dear Brander:

I was very much pleased to catch that half-second's glimpse of you the other day. You are good to have written me. I do hope the mills of the Gods begin to grind some time as regards Wilson—but they are awfully slow about it! I help them when I can!

Faithfully yours,

Theodore Roosevelt

BMP; 1 p.; tls.

To Roosevelt

337 WEST 87TH STREET

Sept 20th 1918

Dear Theodore:

More than twenty years ago you wrote a very flattering review of my little book on American literature and in the course of those years it has sold over 200000 copies.[1] Now I have revised it, adding chapters on "Webster & Lincoln," "Mark Twain" and "Field & Riley".[2] I am sending you a copy of the new edition, thinking that you may care to glance over the brief article on Webster and Lincoln. And I want you to look at p. 213, where you will find a facsimile of the famous letter to Mrs Bixby.[3]

My wife joins me in love to you and Mrs Roosevelt.

Yours Ever

Brander Matthews

TRP; 3 pp.; als.

1. See TR to BM, 6 Dec. 1895, n. 2.

2. BM, *An Introduction to the Study of American Literature* (1896, 1911; rev. ed. New York: American, 1918). As BM states, the 1918 edition includes the chapters "Daniel Webster and Abraham Lincoln" (chap. 16), "Mark Twain" (chap. 17), and "Eugene Field and James Whitcomb Riley" (chap. 18). (The Twain essay was not a new addition—BM had included it in the 1911 rev. ed. of the textbook [chap. 17].) BM's essay on Webster (1782–1852) and Lincoln emphasizes the two statesmen's "single-hearted devotion to the Union," and argues for the "permanent value of their occasional addresses" (206). Twain is extolled as the American West's first important writer, and as one of the 19th century's foremost writers in English (226). Midwesterners Field and Riley (1853–1916) are lauded for producing unpretentious lyrics that aimed to "get close to the hearts of the plain people" (230).

3. See BM to TR, 20 July 1918, n. 2.

To Roosevelt

337 WEST 87TH STREET

Oct 29th 1918

Dear Theodore:

I don't believe that you are a sexagenarian—even if you can prove it by the family Bible![1] None the less, we send you our best wishes for the next sixty years.

And I can congratulate you most cordially on your speech at Carnegie Hall.[2] As you may remember I was a Cleveland Democrat, and as such I voted for you twice. That being the case, you can understand that I was hugely delighted to have you talk out in [meeting?]. You said exactly what I have been thinking and what the people need to be told.

Don't bother to acknowledge this; but give our duplicate loves to Mrs Roosevelt.

Yours Ever
Brander Matthews

TRP; 3 pp.; als.

1. TR celebrated his 60th, and final, birthday on 27 Oct. 1918.
2. On 28 Oct. 1918, TR delivered a two-hour speech to a crowd of 5,000 people at a Republican rally in Carnegie Hall. Wilson had three days earlier urged voters to keep the Democratic party in control of Congress, suggesting that his Republican critics had placed politics ahead of the national interest. In his Carnegie speech, TR issued a scathing indictment of Wilson and the Democratic party, charging that they were guilty of a "complete subordination of national interest to partisan welfare"; he urged not only his fellow Republicans but also Democrats and independents to vote Republican ("Roosevelt Bitter in Beginning War on the President," *New York Times,* 29 Oct. 1918, 1, 7). Republicans did gain control of the Senate in the Nov. election.

To Matthews

THE KANSAS CITY STAR
November 4, 1918.[1]

Dear Brander:

It is good to hear from you always. Many thanks and best wishes.

Faithfully yours,
T. R.

BMP; 1 p.; tls.

1. This is the last dated piece of correspondence between TR and BM; TR died of an embolism on 6 Jan. 1919.

Undated

To Matthews

689 Madison Av

Mar 17th [ca. 1890]

My dear Matthews,

Will you lunch with me again next Friday at 1.30 at Delmonicos to meet Tom Newbold and Frank Stetson—two democratic politicians.[1]

When I get you alone some day I shall endeavor to give you a brief glimps of the very real superiority of the Republican over the Democratic party in N.Y. today—so it is quite a noble act in my asking you to meet two such first class fellows of the opposite faith.

Yours sincerely

Theodore Roosevelt

BMP; 2 pp.; als.

1. Thomas Newbold (d.1929), New York state senator; Francis (Frank) Lynde Stetson (1846–1920), prominent New York City attorney and political figure who opposed the Tweed Ring and supported Samuel J. Tilden.

To Matthews

Washington

March 21st [ca. 1890]

My dear Matthews,

I am sorry to say that for the last two days I have scuttled about in vain on your behalf. Reed left for Italy yesterday.[1] Most of the big men of my own party are sulky and weary, and anxious above all things not to talk, even when given their choice of subjects. Why do'n't you get Mayor Grant[2] or Bourk Cochrane[3] or Crimmins[4] to speak to you on "The real facts about our Municipal Government"?[5] (not that they would tell you the real facts); and then let some kid glove gentleman answer.

I am coming on about the 1st of April, and we'll arrange some dinner or small [spree?] together; and we'll include Sturgis, who seems a very good fellow, and Stedman if we can get him.[6] Is Harrigan acting in any play worth seeing?[7]

Yours faithfully

Theodore Roosevelt

BMP; 4 p.; als.

1. House Speaker Thomas B. Reed; see TR to BM, 10 Feb. 1890, n. 3. This letter was probably written during the wearying debates over the international copyright act.
2. Hugh J. Grant (1852–1910); mayor of New York from 1889 to 1892, and member of the Tammany Hall machine; he was defeated by reform candidate William Strong in the 1894 mayoral election.
3. W. Bourke Cockran (1854–1923); Irish-immigrant lawyer who earned a reputation as Tammany's favorite orator. He was a Democratic congressman (1886–88, 1890–94), but he changed party allegiances several times in later years. In the election of 1912, he supported TR (whom he had verbally attacked in earlier days) and ran for Congress (unsuccessfully) on the Progressive ticket.
4. John Daniel Crimmins (1844–1917); New York City contractor and political figure. He served as the city's park commissioner from 1883 to 1888; Gov. TR appointed him to the Greater New York Charter Revision Commission in 1894.
5. Probably another effort by BM to recruit speakers for a Nineteenth Century Club debate. The club hosted a debate on the topic of municipal government and partisan politics, at Sherry's in New York on 11 Dec. 1895; but none of the people mentioned in this letter was on the four-person panel of speakers ("Politics Their Theme," *New York Times*, 12 Dec. 1895, 3).
6. Probably Russell Sturgis; see TR to BM, 28 Dec. 1890, n. 1.
7. Edward Harrigan (1845–1911); playwright, producer, and actor, whose comic portrayals of New York ethnic—esp. Irish-immigrant—life were very popular during the latter decades of the 19th century. Harrigan wrote and acted the lead role in 39 plays, many of which were performed in his own New York City theaters.

To Matthews

Washington
D.C.
Nov 19th [1892?]

Dear Brander,

The Cosmopolitan outfit is an irritating crew to deal with; without any notice to me they have blandly cut out various sentences and paragraphs from my piece, including, to my especial regret, one in reference to your "Poems of American Patriotism."[1]

I shall be back for several days after Thanksgiving; wo'n't you lunch with me at Del's[2] someday? and I'll ask Howells—and Bunner too, if you say so. Regards to Mrs M.

Yours
Theodore Roosevelt

BMP; 3 pp.; als.

1. TR may be referring to proofs of his article "A Colonial Survival," which appeared in *Cosmopolitan* in Dec. 1892 (see TR to BM, 25 Feb. 1892, n. 1.); if so, this letter was written in 1892.
2. Delmonico's restaurant.

To Matthews

SAGAMORE HILL

Oct 5th [ca. 1895]

Dear Brander,

My sister, Mrs. Cowles, wants you to lunch with her (to meet me! & probably Jacob Riis & Grant La Farge[1]) at 1.30 on Monday the 11th, at 689 Madison Av. so I shall expect to see you then. I am very anxious to see you, about several matters.

Yours always

Theodore Roosevelt

BMP; 2 pp.; als.

1. Christopher Grant La Farge (1862–1938); son of painter John La Farge, Christopher was an architect. His designs include several New York landmarks as well as TR's library at Sagamore Hill. La Farge was also active on advisory committees of the School of Architecture at Columbia.

Selected Bibliography

Unpublished Materials

James Weldon Johnson Collection. Collection of American Literature, Beinecke Rare Book and Manuscript Library, Yale University, New Haven, Conn.

Brander Matthews Papers. Rare Book and Manuscript Library, Columbia University, New York, N.Y.

Theodore Roosevelt Papers. Microfilm. Library of Congress, Washington, D.C.

Charles Scribner's Sons Archives. Princeton University Library, Princeton, N.J.

Books and Articles

Aaron, Daniel. "Theodore Roosevelt as Cultural Artifact." *Raritan* 9 (Winter 1990): 109–26.

Bender, Thomas. *New York Intellect: A History of Intellectual Life in New York City, from 1750 to the Beginnings of Our Own Time.* New York: Knopf, 1987.

Birrell, Augustine. *Essays about Men, Women and Books.* New York: Scribner's, 1894.

Boyesen, H. H. "American Literary Criticism and Its Value." *Forum* 15 (June 1893): 459–66.

Burgess, John W. "Germany, Great Britain, and the United States." *Political Science Quarterly* 19 (1904): 1–19.

———. "Present Problems of Constitutional Law." *Political Science Quarterly* 19 (Dec. 1904): 545–78.

Butler, Nicholas Murray. *Across the Busy Years: Recollections and Reflections.* New York: Scribner's, 1939.

Campbell, Oscar Joseph. "The Department of English and Comparative Literature." In *A History of the Faculty of Philosophy, Columbia University.* Ed. Jacques Barzun. New York: Columbia University Press, 1957. 58–101.

Century Association. *The Century, 1847–1946.* New York: Century Association, 1957.

Cowles, Anna Roosevelt, ed. *Letters from Theodore Roosevelt to Anna Roosevelt Cowles, 1870–1918.* New York and London: Scribner's, 1924.

Cutright, Paul Russell. *Theodore Roosevelt: The Making of a Conservationist.* Urbana: University of Illinois Press, 1985.

Decker, William Merrill. *The Literary Vocation of Henry Adams.* Chapel Hill: University of North Carolina Press, 1990.

Demoor, Marysa, ed. *Friends over the Ocean: Andrew Lang's American Correspondents, 1881–1912.* Rijksuniversiteit Gent, 1989.

Dyer, Thomas G. *Theodore Roosevelt and the Idea of Race.* Baton Rouge: Louisiana State University Press, 1980.

Garland, Hamlin. *Companions on the Trail: A Literary Chronicle.* New York: Macmillan, 1931.

———. *Crumbling Idols: Twelve Essays on Art Dealing Chiefly with Literature, Painting, and the Drama.* 1894; rpt. ed. Cambridge, Mass.: Harvard University Press, 1960.

———. *Main-Travelled Roads.* 1891, 1922; rpt. ed. New York: Signet, 1962.

Garraty, John A. *Henry Cabot Lodge: A Biography.* New York: Knopf, 1965.

Gibson, William M. *Theodore Roosevelt Among the Humorists: W. D. Howells, Mark Twain, and Mr. Dooley.* Knoxville: University of Tennessee Press, 1980.

Giddings, Franklin H. "The American People." *International Quarterly* 7 (June 1903): 281–99.

———. "Sovereignty and Government." *Political Science Quarterly* 21 (Mar. 1906): 1–27.

Gould, Lewis L. *The Presidency of Theodore Roosevelt.* Lawrence: University Press of Kansas, 1991.

Hamilton, Clayton. "Brander." *Scribner's Magazine* 86 (July-Dec. 1929): 82–87.

Howells, William Dean. *Selected Letters of W. D. Howells.* Ed. Thomas Wortham et al. Boston: Twayne, 1981.

Johnson, James Weldon. *Along This Way: The Autobiography of James Weldon Johnson.* New York: Viking, 1933.

———. *The Autobiography of an Ex-Coloured Man.* Boston: Sherman, French, 1912.

———. *Fifty Years & Other Poems.* Boston: Cornhill, 1917; rpt. ed. New York: AMS, 1975.

Kipling, Rudyard. *Something of Myself for My Friends Known and Unknown.* New York: Doubleday, 1937.

Lang, Andrew. *Essays in Little.* New York: Scribner's, 1891.

———. *Letters to Dead Authors.* New York: Scribner's, 1886.

Langford, Gerald. *The Richard Harding Davis Years: A Biography of Mother and Son.* New York: Holt, Rinehart, 1961.

Lanson, Gustave. "Deux 'Lectures' Académiques à New York." *Revue des Deux Mondes* 37 (Feb. 1917): 800–812.

Leech, Margaret. *In the Days of McKinley.* New York: Harper, 1959.

Lemaître, Jules. *Théories et Impressions.* Paris: Société Française d'Imprimerie et de Librairie, 1903.

Lodge, Henry Cabot. *Certain Accepted Heroes and Other Essays in Literature and Politics.* New York: Harper, 1897.

———. *Early Memories.* New York: Scribner's, 1913.

———. *Historical and Political Essays.* 1892; rpt. ed. Freeport, N.Y.: Books for Libraries Press, 1972.

———. *Studies in History.* 1884; rpt. ed. Freeport, N.Y.: Books for Libraries Press, 1972.

———, ed. *Selections from the Correspondence of Theodore Roosevelt and Henry Cabot Lodge, 1884–1918.* 2 vols. New York: Scribner's, 1925.

Lounsbury, Thomas R. "Confessions of a Spelling Reformer." *Atlantic Monthly* 99 (May 1907): 614–31.

McCutcheon, John Tinney. *T. R. in Cartoons.* Chicago: McClurg, 1910.

Matthews, Brander. *American Authors and British Pirates.* New York: American Copyright League, 1889.

———. *The American of the Future and Other Essays.* New York: Scribner's, 1909.

———. "American Scholar: Thomas Raynesford Lounsbury." *Century Magazine* 55 (Feb. 1898): 560–65.

———. "Americanism." *Harper's Round Table,* 6 July 1897, 873–74.

———. *Americanisms and Briticisms: With Other Essays on Other Isms.* New York: Harper, 1892.

———. "Andrew Lang." *Century Magazine* 47 (Jan. 1894): 375–81.

———. "As to 'American Spelling.'" *Harper's Monthly* 85 (July 1892): 277–84.

———. *Aspects of Fiction.* 1896; rpt. ed. Upper Saddle River, N.J.: Gregg, 1970.

———. *Bookbindings Old and New: Notes of a Booklover, with an Account of the Grolier Club of New York.* New York: Macmillan, 1895.

———. *Books and Play-books: Essays on Literature and Drama.* London: Osgood, McIlvane, 1895.

———. "Briticisms and Americanisms." *Harper's Monthly* 83 (July 1891): 215–22.

———. "A Cameo and a Pastel." *Harper's Monthly* 86 (Dec. 1892): 130–35.

———. "Can English Literature Be Taught?" *Educational Review* 3 (Apr. 1892): 337–47.

———. *Cheap Books and Good Books.* New York: American Copyright League, 1888.

———. "Concerning Certain American Essayists." *Cosmopolitan* 13 (May 1892): 86–91.

———. *The Decision of the Court: A Comedy.* New York: Harper, 1893.

———. "A Decoration Day Revery." *Century Magazine* 40 (May 1890): 102–5.

———. "The Dramatization of Novels." *Longman's Magazine* 14 (Oct. 1889): 599–603.

———. "English at Columbia College." *Dial* 16 (16 Feb. 1894): 101–2.

———. "The Evolution of Copyright." *Political Science Quarterly* 5 (Dec. 1890): 583–602.

———. *A Family Tree and Other Stories.* New York: Longmans, Green, 1889.

———. "Foreign Words in English Speech." *Harper's Monthly* 107 (Aug. 1903): 476–79.

———. *French Dramatists of the Nineteenth Century.* New York: Scribner's, 1881. Rev. eds. 1891 and 1901.

———. "The Frog that Played the Trombone." *Harper's Monthly* 87 (Nov. 1893): 911–17.

———. *Fugitives from Justice.* New York: Corlies, Macy, 1912.

———. "The Function of Slang." *Harper's Monthly* 87 (July 1893): 304–12.

———. "The Future Literary Capital of the United States." *Lippincott's Magazine* 37 (Jan.–June 1886): 104–9.

———. *Gateways to Literature and Other Essays.* 1912; rpt. ed. Freeport, N.Y.: Books for Libraries Press, 1968.

———. "'Hamlet' with Hamlet Left out." *Yale Review* 5 (Oct. 1915): 117–26.

———. *His Father's Son: A Novel of New York.* New York: Harper, 1895.

———. *The Historical Novel and Other Essays.* New York: Scribner's, 1901.

———. *In the Vestibule Limited.* New York: Harper, 1892.

————. Introduction. *Bunker-Hill; or, The Death of General Warren: An Historical Tragedy.* By John Burk. 1797; rpt. ed. New York: Dunlap Society, 1891. 1–14.

————. Introduction. *Fifty Years & Other Poems.* By James Weldon Johnson. 1917; rpt. ed. New York: AMS, 1975. xi–xiv.

————. *An Introduction to the Study of American Literature.* New York: American Book, 1896. Rev. eds. 1911 and 1918.

————. "Irish Plays and Playwrights." *Scribner's Magazine* 61 (Jan. 1917): 85–90.

————. "A Letter of Farewell." *Scribner's Magazine* 19 (May 1896): 644–48.

————. "Memories." *Scribner's Magazine* 6 (Aug. 1889): 168–75.

————. "Mugwumps." *Saturday Review* (London) 58 (24 Nov. 1884): 658–59.

————. "The Muses of Manhattan." *Cosmopolitan* 14 (Jan. 1893): 324–32.

————. "New York as a Historic Town." *Century Magazine* 41 (Jan. 1891): 476–77.

————. *Notes on Speech-making.* New York: Longmans, Green, 1901.

————. *Outlines in Local Color.* 1897; rpt. ed. Freeport, N.Y.: Books for Libraries Press, 1969.

————. *Parts of Speech: Essays on English.* New York: Scribner's, 1901.

————. *Pen and Ink: Papers on Subjects of More or Less Importance.* 1888; New York: Scribner's, 1902.

————. *Recreations of an Anthologist.* New York: Dodd, Mead, 1904.

————. "Reform and Reformers." *North American Review* 183 (21 Sept. 1906): 461–73.

————. *Royal Marine: An Idyl of Narragansett Pier.* New York: Harper, 1894.

————. *Shakspere as a Playwright.* New York: Scribner's, 1913.

————. "The Spelling of Yesterday and To-morrow." *Outlook* 82 (14 Apr. 1906): 848–53.

————. *The Story of a Story and Other Stories.* 1893; rpt. ed. Freeport, N.Y.: Books for Libraries Press, 1969.

————. *Studies of the Stage.* New York: Harper, 1894.

————. *A Study of Versification.* Boston: Houghton Mifflin, 1911.

————. "The Supreme Leaders." *Munsey's Magazine* 34 (Jan. 1906): 460–65.

————. *The Theatres of Paris.* New York: Scribner's, 1880.

————. "Theodore Roosevelt as a Man of Letters." In *The Works of Theodore Roosevelt: National Edition,* ed. Hermann Hagedorn. New York: Scribner's, 1926. 12:ix–xx.

————. *These Many Years: Recollections of a New Yorker.* New York: Scribner's, 1917.

————. *Tom Paulding: The Story of a Search for Buried Treasure in the Streets of New York.* New York: Century, 1892.

————. *Vignettes of Manhattan.* New York: Harper, 1894.

————, ed. *American Familiar Verse.* New York: Longmans, Green, 1904.

————, ed. *Poems of American Patriotism.* New York: Scribner's, 1882.

————, ed. *The Poems of H. C. Bunner.* New York: Scribner's, 1896.

Miller, Nathan. *Theodore Roosevelt: A Life.* New York: William Morrow, 1992.

Morris, Edmund. *The Rise of Theodore Roosevelt.* New York: Coward, McCann and Geoghegan, 1979.

Morris, Sylvia Jukes. *Edith Kermit Roosevelt: Portrait of a First Lady.* 1980; rpt. ed. New York: Vintage, 1990.

Norton, Aloysius A. *Theodore Roosevelt.* Boston: Twayne, 1980.

Oliver, Lawrence J. "Brander Matthews." *Bibliography of American Fiction, 1866–1918.* Ed. James Nagel and Gwen Nagel. New York: Manly, 1993. 282–84.

———. *Brander Matthews, Theodore Roosevelt, and the Politics of American Literature, 1880–1920.* Knoxville: University of Tennessee Press, 1992.

Peck, Harry Thurston. "American Newspapers." *Living Age* 215 (11 Dec. 1897): 761–62.

Rand, Laurance B. *High Stakes: The Life and Times of Leigh S. J. Hunt.* New York: Peter Lang, 1989.

Repplier, Agnes. "Pastels—A Query." *Cosmopolitan* 16 (Apr. 1894): 762–64.

———. "The Praises of War." *Atlantic Monthly* 68 (Dec. 1891): 796–805.

———. "Wit and Humor." *Atlantic Monthly* 70 (Dec. 1892): 801–8.

Riis, Jacob A. *Theodore Roosevelt, the Citizen.* New York: Outlook, 1904.

Roosevelt, Theodore. *The Letters of Theodore Roosevelt.* Ed. Elting E. Morison et al. 8 vols. Cambridge, Mass.: Harvard University Press, 1951–54.

———. *The Works of Theodore Roosevelt: National Edition.* Ed. Hermann Hagedorn. 20 vols. New York: Scribner's, 1926.

Shaler, Nathan S. "The Natural History of War." *International Quarterly* 8 (Sept. 1903): 17–30.

Slotkin, Richard. "Nostalgia and Progress: Theodore Roosevelt's Myth of the Frontier." *American Quarterly* 33 (1981): 608–37.

Spector, Ronald. *Admiral of the New Empire: The Life and Career of George Dewey.* Columbia: University of South Carolina Press, 1974.

Sproat, John G. *"The Best Men": Liberal Reformers in the Gilded Age.* New York: Oxford University Press, 1968.

Steffens, Lincoln. *The Autobiography of Lincoln Steffens.* New York: Harcourt, Brace, 1931.

Trent, William P. "Mr. Brander Matthews as a Critic." *Sewanee Review* 3 (May 1895): 373–84.

———. "The Teaching of English Literature." *Sewanee Review* 1 (May 1893): 257–72.

———. "Theodore Roosevelt as a Historian." *Forum* 21 (July 1896): 566–76.

Wharton, Edith. *A Backward Glance.* New York: Scribner's, 1933. Rpt. ed. 1964.

Wister, Owen. *Roosevelt: The Story of a Friendship 1880–1919.* New York: Macmillan, 1930.

Index

Aaron, Daniel, xvii
Abbot, Lyman, 190n
Adams, Charles Francis, 10, 11n
Adams, Henry, xvii, 52n, 78, 79n;
    Roosevelt's opinion of Adams's *De-
    mocracy,* 163
Adler, Felix, xxiii
Albert, Kaiser Friedrich Wilhelm, 212
Alden, Henry M., 210–11
Aldrich, Thomas Bailey, 12n, 55n
Alger, Russell Alexander, 124, 125n
Allen, James Lane, 103
Allston, Washington, 50–51
American Academy of Arts and Letters, xx,
    157, 158n, 200, 202–3, 206, 209n, 215
American Copyright League, 8n
American Historical Association, 199, 209n
Americanism, xvii, xxiv–xxv, 16, 26, 28, 31,
    35, 52n, 54, 64, 81, 85, 107–8, 212n
Ammon, John Henry, 16
Anti-Semitism, 140, 141n, 218n
Archer, William, 61, 115
Arnold, Sir Edwin, 56
Arnold, Matthew, xix
Association for International Conciliation,
    208n
Athenaeum Club, 128
Atkinson, Edward, 94
Atlantic Monthly, 51–52, 77, 82, 99, 179, 181
Aubert, Louis, 141, 142n, 143, 172, 173n
Authors Club, 25

Bacon, Sir Francis, 110n, 161, 162n
Bartlett, Edward T., 63, 64n
Beardsley, Aubrey, 84n
Bernini, Giovanni Lorenzo, 189
Bierce, Ambrose, 33, 34n
Birrell, Augustine, 72, 74, 75n
Bixby, Lydia Parker, 220n; and letter to
    Abraham Lincoln, 222
Black, William, 152, 153n
Blaine, James G., 5
Bloch, Ivan, 152n

Boas, Franz, xxiii–xxiv, 207, 208n
Boissier, Gaston, 185, 208
Bookman, The (magazine), 101
Boone and Crockett Club, 24, 65, 73–74, 121
Booth, Agnes, 56
Booth, Edwin, 13n, 56n; memorial tribute
    for, 63
Booth, Mary Louise, 6
Borrow, George Henry ("Lavengro"), 188n
Boulanger, Georges Ernest, 124, 125n
Boulger, Demetrius Charles, 133, 134n
Boyesen, Hjalmar Hjorth, 15, 58, 59n
Boynton, Edward Carlisle, 127
Brander Matthews Dramatic Museum, 211n
Brieux, Eugène, 205, 206n
Brown, Charles Brockden, 100
Brown, John, 133, 134n
Brownell, William Crary, 169
Brunetière, Ferdinand, 154–57
Buller, Sir Redvers, 124, 125n
Bunner, Henry Cuyler, xxiii, 5, 6n, 41, 45,
    54, 55n, 57, 66, 69, 75, 146, 156, 158–59,
    225
Bunyan, John, 171n
Burden (I. Townsend) robbery, 101
Burgess, John W., xxiii, 144–45, 149, 154
Burk, John, 30
Burroughs, John, 130, 131n
Butler, Nicholas Murray, xxiii, 114, 118, 119n,
    128, 137, 142–43, 146, 148, 150, 157, 159,
    160n, 166, 169, 183
Butler, Rosa, 158n
Byron, George Gordon, 81

Campbell, Douglas, 41
Carlisle, John Griffin, 14
Carlyle, Thomas 208, 209n, 212
Carmencita, 49
Carnegie, Andrew, xix, 152, 153n, 172n, 178n–
    79n
Carr, Joseph W. Comyns, 60, 61n
Catiline, 185
Century Club, 46–47, 217, 218n

Century Magazine, 52
Chanler, Winthrop Astor, 60, 61n, 69
Charles Scribner's Sons, 205, 210
Chicago World's Fair. *See* Columbian Exposition
Choate, Joseph Hodges, 159, 160n
Cicero, Marcus Tullius, 185
Cleveland, Grover, 3n, 5n, 60n, 62n, 66n, 84n, 222
Cochrane, Bourk, 224, 225n
Coler, Bird Sim, 118, 119n
Columbia College/University, xxiii, 18n, 27n, 52n, 53n, 107n, 115n, 143n, 149, 162, 165n, 196n, 207, 209n, 210n, 212n, 217
Columbia University Quarterly, 169
Columbian Exposition, 58, 59n
Cooper, James Fenimore, xxv, 27n, 31n, 169–70, 179–81, 182n
Cooper Union for the Advancement of Science and Art, 31, 32n
Copyright Act of 1891 (Platt-Simmonds Act), 8n, 9, 14, 25; *see also* Matthews and Roosevelt subheadings
Coquelin, Benoit Constant, xix, 119–20
Cosmopolitan Magazine, 225
Coudert, Frederic Rene, 15
Cowles, Anna. *See* Roosevelt, Anna
Cowles, William Sheffield, 169
Crane, Stephen, 84n
Crawford, Francis Marion, 85
Crimmins, John Daniel, 224, 225n
Critic (magazine), 50–51, 52n, 54–55
Cullum, George Washington, 127

Dallin, Cyrus E., 59n
Daly, Augustin, 211
Darwin, Charles, 210n
Davis, Cushman Kellogg, 81
Davis, Henry Charles, Jr., 65, 66n
Davis, Richard Harding, 33, 34n, 46, 60, 70, 71n
Delano, Francis H., 133
Delano, P. W., 133–34
De Nevers, M. Edmond, 155n
Derby, Richard, 201–2
Dewey, George, 117, 118n, 123n, 203
Dial (magazine), 68, 75n
Dow, Charles M., 168
Downes, William Augustus, 217, 218n
Doyle, Arthur Conan, 147, 148n

Draper, Andrew, 35
Dreyfus, Alfred, 119, 120n, 140
Dunlap Society, 30
Dunphy, John Edward, 17
Durand, E. Dana, 138n

Eagan, Charles Patrick, 124, 125n
Emerson, Ralph Waldo, 93, 110n
Emmet, Thomas Addis, 5, 6n
Everett, William, 70, 71n

Faguet, Émile, 193
Fairlie, John A., 117n
Farragut, David Glasgow, 117, 118n
Fassett, Jacob Sloat, 27
Fawcett, Edgar, 17, 83
Ferguson, Patrick, 57
Field, Eugene, 45, 222
Field, Kate, xix
Fish, Hamilton, Jr., 115n
Fisher, Sydney G., 68n
Fiske, John, 41
Flagg, Jared Bradley, 51n
Ford, Henry Jones, 154
Ford, James Lauren, 88
Forest and Stream (magazine), 73
Forum, The (magazine), 99, 110
Fox, John, Jr., 93
Franklin, Benjamin, xx–xxi, 70, 71n, 93n, 158
Frederick the Great, 209n, 212
French, Daniel C., 59n
Fur and Feather (book series), 73–74

G. P. Putnam's Sons, 105–6, 107n
Garland, Hamlin, xvii, xxvi, 81–83, 84n, 89–90, 91n, 103, 108n, 201
Gausseron, B. H., 80n
George, Henry, 103
Gibbon, Edward, 208, 209n
Giddings, Franklin H., xxiii–xxiv, 131, 133, 170, 182–83
Gilder, Jeanette, 52n
Gilder, Joseph, xxii, 52n
Gilder, Richard Watson, xxiii, 7, 24, 33, 41, 52n, 53, 88
Gillette, William H., 95
Gilman, Daniel Coit, 74
Gladstone, William, 133, 134n
Godkin, Edwin Lawrence, 69n, 104n, 163n
Gordon, Charles, 133–34

Gordon, John Campbell Hamilton (Lord
    Aberdeen), 95
Grant, Hugh J., 224, 225n
Grant, Ulysses S., 20
Greene, Nathanael, 57
Gresham, Walter Q., 62n
Grinnell, George Bird, 73–74
Guild, Curtis, Jr., 107n

Hague Tribunal, 161, 162n
Hall, Fitzeward, 70
Halstead, Murat, 9, 24
Hamilton, Clayton, 4n
Hannay, David, 114n
Harcourt, Vernon, 171–72n
Harper's Monthly, 210
Harper's Weekly, 133
Harrigan, Edward, 224, 225n
Harris, Joel Chandler, 83, 84n
Harrison, Benjamin, 3n
Harrison, Frederic, 13n
Hart, Albert Bushnell, 46, 47n, 53, 136
Harvard University, xvii, 78, 79n, 137, 138n, 158n
Hawley, Joseph Roswell, 24
Hawthorne, Julian, 37, 38n
Hawthorne, Nathaniel, 38n
Hay, John, 97, 151n, 158n, 161, 162n, 163
Hayes, Rutherford B., 203
Hazen, Mildred, 117n
Hazen, William B., 117
Hearst, William Randolph, 146–47, 187n
Henderson, George F. R., 193, 194n
Heney, Francis Joseph, 181, 182n
Herbert, Hilary, 65, 66n
Herford, Oliver Brooke, 149, 152
Higginson, Thomas Wentworth, 31, 32n,
    35n, 37
Hill, David Bennet, 64n, 118, 119n
Holmes, Oliver Wendell, 46
Holt, Harrison Jewell, 137
Homer, 41n, 82, 163–64
Howells, William Dean, xvii, 17, 18n, 31, 33–
    34, 37, 41, 42n, 46, 53, 103, 108n, 126–27,
    158n, 161, 162n, 163, 225; *Boy's Town*, 23;
    Roosevelt's criticism of, 89, 90n
Hubert, Sir Walter, 216
Hughes, Charles Evans, 187
Hunt, Leigh S. J., 123–24, 131–33, 159, 161;
    director of Sudan Plantations Syndi-
    cate Board, 160n

Immigration, 82, 83n–84n, 131n
Independent (magazine), 182
International Quarterly, 131–32, 137

James, Henry, 15n, 80n, 84n, 128n;
    Roosevelt's disdain of, 83
Jameson, John Franklin, 11n
Jefferson, Joseph, 157, 158n, 159
Jefferson, Thomas, xx, 157
Jeffries, James J., 177
Jenkins, Fleeming, 212n
Jerome, William Travers, 182n
Jewett, Sarah Orne, 36, 37n
Johnson, James Weldon, xix, xxiv, 190, 197,
    198n, 199–200, 218–19
Johnson, Robert Underwood, 202
Johnston, George D., 60n
Jones, Charles H., 9n
Jusserand, Jean Jules, 161–62, 177, 182, 186

Kansas City Star, 219n
Kipling, Rudyard, xvii, 36, 46, 47n, 58, 77,
    78n, 83, 90, 91n, 97, 100, 128, 199n; let-
    ter to Matthews about Roosevelt, 191;
    Roosevelt's first meeting with, 96
Kitchener, Horatio, 128
Kyle, James Henderson, 90–91n

Ladies' Home Journal, 208, 209n
La Farge, Grant, 226
La Farge, John, 165
Lang, Andrew, 8, 10–13, 25, 30, 34, 37, 41, 43,
    49, 50n, 51, 55, 57, 67, 69n, 77–78, 88n,
    181
Lanson, Gustave, 215
Lavengro, 188
Lawrence, William L., 195–96
League of Nations, 221n
Lee, Alice Hathaway, 3
Lee, Henry ("Light-Horse Harry"), 57
Lee, Robert E., 12n, 56
Lehlbach, Herman, 16
Lemaître, Jules, 139–42
Library of the World's Best Literature
    (Warner's), 214, 216
Lincoln, Abraham, xx–xxi, 73n, 94n, 109,
    117, 130, 212n, 220n, 222
Littell, Eliakim, 76n
Living Age (magazine), 76
Lodge, George ("Bay"), 147, 148n

Lodge, Henry Cabot, xix, 3, 4n, 9, 14, 21, 24–25, 27–28, 31, 35, 41, 46–47, 52, 56, 61–66, 68, 70, 75, 77–78, 80, 82, 92, 110n, 111, 154n, 182n; Certain Accepted Heroes and Other Essays, 108, 109n; "Colonialism in the United States," 28; Early Memories, 203; Hero Tales from American History, 85n–86n, 97; "The Opportunity of the Republican Party," 72, 73n

Loeb, William, 173, 174n

Longfellow, Henry Wadsworth, 19, 197, 198n

Longman, Charles James, 7

Loubat, Joseph Florimond, 52n; see also Loubat Prize

Loubat Prize, 52–53

Louis XIV, King, 189

Lounsbury, Thomas Raynesford, 39, 40n, 74, 75n, 101, 113, 158, 182n; and simplified-spelling movement, 40n, 178–80, 180n

Low, Seth, 31, 32n, 52n

Lowell, James Russell, 65, 66n, 110n

Lummis, Charles Fletcher, 183, 184n

Mabie, Hamilton, 146, 147n

Macaulay, Thomas Babington, 208, 209n, 212

MacDowell, Edward, 143n

Maclay, Edgar Stanton, 123n

Macy, Nelson, 169

Mahan, Alfred Thayer, 53, 54n, 82, 83n, 107, 108n, 166

Mahone, William, 7

Manderson, Charles Frederick, 90, 91n

Matthews, Ada, 4, 25, 62, 130, 151–52, 182, 184, 193, 197, 205 and passim

Matthews, Brander: advisory editor to Harper and Brothers, 105n; awarded French Legion of Honor, 177; Cleveland Democrat, 222; and Columbia College/University, xviii, 76n, 119n, 162; on heroic ideal, 133; influence on Roosevelt, xxii–xxiii; and jingoism, 107n; and Rudyard Kipling, 36n; and literary Americanism, 34n, 38n, 84n, 162n; and literary centers, 17, 18n, 84n; and literary clubs, xviii, 38n, 128; on "melting pot," 195; and the Nation,

47n, 69n; on New York City, 87n; racial ideology, 150, 160, 195, 205; and Agnes Repplier, 35, 47; and simplified spelling, 38; and Southern literature, 42n; testimonial dinner for, 66; and William P. Trent, 75

—Writings: American Authors and British Pirates, 8n; "American Character," 162, 169–70; "American Epigrams," 153n; American Familiar Verse, 158–59; The American of the Future, 155n; "An American Scholar: Thomas Raynesford Lounsbury," 113; "Americanism," 107–8; Americanisms and Briticisms, 24n, 40n, 52n, 55n, 58, 70n, 72n, 94, 99n; "Andrew Lang," 12n, 67, 71; "Apology for Technic," 160n; "As to 'American Spelling,'" 38, 39n, 40n; "At a Private View," 87n; "Before the Break of Day," 84n; "Benjamin Franklin," 70, 71n, 72, 73n; "Bookbindings of the Past," 78, 79n; "Briticisms and Americanisms," 26, 31n, 41, 59, 72; "A Cameo and a Pastel," 49, 77; "Can English Be Taught?" 34n; Cheap Books and Good Books, 8n; "Concerning Certain American Essayists," 32n, 35n, 37n; "Concerning Certain Contemporary Essayists," 110; The Decision of the Court, 55–56; "A Decoration Day Revery," 14; "The Dramatizatioin of Novels," 8, 95n; "English at Columbia College," 76; "The Evolution of Copyright," 10n, 12n; "Fenimore Cooper," 181; "Foreign Words in English Speech," 135; French Dramatists of the Nineteenth Century, 22n, 28n; "The Frog that Played the Trombone," 58, 62; Fugitives from Justice, 197n; "The Function of Slang," 59, 60n; "'Hamlet' with Hamlet Left out," 211n; His Father's Son, 99n; The Historical Novel and Other Essays, 122n; "Ignorance and Insularity," 12n–13n, 50n, 55n; "In the Little Church down the Street," 87n; "In the Midst of Life," 66, 67n; "In the Vestibule Limited," 33n; In the Vestibule Limited, 32, 33n; An Introduction to the Study of American Literature, xviii, xxii, 38n, 88n, 99n, 100, 136, 220n,

222; "Irish Plays and Irish Playwrights," 214n; "A Letter of Farewell," 101, 102n; "Literary Independence of the United States," 28n; "Memories," 5, 6n; "More American Stories," 34n; "The Muses of Manhattan," 49; "New York as a Historic Town," 23; "A Note on Recent Briticisms," 91, 92n; *Notes on Speech-making*, 122n, 193, 194n; "Of Women's Novels," 19n; *Outlines in Local Color*, 107–9; *Parts of Speech: Essays On English*, 122n, 135, 136n; "The Penalty of Humor," 48n, 102n; "Picturesque New York," 49, 50n; *Poems of American Patriotism*, 88n, 97, 225; *The Poems of H. C. Bunner*, 156n; "Ralph Waldo Emerson," 93; *Recreations of an Anthologist*, 152, 153n, 155–56, 158; "Reform and Reformers," 174–75; review of Roosevelt's *Autobiography*, 203, 205; "Robert Louis Stevenson," 93; "Royal Marine: An Idyl of Narragansett Pier," 84, 85n; *The Royal Marine: An Idyl of Narragansett Pier*, 88, 90n; *Shakspere as a Playwright*, 204, 206; "Some Personal Preferences," 88n; "Songs of the Civil War," 31n; "The Speech of the Evening" 62n; "The Spelling of Yesterday and To-morrow," 172n; *A Study of Versification*, 193, 194n, 195; "The Supreme Leaders," 166; *The Theatres of Paris*, 22n; "Theodore Roosevelt as a Man of Letters," xx, 214n; *Tom Paulding*, 32; "The True Theory of the Preface," 21n; "Two Studies of the South," 41–43; *Vignettes of Manhattan*, 67n, 77, 79, 80n, 83, 86, 87n, 189n; "The Whole Duty of Critics," 60n
Matthews, Edith Brander, 96, 130, 169
Matthews, Edward, xviii
Matthews, John, 143n
Matthews, Nathan, 20
Matthews, Virginia Brander, 44, 45n, 49, 139
Maynard, Isaac H., 63, 64n
McAllister, Samuel Ward, 19, 94
McClure's Magazine, 165
McCutcheon, John Tinney, 150
McGaffey, Ernest, 55
McKim, Charles Follen, 149

McKinley, William, 14, 117n, 122n, 125n
Metropolitan Club, 121
Metropolitan Magazine, 215n
Meyer, George von Lengerke, 154–55
Miles, Nelson A., 124, 125n
Mills, Roger Quarles, 14
Milton, John, 82
Mitford, William, 81, 82n
Modern Language Association, 199
Mohonk conference on Indian affairs, 43–45
"Molly Pitcher" (Molly Ludwig), 87, 88n
Morse, Anson Daniel, 42, 43n
Motley, John Lothrop, 53
Moxie (soft drink), 133–36
Mugwumps, 5, 6n, 187n
Munsey's Magazine, 166–67
Museum of War and Peace (Lucerne), 152

Nation, The (magazine), 69n, 107, 108n
National Academy of Arts and Letters. *See* American Academy of Arts and Letters
National Institute of Arts and Letters, xxv, 158n, 199–201, 203, 206
Nationalism. *See* Americanism
Naval Academy, 167–68
Needham, Henry Beach, 165n
Nelson, Horatio, 133, 134n, 212, 213n
New York Evening Post, 69, 103, 104n, 111, 142–43, 145, 156, 157n, 163, 174, 195
Newbold, Thomas, 224
Niagara Falls, 167, 168n, 169n
Nineteenth Century Club, xix, 9n, 15, 19n, 20–21, 23, 32, 43n, 225n
North American Review, 174–77
Norton, Charles Eliot, 158

O'Laughlin, John Callan, 192n
O'Reilly, John Boyle, 15–16
Osborne, Henry Fairfield, 210
Ottendorfer, Oswald, 16
Out West (magazine), 183, 184n
Outing (magazine), 73
Outlook (magazine), 167, 190n
Overland Monthly, 82, 84n

Page, Thomas Nelson, 36, 37n, 41, 42n
Paine, Henry Gallup, 133
Parkman, Francis, 38, 39n, 53n, 68n, 214
Parsons, Herbert, 175n

Parton, James, 10, 11n
Patch, Sam, 161, 162n
Pater, Walter, 13n, 91, 92n
Patmore, Coventry, 91, 92n
Pauncefote, Sir Julian, 95
Payson, Lewis R., 14n
Peck, Harry Thurston, 100n, 111n
Peffer, William Alfred, 90, 91n
Periodical Publishers Association, 145
Phillips, David Graham, 17n
Platt, Thomas Collier, 27n, 119n
Players Club, 13, 36, 64n, 66, 67n, 149n, 158n
Poe, Edgar Allan, 67
Political Science Quarterly, xxiii, 116, 137–38, 144–45, 154–56, 185–86
Populism, 90, 91n
Porter, Horace, 154
Progressivism, xxiii, xxv, 197n
Puck (magazine), 146, 156, 196, 197n
Putnam, George Haven, 106, 109n

Quigg, Lemuel Ely, 174, 175n

Race and racism, xxiii–xxiv, 131n, 132, 133n, 138n, 144n, 207, 208n
Raynor, Lester, 80n
Reckitt, Sir James, 146, 147n
Reed, Thomas Brackett, 10, 12n, 14, 26, 61, 224, 225n
Reeves, William Pember, 128
Remington, Frederic, 45
Repplier, Agnes, 30–31, 35–37, 47, 50n, 52, 54–55, 71n, 72, 77, 81, 87, 88n
Revue des Deux Mondes, 215
Revue Encyclopédique, 80
Richards, Laura E., 32, 33n
Riis, Jacob A., 179, 226
Riley, James Whitcomb, 222
Ripley, William Z., 185n
Roberts, Frederick S., 128
Robinson, Edwin Arlington, 164
Rockefeller, John D., 177
Rockhill, William Woodville, 97, 98n
Roosevelt, Alice, 69
Roosevelt, Anna ("Bamie"), 27, 76, 169n, 226
Roosevelt, Anna (Hall), 47, 48n
Roosevelt, Archibald Bulloch, 78
Roosevelt, Corinne (Mrs. Douglas Robinson), 27, 120n, 197
Roosevelt, Edith Kermit, 20, 21n, 27, 29, 32, 40, 49, 56, 70, 78–79, 96, 101, 112–13,

118, 130, 137, 139, 148n, 152, 157, 172, 182, 184, 193, 195–96, 206, 211, 212 and passim
Roosevelt, Ethel, 200, 201n
Roosevelt, Kermit, 7
Roosevelt, Quentin, 219, 220n
Roosevelt, Theodore: and American Revolution, 57; and Anglo-American relations, 115; on art, 189; on Aryan race, 181; assistant secretary of the navy, 105–13 passim; and Berkeley addresses, 193, 194n; and Boone and Crockett Club, 24, 65, 73–74, 121; and Brazilian expedition, 206n; Carnegie Hall speech, 222, 223n; Civil Service Commissioner, 4–98 passim, 102n; and coal strike, 137, 138n; and "colonial" Americans, 31, 50, 68–70, 100; contributing editor to *Outlook*, 190n–91n; and copyright law, 9–10, 12, 14; on cowboy life and literature, 45–46, 61, 62n, 89, 95; on dialect in fiction, 78; on Egypt, 191; elected to Academy of Arts and Letters, 157, 158n; foreign policy, 160n; on French authors, 21, 22n, 65, 66n; governor of New York, 114–21 passim; and Harvard-Yale debate, 78–79n; and Haymarket Square affair, 13n–14n; honorary LL.D. from Columbia College, 115n; on immigration restriction, 82, 84n; and imperialism, 127n, 141, 144n, 191n; on Indians in Cooper's fiction, 179–80, 181n; and intercollegiate athletics, 65; and labor question, 90, 132; lectures and addresses at Columbia College, 62–65, 115n; and literary Americanism, xxiv–xxv, 9, 30, 35, 37–38, 51–52, 53n, 78–81, 82–83, 109; literary career, 20; on literary centers, 82; on literary clubs, 17; London visit and speech, 191; and muckrakers, 171; and navy, 12, 13n, 54n, 123–27 passim, 133–34, 203, 204n; on "Negro Problem," 132, 133n, 138n, 200; on New York City, 52, 82, 86, 88, 103–4, 188, 189n; Nobel Peace Prize, 155n; Police Commissioner (New York City), 98–105 passim; President of the U.S., 121–90 passim; and Progressive Party, 197n, 199; and railroad regulation, 185n; review of Matthews's *An Introduction to*

the *Study of American Literature,* 100–
101; review of E. A. Robinson's *Children of the Night,* 164n; and Rough
Riders, 113, 114n, 137n, 188; on
Shakespeare, 82, 204; on social reformers, 89, 103, 171; travels in Africa and
Europe, 188n; and *Vignettes of Manhattan* dedication, 79, 86, 87n; on Wall
Street, 181, 184n
—Writings and addresses: *American Ideals
and Other Essays,* 105–8, 109n; "Americanism in Politics," 15n, 23n; *Autobiography,* xx, 62n, 96n, 197, 198n, 203; "Books
That I Read, and When and How I Do
My Reading," 209n; "A Colonial Sur-
vival," 31n, 36n, 37, 41, 46, 49, 50n, 226n;
"The Foreign Policy of President
Harrison," 42, 43n; "The Foundation of
the Trans-Allegheny Commonwealth,"
64n; "Francis Parkman's Histories," 38,
39n, 41; "The Fur Seal Fisheries," 78n;
Hero Tales from American History, 57n,
85, 86n, 97; *History as Literature and
Other Essays,* xx, 203; "How Not to
Help Our Poorer Brother," 107n; "How
Old Is Man?," 210n; *Hunting Trips of a
Ranchman,* 80n; "In Cow-boy Land,"
58; *Life-Histories of African Game Animals,* 205; "The Man with the Muck-
Rake," 171; "The Monroe Doctrine,"
115n; "Nationalism in Literature and
Art," xxii, 215n; *The Naval War of 1812,*
114n; *New York,* xix–xx, 3–6, 10, 17, 18n,
21n, 23, 32n, 57n, 139–40; "Our Common Schools," 65n; *Outdoor Pastimes of
an American Hunter,* 163n; "President
Harrison's Foreign Policy," 107n; "Public Life," 14n; "The Puritan Spirit and
the Regulation of Corporations," 183n;
Realizable Ideals, 194n; review of Albert
Bushnell Hart's *Formation of the Nation,* 46, 47n, 53; "The Strenuous Life,"
129n; *Through the Brazilian Wilderness,*
206; "True American Ideals," 94;
"True Americanism," 13; "Value of an
Athletic Training," 66n; "The Westward Growth of the United States
during the Revolution," 62n; *The Wilderness Hunter,* 58, 59n, 180; *The Winning of the West,* xxi, 52, 57n, 80n, 107–
8, 109n, 180, 214, 216n

Roosevelt, Theodore, III (Ted), 69, 126, 191
Root, Elihu, 149
Ruskin, John, 13n
Russo-Japanese War, 155n, 160n, 161, 162n

Saint-Gaudens, Augustus, 188–89
Saintsbury, George, 13n
Saltus, Edgar, 17
Sampson, William T., 123–24, 125n
Sandys, Edwin, 73–74
Sanger, William Cary, 128
Savile Club, 128
Savine, Albert, 139, 140n
Schley, Winfield Scott, 123–24, 125n, 126, 127n
Scribner, Charles, xix
Scribner's (magazine), 169–70
Scudder, Horace E., 77n
Seligman, Edwin R., xxiii
Sewanee Review, 54; *see also* Trent, William P.
Seymour, Edward, 128
Shakespeare, William, 82, 204
Shaler, Nathaniel S., 137, 138n
Siddons, Sarah Kemble, 211, 212n
Simplified Spelling Board, 40n, 172n, 173n,
    178, 179n, 183, 184n; and Andrew
    Carnegie, 153n; *see also* simplified spell-
    ing movement
Simplified-spelling movement, 39, 40n, 78,
    172–76, 178, 183, 184n
Sloane, William Milligan, 208, 209n
Smalley, George Washburn, 39, 40n
Smith, Edmund Munroe, 116, 117n
Smith, Robertson, 13n
Southey, Robert, 133, 134n, 213n
Spanish-American War, 113, 138n, 158n
Sprague, Frank, 167–68
Spring-Rice, Cecil Arthur, 26n
St. Nicholas Magazine, 32n, 38n, 85
Stedman, Edmund Clarence, 17, 224
Steffens (Joseph) Lincoln, 103–5, 154
Stephen, Leslie, 13n
Stetson, Frank Lynde, 224
Stevenson, Robert Louis, 13n
Stickney, Albert, 170
Stillings, Charles Arthur, 173n
Stockton, Francis R., 56n
Strong, William L., 98n, 225n
Sturgis, Russell, 21, 24, 224, 225n
Sullivan, John L., 188
Swinburne, Algernon, 13n
Symonds, John Addington, 13n

Taft, William Howard, 187n
Taine, Hippolyte, 208, 209n
Tammany Hall, 118, 119n, 225n
Temps, Le (newspaper), 129
Thomas, Alfred Edward, 73n
Thompson, Daniel Greenleaf, 42, 43n, 46–47, 63n
Torquemada, Tomas de, 133, 134n
Trent, William P., xxv, 41, 42n, 43, 44n, 53–54, 59, 60n, 74–77, 94, 105, 112, 205; on Matthews as a literary critic, 98; on Roosevelt as a historian, 102–3n
Trevelyan, George, 147, 148n
Twain, Mark, xix, 10n, 13n, 48n, 60, 67n, 83, 126–27, 158n, 222

Union League Club, 8, 25, 66

Van Alen, James J., 61, 62n
Van Horne, John D., 56
Voltaire, 208, 209n

Walker, John Brisben, 41, 42n, 49
Wanamaker, John, 6n
Warner, Charles Dudley, 214n
Washington, Booker T., 131, 132n; supports sending African Americans to Sudan plantations, 160n
Washington, George, 58, 59n, 94n, 130, 132, 189n, 212n

Watts, Theodore, 13n
Wayne, "Mad Anthony," 57
Webster, Daniel, 222
Wellington, 1st Duke of, 213
West, Benjamin, 50–51
Wharton, Edith, xviii, 147, 148n
Whitcomb, Selden Lincoln, 74, 75n, 87, 88n
White, Stewart Edward, 131–32
Whitman, Walt, 49n
Whittier, John Greenleaf, 129, 130n
Wilson, Woodrow, 197n, 203n, 211, 212n, 218n, 221, 223n
Wister, Owen (Dan), xviii, 69, 83, 84n, 97, 98n, 107n, 132n
Wolcott, Edward Oliver, 90, 91n
Wolseley, Garnet Joseph, 133, 134n, 147
Wood, Leonard, 129
Woodberry, George, 165
Woodward, Benjamin, D., 144–46
World War I, 207, 208n, 209n, 211, 212n, 218n, 220n
Wotherspoon, William Wallace, 45

Yale Review, 211
Yellow Book, The (magazine), 83, 84n

Zola, Émile, xxii, 22n; and Dreyfus affair, 120n